NOT A
PASSING
PHASE

Also of interest by members of the Lesbian History Group from The Women's Press:

Anticlimax: A Feminist Perspective on the Sexual Revolution Sheila Jeffreys (1990)
A World of Girls: The Appeal of the Girls' School Story Rosemary Auchmuty (1992)

Other titles of interest from The Women's Press:

Surpassing the Love of Men: Romantic Friendship and Love between Women from the Renaissance to the Present Lillian Faderman (1985)
Lesbian Mothers' Legal Handbook Rights of Women Lesbian Custody Group (1986)
A Passion for Friends: Toward a Philosophy of Female Affection Janice Raymond (1986)
A Corridor of Mirrors Rosemary Manning (1987)
The Life and Rebellious Times of Cicely Hamilton Lis Whitelaw (1990)
What Lesbians do in Books eds Elaine Hobby and Chris White (1991)
Women Like Us Suzanne Neild and Rosalind Pearson (1992)

NOT
A PASSING
PHASE

◆

Reclaiming Lesbians in History 1840-1985

◆

Lesbian History Group

First published by The Women's Press Ltd, 1989
A member of the Namara Group
34 Great Sutton Street, London EC1V 0DX

Reprinted and updated 1993

British Library Cataloguing-in-Publication Data
Not a passing phase: reclaiming lesbians in history.
  1. Lesbianism, history
  I. Lesbian History Group
  306.7'663'09

ISBN 0 7043 4175 1

Phototypeset by MC Typeset Ltd, Gillingham, Kent and Intype, London
Printed and bound in Great Britain by Cox & Wyman, Reading, Berks

Contents

Introduction

Why lesbian history?

For many people the idea of lesbian history must seem as
unlikely a subject for study as women's history once seemed.
Twenty years ago it was thought that women did not have a
history worth recounting: that all the important things in the past
had been done by men, or else that women's history was insep-
arable from men's. If women did appear in the history books it
was as heroines who had made it on men's terms. The interven-
ing years have seen a swing away from traditional history towards
an acknowledgement of the experience of minorities, which has
led to a limited rewriting of history, putting in the working-class,
Black people and women, but there has still been no mention of
lesbians, despite our existence within all these groups.

Feminist history has evolved from simply seeing women as a
group that has been excluded, to studying the history of women
in relation to men, focusing on what the Feminist History Group
have called *The Sexual Dynamics of History*.[1] The central
question of feminist history is 'How have men managed to keep
women in subordination?'. This is never even posed as an issue
by traditional historians, who take women's subordination for
granted. But if the position of women generally in history has
been diminished, that of lesbians has simply been ignored.
Regrettably not only traditional historians but many feminists
seem to have difficulty in acknowledging the lesbianism of
women they study, let alone understanding its significance.

A knowledge of lesbian history is essential to everyone
because we will never have more than a sketchy and distorted

1

view of the past until history tells the experience of *all people*, including lesbians. Lesbians have existed throughout the centuries and we need to know about their lives. We also need to know about the social structures and ideas which shaped their experiences in their own particular era. Such knowledge will cast light not only on the lives of the minority group but also on the values and beliefs of the ruling class who wish to keep us a minority.

For lesbians themselves, the need for lesbian history is self-evident. Every social group needs access to its own history. Knowledge of our past gives us cultural roots and a heritage with models and experiences to learn from and emulate, or to choose not to follow. Lesbians have been deprived of virtually all knowledge of our past. This is deliberate since it keeps us invisible, isolated and powerless. Just as many lesbians today are ignorant of the existence of other lesbians in their own community because society has placed an effective ban on the spread of any information about them, so societies in the past have also cut women off from knowledge of lesbianism. For instance, during an attempt to criminalise lesbian acts in Britain in 1921 several MPs argued that it was better to remain silent about the subject than to publicise the fact that lesbianism existed by passing a law against it.[2] Recent legislation to prohibit the 'promotion' of homosexuality in schools and elsewhere[3] is a recognition of the fact that the attempt to conceal lesbianism has not been completely successful; the law has been created to enforce the ignorance which prevents people from making free and informed decisions about their lives. The suppression of lesbianism extends beyond the control of contemporary images and information to include control of historical knowledge so that, for instance, the lives of women who were lesbians are rewritten to a more acceptable script which focuses on a man or men.[4]

Knowledge of our history gives us a context in which to place ourselves in the world and a basis for our efforts to change things. Lesbian history is important both for lesbians, who may gain strength and hope from learning about experiences shared with women in the past, and for all other women and girls, who may reassess their own lives and the choices available to them in the light of learning that some of the women they have been taught to admire were – unthinkable as it may seem – *lesbians*. As Adrienne Rich has written,

> The denial of reality and visibility to women's passion for women, women's choice of women as allies, life companions, and community; the forcing of such relationships into dissimulation and their disintegration under intense pressure have meant an incalculable loss to the power of all women *to change the social relations of the sexes, to liberate ourselves and each other.*[5]

Difficulties of writing lesbian history

Writing the history of women is difficult because in a patriarchal society (i.e. one organised in the interests of men) fewer sources concerning women exist and those that do have often been ignored as 'unimportant', or have been altered. The task of the feminist historian is first to rescue women from oblivion, and then to interpret women's experience within the context of the society of the time.

This is also true for the lesbian historian. In her case, however, the problem of sources is magnified a thousandfold. First, there is relatively little explicit information about lesbian lives in the past, though probably much more than we know about at the moment. Second, much important material has been suppressed as irrelevant, or its significance overlooked by scholars pursuing a different theory. Material may have been omitted as 'private' or likely to embarrass the family or alienate the reader. Much of the evidence we do have has been distorted by historians who wilfully or through ignorance have turned lesbian lives into 'normal' heterosexual ones. Women can be ignored, but lesbians must be expunged.

Lesbians do not usually leave records of their lives. Those who do may not include any details which would identify them unmistakably as lesbians. They may confine themselves to information about their 'public' lives. They may be aware of the dangers of being too forthright in a climate hostile to lesbians: the autobiographies of several well-known lesbians of the 1930s, for example, are so circumspect as to be misleading.[6] They may not identify their experience as lesbian because it does not coincide with the current definition of lesbianism. For example, it is not certain that Eva in *Dear Girl* recognised herself in Edward Carpenter's version of the female 'invert'.[7]

Even where the documents exist, their suppression may begin immediately after the author's death. Family members and literary executors withhold access to incriminating papers and sanction safe biographies. One of Constance Maynard's executrices apparently destroyed a particularly revealing portion of her intimate diaries.[8] Scholars select material for publication to fit their preconceptions, often overlooking vital references because they are simply not equipped to see their significance. Publishers too will pander to market prejudice and omit controversial documents which may have legal repercussions.

From suppression to actual distortion is only a small step. There are many ways to 'normalise' a lesbian. One is to deny any close relationships she may have had with other women. This is not difficult. Biographies and history books are mostly about people who have been famous in public life, a world dominated by men. Moreover, a woman's position in society is largely determined by her relationship to men: father, husband, son, mentor, colleague. As a result, biographies of women are mostly about the men they knew. Since women are correspondingly absent from public life, and friendship is not yet a topic of much fascination for conventional historians (compared with, say, marriage, love, sex or children), women's relationships with other women are largely ignored in biographies and history books. Regarding them as insignificant, or perhaps reluctant to accord to them the significance the primary sources suggest, historians remain extraordinarily indifferent to the strength of women's feelings for other women. Occasionally the historian's blinkers will lead to howlers such as that perpetuated by Tristram Powell, who did away with the most famous lesbian in

British history in one ill-informed sentence: 'Laura Troubridge had a son Ernest who married Una Taylor who later married John Radcliffe Hall and wrote "The Well of Loneliness" '.[9]

Hand in hand with the diminishing of women's feelings about other women goes the compensating exaggeration of women's feelings about men. Gifford Lewis states that Edith Somerville, who lived and wrote in partnership with Violet Martin, became a 'singular woman' as a result of a male ex-suitor's marriage to another woman.[10] Octavia Hill's passionate friendship with Sophia Jex-Blake was written out of mid-twentieth-century biographies, while a hasty engagement which lasted exactly one day was elevated into the romance of her life, with Hill holding the young man's memory 'sacred to her heart till the end of her life'.[11] In fact she lived for the last 35 years of her life with another woman, Harriot Yorke.

A third tactic in the 'normalising' process is the outright denial. Biographers have shown great ingenuity in deflecting suggestions that their subjects may have been lesbians. It is in this respect that writing lesbian history differs most sharply from writing the history of most other oppressed groups. While it may not be easy to locate women or Black or working-class people in history, once you have found them there can be little question as to their identity as women, Black or working-class people. It is unlikely (though not impossible) that anyone is going to read your research and say, She must have been a man really, or She can't have been Black, because . . . . But to claim *lesbians* in history is to invite denial on all sides.

It will, for instance, be seen as conclusive proof that a woman was *not* a lesbian if she was attractive to men (we all know that lesbians are so unattractive they cannot get a man), 'feminine' (lesbians are assumed to be 'mannish'), or if she liked men (lesbians are 'man-haters'). Likewise, the marriage or mother-hood of any woman is considered to be proof against the accusation. There is, it is true, a species of biographer who delights in ascribing a deviant sexuality to his female subjects. What is clear about these scholars, who are usually men, is that they dislike the women they are writing about, who are often strong

5

spinsters with feminist leanings. R.K. Webb, for example, wrote of Harriet Martineau's 'sexual uncertainties':

> She was afraid, she said in her autobiography, of being unable to justify dependence on herself, as she was afraid of loving her own [hypothetical] children too much or of being too devoted to her [hypothetical] husband; behind these fears lay more basic insecurities which must inform too her hysterical self-righteousness when she was faced later in life with some instances of sexual attachment among her friends and acquaintances – W.J. Fox, George Eliot, and John Stuart Mill. . . . It would be a guess with more than a little justification that Miss Martineau was latently homosexual.[12]

Aside from these wholly negative portrayals, why is it so difficult for historians and biographers to name the women they are writing about as lesbians? One reason is that the word is perceived as an insult. It suggests abnormality: at worst a perversion, at best a pitiful handicap. There are even lesbians today who find it hard to speak directly of women in history as lesbians, so strong is the influence of the heterosexist culture we live in. Some of us might feel very positively about our *own* lesbian identity but we still fall over ourselves not to libel the dead or offend our heterosexual contemporaries.

Our anxiety arises partly from a related belief, which is that the term 'lesbian' refers solely to a sexual practice, and not to a mode of life in which a woman's political, intellectual, emotional, social and sexual energies are focused on other women. Words associated with a heterosexual mode of life, for instance 'marriage', do not carry this overriding connotation of sexual activity. (In any case, heterosexual sexual behaviour is regarded by society as 'natural', even where its form is manifestly oppressive, while lesbian behaviour is not simply overtly sexual but *perverted*.) Thus to describe someone as 'lesbian' may be perceived as limiting one's viewpoint to a narrow, abnormal aspect of otherwise 'normal' lives, and scholars will go to great lengths to find some other expression for that person's relationships. For instance, Elizabeth Mavor writes of the Ladies of Llangollen:

> I have preferred the terms of romantic friendship (a once flourishing but now lost relationship) as more liberal and inclusive and better suited to the diffuse feminine nature. Edenic it seems such friendships could be before they were biologically and thus prejudicially defined. . . . Indeed, much that we would now associate solely with a sexual attachment was contained in romantic friendship: tenderness, loyalty, sensibility, shared beds, shared tastes, coquetry, even passion.[13]

By denying their subjects' lesbianism, these authors end up denying the possibility of a sexual dimension to their relationships.[14]

The other major stumbling block which stands in the way of naming lesbians may be called *the standard of proof*. Because of society's reluctance to admit that lesbians exist, a high degree of certainty is expected before historians or biographers are allowed to use the label. Evidence that would suffice in any other situation is inadequate here. There are plenty of clues in women's lives which might alert scholars to the possibility of lesbianism. Lesbians were often to be found in feminist or other rebellious movements; in employments where women worked (and sometimes lived) together, such as teaching, nursing, or settlement work;[15] in social activities where they could meet and associate with other women, like folk-dancing.[16] A woman who never married, who lived with another woman, whose friends were mostly women, or who moved in known lesbian or mixed gay circles, may well have been a lesbian. And there are many other circumstances, some raised by the chapters in this volume, which might constitute evidence supporting such a hypothesis.

But this sort of evidence is not 'proof'. What our critics want is incontrovertible evidence of sexual activity between women. This is almost impossible to find. How many of us, heterosexual or lesbian, keep a written or photographic account of our sexual experiences for posterity? More to the point, would we expect this standard of proof of heterosexuality? Of course not. No one thinks twice if a historian or biographer assumes that his or her subject is heterosexual, though there may be no grounds whatsoever for this assumption. No one expects the historian to provide evidence for this, let alone proof.

In attempting to re-create and explain the past, historians are inevitably limited by their sources; they are sometimes forced to fill in gaps or infer causes or effects for which there is no conclusive evidence. The past does not speak for itself; historians must interpret their material and try to suggest reasons why particular events occurred and particular people behaved as they did. Hypotheses are as much a part of the historian's stock in trade as of the scientist's. We should feel free to examine all the evidence and make our interpretation based on *all* the relevant issues: lifestyle, friends, work, interests, ideas, politics, as well as sexuality. If we cease to consider the word 'lesbian' as an insult or to imagine that it refers solely to sexual practice, there can be no problem in hypothesising from the evidence that a given woman may have been, or probably was, a lesbian.

What is a lesbian?

Historians have different definitions of what a 'lesbian' is. This naturally influences the way they write history. Most historians work with a sexological model created in the late nineteenth century, seeing lesbians as a small group of sexual deviants with a faulty biology. This leads to their acknowledgement of only those most flamboyant and unlikely individuals who conform to this narrow prescription. Lesbian feminists have a much broader definition, which includes many women who would appear to traditional historians to be 'patterns for their sex'. The problems of definition are addressed in all the chapters in this book, but a brief outline of traditional and lesbian–feminist views follows here.

Of the definitions of lesbianism in currency today, the most commonly encountered is the *deviant sexuality* model. Here the lesbian is seen as a woman who has an 'abnormal' sexual orientation towards women instead of the 'normal' one towards men. Different explanations may be offered for this. Some of the late nineteenth-century sexologists believed that it was congenital, that is, that a (small) proportion of females were born with this abnormal nature. As well as having an 'inverted' sexual nature, such women had other characteristics of the opposite sex. This led Edward Carpenter to call them, with homosexual men, an 'Intermediate Sex':

> in bodily structures there is no point which will certainly distinguish the subjects of our discussion from ordinary men and women; but if we take the general mental characteristics it appears from almost universal testimony that . . . the female is . . . fiery, active, bold and truthful, with defects running to brusqueness and coarseness. Moreover, the mind . . . is more logical, scientific, and precise than usual with the normal woman.[17]

Karl Ulrichs called homosexuals 'Urnings' or Uranians, men with the souls of women and women with the souls of men. Both Carpenter and Ulrichs were themselves homosexual and at pains to emphasise that the people they described were merely *different* from ordinary people and in no way inferior to them; indeed, they were often superior, as was evident from the fact that Michelangelo, Shakespeare and Alexander the Great were homosexual in their inclinations – and also Queen Christina and Sappho.

Krafft-Ebing, author of *Psychopathia Sexualis* (1886), shared their view that homosexuality was congenital, but felt that it was an unmistakable sign of degeneration and inherited vice, on a par with all the other perversions he studied. It was to counter this view, shared by most medical authorities of the day, that Havelock Ellis undertook to survey the whole range of sexual practices in his seven-volume *Studies in the Psychology of Sex* (1896–1928), beginning with *Sexual Inversion*. Ellis, perhaps the most important influence on British views of homosexuality, distinguished between 'true' and 'pseudo-inverts'. 'True' inverts were born that way, and nothing could make them normal. Pseudo-inverts (whom confusingly he labelled as 'homosexuals') were people who got involved in inverted behaviour through circumstances rather than natural inclination, and were really normal heterosexuals.

> This kind of homosexuality is specially fostered by those employments which keep women in constant association, not only by day, but often at night also, without the company of men. This is, for instance, the case with the female servants in large hotels, among whom homosexual practices have been found very common. . . . The circumstances under which numbers of young women are employed during the day in large shops or factories, and sleep in the establishment, two in a room or even two in a bed, are favorable to the development of homosexual practices.[18]

The fact that Ellis's wife was a lesbian and his own sexual preference was for watching women urinate may account for the avowed spirit of medical objectivity and liberal toleration of all deviations with which he wrote.[19] Nevertheless, he saw no reason to encourage pseudo-homosexuality, which had no congenital excuse; and his followers, especially the sex reformers like Stella Browne and Marie Stopes, chose to use his findings as evidence for the superiority of 'normal' heterosexual behaviour over all deviant forms. Lesbianism they singled out for particular attack as a serious threat to marriage. In one of her popular marriage manuals, the ambiguously titled *Enduring Passion* (1923), Stopes wrote:

> Another practical solution which some deprived women find is in lesbian love with their own sex. The other, and quite correct, name for what is euphemistically called lesbian love is homosexual vice. It is so much practised nowadays, particularly by the 'independent' type of woman, that I run the risk of

10

being attacked because I call the thing by its correct name. . . . If a married woman does this unnatural thing, she may find a growing disappointment in her husband and he may lose all natural power to play his proper part. . . . No woman who values the peace of her home and the love of her husband should yield to the wiles of the lesbian whatever the temptation to do so.[20]

It is no accident that these arguments appeared in the 1920s when there was a backlash against the gains of the first wave of feminism.

Freud's influence on Western ideas about homosexuality is less than he has generally been credited with, and indeed he relied to some extent upon the published research of Havelock Ellis in formulating his theories on the subject. Freud proposed that the normal sexual development for men and women was essentially heterosexual. He described how girls take the difficult path to femininity by giving up their mothers as love object and transferring their attentions to men in their search for the penis that has been denied them. Failure to negotiate this route successfully might lead to lesbianism: 'They might remain arrested in their original attachment to their mother and never achieve a true change-over to men'. Or they might fall victim to the 'masculinity complex': 'Thus a girl may refuse to accept the fear of being castrated, may harden herself in the conviction that she *does* possess a penis, and may subsequently be compelled to behave as though she were a man'. 'The extreme achievement of such a masculinity complex would appear to be the influencing of the choice of an object in the sense of manifest homosexuality.'[21] Freud's followers held, therefore, that lesbianism was an 'illness' which could be 'cured' by psychoanalysis.

Out of Freud's theories grew the notion that homosexuality and lesbianism were simply forms of arrested sexual development, representing a failure to progress satisfactorily to mature heterosexuality. Later this came to be seen as a stage that young people passed through in their teens, manifesting itself in harmless 'hero-worship' and 'raves' which gave way to normal heterosexual attachments in adulthood. Later still adolescent homo-

11

sexuality became a cause for anxiety, critics suspecting that some young people remained arrested in their youthful patterns of sexual attraction. It was this suspicion that fuelled the attacks on spinster teachers and single-sex schools in the interwar and postwar years.[22]

Another theory of lesbianism is the religious one, of much greater antiquity but still surprisingly pervasive in a largely secular society. It was much in evidence in the debates on Section 28 of the Local Government Act 1988 and in the discussions within the Church of England about homosexual priests in the same year. It has long been the attitude of the Roman Catholic Church. In this view lesbianism is *sinful* and lesbians deserve social condemnation. The sexologists, by distinguishing between true and pseudo-inverts, fed into the religious fear that innocent normal people might be led into sin by predatory lesbians and homosexuals. The same reasoning helped provide spurious justification for laws against homosexual behaviour and the 'promotion' of homosexuality, and the continuing discrimination against lesbians and gays.

The Anglican Church's emphasis on free will helps to explain its approach to the 'problem'. While accepting the view that homosexuals cannot help themselves (because they were born this way, or became so at so early a time that it cannot be rectified), religious critics nevertheless contend that people should not be allowed to indulge in homosexual behaviour. Everyone has the choice, it is argued, and the right choice is heterosexuality within marriage – or not acting upon one's sexuality at all.

Sexual liberals, on the other hand, believe that homosexuality is but one of the many varieties of human sexual behaviour, a matter of personal preference, and in no way better or worse than heterosexuality. The idea of sexual preference is that some people happen to prefer to relate sexually to members of either their own or the opposite sex. A definition of lesbianism based solely on this idea has limited usefulness in any society like our own where the choice is not a free or equal one.

In all these cases sexuality is seen as a personal issue; thrust

12

upon one by birth or upbringing, or freely chosen by individual preference. This idea is refuted by the lesbian–feminist theory.

Lesbian feminists do not recognise heterosexuality as either 'normal' or 'natural' but as socially constructed in order to organise social relationships under male supremacy. Heterosexuality, as an institution, not just a sexual preference, exists to subordinate women and wrest from them their physical and emotional energies for men's use. To create this political institution women, born with the capacity to relate emotionally and sexually to persons of either sex, are deliberately conditioned into heterosexuality by being deluged with heterosexual images and role models (lesbian images and models being systematically excluded or distorted), and by being taught that heterosexuality is normal and natural. This ensures that women as a rule 'fall in love' with and attach themselves to men. However, this socialisation does not always work. There are lesbians who against all odds have never been interested in men, and others for whom heterosexuality is only a passing phase.

Adrienne Rich has suggested that all women are included within a lesbian continuum, ranging from those who may be in relationships with men but have emotional ties to other women to those with a full emotional, sexual and political commitment to women.[23] This implies that not only can all women be lesbians, all women *are* in some sense lesbians. Other feminists are critical of this definition because it does not distinguish between women who are still helping to maintain patriarchy by serving men in heterosexual relationships and those who challenge patriarchy by choosing to put their energies into women. But most lesbian feminists would agree with Rich's assertion that male supremacy has to pathologise or criminalise lesbianism in order to enforce heterosexuality. Lesbians are seen as a threat not so much because of our sexual deviance as because of our political deviance.

The definitions in practice

Different theories of lesbianism, when applied to the past, result in different interpretations of lesbian history. One area in which this is most apparent is in the identification of lesbians. Those using a sexological definition identify very few women as lesbians. Even amongst lesbian historians there is disagreement on this issue.

Some argue that it is wrong to apply the term 'lesbian' to women who would not have taken on such a definition themselves and might have experienced their love for women in a very different way from contemporary lesbians. But we believe that to confine the use of the word to those who accepted it would be to 'disappear' lesbians from history even further. It would mean that another word would have to be used for virtually all 'lesbians' before the twentieth century and for those who did not have a sexological view of themselves. Yet such women often acknowledged their essential difference from other women in their own way, and that arguably is what counts. For instance, Anne Lister wrote in 1821, with no sexological theories or models to follow: 'I love and only love the fairer sex and thus beloved by them in turn, my heart revolts from any love but theirs'.[24] We believe it is important to reveal and reclaim women's love for each other throughout history and to place ourselves as lesbians today in a line of descent from those women of all times who placed importance on their love for women.

Lesbian experience varies not only from era to era but from individual to individual according to both the prevailing theories of lesbianism and each woman's acceptance or rejection of them. We must bear in mind that many lesbians past and present accepted sexological or sexual preference interpretations and internalised these models. There can never be a fixed description of what it means to be a lesbian. The task for historians is to try to recreate the past as women living then would have experienced it and to locate lesbians within it. But we must also try to reinterpret the past in the light of our own lesbian–feminist understanding of what was going on and why particular lesbians in a particular era, such as Queen Christina or Radclyffe Hall, thought and acted in the way they did.

14

Do we define 'lesbian' as only applying to women who had genital connection with each other? Or only to women who prioritised their love for women and made it central to their existence, refusing to organise their lives around men as society demanded? Writers in this collection answer the question differently. It is a discussion which will continue, hinging as it does on contemporary political definitions of lesbianism. But we all agree on including women who loved other women within the scope of lesbian history.

It would be difficult to insist on a narrow sexual definition for lesbians in history simply because we have so little evidence as to whether they 'did it'. We might not even agree as to what 'it' was. But a woman who gives her primary energies to women, who puts on record that she lived with or loved another woman, can be assigned a lesbian identity with rather more validity than many of the heterosexual ones that biographers have scattered about. We want to expand the scope of lesbian history rather than narrow the field.

The scope of lesbian history

Just as feminist historians began by reclaiming women's role in history and pointing out their contributions to history, so lesbian historians have started out by rediscovering the lesbianism of women who were known historical figures. We have already seen, however, that even well-known women who did leave records may not have recorded their experiences as lesbians. And just as feminist historians have had difficulty finding and revalidating the lives of women who were not prominent and did not write about themselves, or who were oppressed in terms of race or class as well as gender, so lesbian historians have difficulty finding out about lesbians who were not famous and did not write about themselves. We recognise that this collection has made little progress in solving the problem of writing the history of lesbians who are not already well known in the dominant white culture. But we hope that as the territory is more

15

thoroughly explored its parameters will be expanded. This is very much a pioneering study and there is much more ground to cover.

Gratifying though it is to discover our lesbian sisters in the past, this is not all there is to lesbian history, nor even the most important part. Lesbian history is also *an approach to history*. Lesbian feminists see heterosexuality as a political institution, which must be maintained by the repression or stigmatising of those who challenge it. Thus lesbian history is also concerned with studying how anti-lesbianism has operated in history.

A society organised in the interests of men must enforce heterosexuality as a means of ensuring the control of women by men. This means that lesbianism has to be defined as a perversion, and lesbian experience must be deliberately and systematically suppressed and/or distorted. We have to understand the mechanics of oppression in every age, the prevailing attitudes, laws and medical theories, before we can understand the experience of lesbians, and of women generally, at any given time. If feminist history is about the sexual dynamics of history, lesbian history concerns the heterosexual dynamic of history: how men have kept women in subordination through the imposition of *compulsory heterosexuality*.

Studies of the treatment of lesbians and celibate women throughout history reveal with what contempt and brutality women who tried to exist without men have been treated. Consider the popular press's reaction to the Greenham Common campaigners, for example. The historian who takes a lesbian perspective will see heterosexuality as a problem for women instead of an inevitable and unquestionable way of life. She will examine the role of heterosexuality as an institution of political control in every aspect of history. The techniques used to enforce compulsory heterosexuality have varied according to circumstance: in some contexts lesbian activity may be forbidden by law (as it is in the British armed forces, for example); lesbian literature may be withdrawn from circulation (as happened when *The Well of Loneliness* was banned in 1928, and more recently when customs officers seized imported volumes destined for

Gay's the Word bookshop in London); lesbians may lose their jobs, or be cowed into silence and denial; in other eras they have been burnt at the stake; in other places, stoned to death. And these are only the public sanctions.

In terms of lesbian history, as well as understanding the mechanics of suppression and distortion that are applied retrospectively by historians, we need to understand the suppression and distortion that went on at the time and moulded women's responses to their lesbianism. The deviant who is 'normalised' through denying, ignoring or distorting her lesbian existence becomes acceptable to a heterosexist society. Those who read about her are left in no doubt that there is only one possible sexual choice for women. If there were famous, happy, successful lesbians as positive role models, then maybe women and girls might be tempted to emulate them – and then where would the patriarchy be!

The Lesbian History Group

The Lesbian History Group was set up after the Lesbian Studies Conference in the summer of 1984, where it became clear that many women were enthusiastic about the idea of a forum where we could study our own history in a supportive environment. Some of the founder members had been involved with the London Feminist History Group which, though it did not ignore lesbian history, only devoted a small proportion of its programme to this field. At the same time we were aware that a good deal of so-called feminist historical research ignored lesbians completely. We knew that the information was there, though it had been overlooked and sometimes deliberately suppressed, and we wanted to investigate and share it with other lesbians.

We meet fortnightly on Friday evenings at the London Women's Centre, Wesley House, Wild Court, London WC2. Sometimes we listen to informal presentations given by women on research they have been doing or aspects of their lives which are part of lesbian history; sometimes we have general discussions on particular issues in lesbian history; sometimes there are lighter sessions with poetry, slides or quizzes. We have done Lesbian Historical Walks in London and visited places associated with lesbians in the past outside London. We have sponsored larger meetings addressed by well-known lesbian writers including visitors from other countries such as Jane Rule and Lillian Faderman. We have helped to launch a number of books on lesbian history and have provided a space for writers to talk about and publicise new work in the field: for example, Diana Souhami came to speak about both her book on Gluck and her book on Gertrude Stein and Alice B. Toklas when each was newly published.

In 1992 we inaugurated an occasional series of events called The Lesbian Idea which are a forum for lesbian-feminist debate across a range of fields from psychology to film-making, and from hotel management to politics. This venture takes us beyond history, but we felt that although there are now plenty of social outlets for lesbians in London, opportunities for intellectual discussion of lesbian feminism were still limited. These meetings have generally been very successful, attracting large numbers of new women who would not normally come to the Lesbian History Group, as well as regular attenders.

Though most of us are not professional historians, some have been inspired by the Group to undertake research, to attend and to teach classes in lesbian history. This book represents some early fruits of our work and was our first joint publication.

1
Does It Matter If They Did It?

Sheila Jeffreys

An earlier version of this piece appeared in Trouble and Strife, *No. 3 (Summer 1984), 25–9*

In her book *Surpassing the Love of Men*,[1] Lillian Faderman showed that passionate friendships with other women were a crucial part of the lives of middle-class women in the eighteenth and nineteenth centuries. She, in common with other American feminist historians, found that the diaries and letters of these women would almost inevitably reveal a same-sex friendship which was likely to have involved passionate embraces and kisses, declarations of love, sharing a bed for a night of cuddles and intimacies, and which would last, often, from childhood to old age. These relationships were so socially acceptable to contemporaries that a woman could write to the fiancé of the woman she loved and tell him that she felt just like a husband to his betrothed, and loved her to distraction and could not help but be very jealous. Men tended to see these relationships as very good practice for their future wives in the habit of loving. Sometimes the women friends could not bear to be parted even on the honeymoon and the husband would have to spend his honeymoon with both of them.

To modern eyes the passionate declarations of eternal devotion and descriptions of highly sensual interaction are startling because we have been trained to see such behaviour as indicative of lesbianism and not part of the everyday lifestyle of the majority of married middle-class women. Faderman shows how sexologists in the late nineteenth century started to create a stereotype of the lesbian in which such passionate interactions were included, and how the acceptable form of friendships between women became more and more circumscribed. Strong emotional and physical intimacy was allowed only to those who were classified as lesbian. She attributes this change to the greater necessity of controlling woman which resulted from the development of a really strong women's movement, and social and economic changes which threatened men's power over women. Emotional relationships between women were harmless only when women had no chance to be independent of men, and became dangerous when the possibility of women avoiding heterosexuality became a reality. Faderman's work deservedly earned her many admirers, but it also provoked some critics to a storm of protest. It is important to our understanding of ourselves that we understand what the controversy was all about.

The problem seems to be that Faderman includes these passionate friendships specifically within the history of lesbianism. She assumes that the women involved were unlikely, because of nineteenth-century views on women's lack of an active sexuality, to have engaged in genital contact, and her definition of lesbianism does not include compulsory genital activity:

'Lesbian' describes a relationship in which two women's strongest emotions and affections are directed toward each other. Sexual contact may be a part of the relationship to a greater or lesser degree, or it may be entirely absent. By preference the two women spend most of their time together and share most aspects of their lives with each other.

'Romantic friendship' described a similar relationship.[2]

Faderman is aware that the suggestion that lesbian identity need not include genital contact is controversial. She recognises that 'It is no doubt unlikely that many women born into a sex-conscious era can conduct a lesbian relationship today without some sexual exchange. The pressure is on in our culture if we want to be physically and mentally healthy . . .'.[3] She quotes a number of lesbian writers who reject what they see as the male definition of lesbianism as defined by and focused upon genital contact.

In discussions, workshops, on the pages of the *Guardian* and elsewhere, lesbians have voiced hostile reactions to Faderman's assumptions. There seem to be two main grounds for the opposition. One objection is that Faderman has made a false reading of history and has somehow been disloyal to the memories of the women she describes as having passionate friendships by imputing to them lesbianism when they would not have recognised themselves as lesbians. Another is a sense of betrayal. Faderman's definition is seen as watering down lesbianism by playing down the sexual content. An example of a fairly standard attack is an article by Sonja Ruehl in the Women's Press collection *Sex and Love* (1983) in which she dismisses Faderman's work as being of any use to feminist theory because, she says, Faderman 'desexualises' lesbianism.[4]

Ruehl and other critics take a particular contemporary definition of lesbianism – the one which lies closest to the hearts of the male sexologists – and they deny that women's passionate friendships can have anything to do with lesbianism because, not surprisingly, they don't match up to this definition. They want to uphold a particular lesbian identity and subculture which they see as being threatened by admitting those who have not gone through the initiation ceremony of genital contact. (They clearly define 'sex' as genital contact.) All the intense sensual activity, kissing and fondling which nineteenth-century passionate friends went in for is classed as wishy-washy and 'not' lesbianism.

Some of their anxiety is well grounded. It is true that the uniqueness of lesbianism and the lesbian identity has been under threat from the concept of sisterhood. During the 1970s and 1980s lesbians within the women's liberation movement have considered it necessary to play down their passions and sexuality so as not to give offence to the heterosexual women who are still the bulk of the movement; and little attention has been given to lesbianism or any issues connected with it. Lesbianism cannot be subsumed beneath the good feelings of hand-holding sisterhood. This leaves no space to talk about specifically lesbian oppression and gives us little chance to build up the history and culture of lesbianism which we need for our pride and our survival. In this context Adrienne Rich's idea of the lesbian continuum is problematic; her argument that all women's friendships with women are some shade or gradation of lesbianism inevitably confuses attempts to analyse lesbian oppression.[5] Women who simply have 'best friends' who are women share neither lesbian oppression nor lesbian experience. So long as we keep the definition of lesbianism open enough to include heterosexual women who love their women friends, it will be hard to articulate what is specific about the experience and oppression of lesbians and to develop the strength to fight compulsory heterosexuality and the invisibility of lesbians.

Passionate friendships and the history of lesbianism

However, if we accept that proof of genital contact is required before we may include any relationship between two women in the history of lesbianism, then there is a serious possibility that we will end up with no lesbian history at all. The history of heterosexuality – and that is the only history we have been offered to date – does not rely on proof of genital contact. Men and women are assumed to be heterosexual unless there is 'genital' proof to the contrary. Women who have lived in the

22

same house and slept in the same bed for thirty years have had their lesbianism strongly denied by historians. But men and women who simply take walks together are assumed to be involved in some sort of heterosexual relationship.

If we see the creation of a lesbian history as important then we must be prepared to assert that certain women were involved in relationships which have some relationship to lesbianism, even though in any historical period before the 1920s we are likely to have difficulty locating women who would be recognisably part of a subculture and lesbian identity which would fit with current definitions. It is surely dubious to argue that it is insulting and unfair to identify as lesbian those women who did not see themselves as lesbian. First, if they lived in periods before sexological theories became fashionable, their general frames of reference, as well as their particular views regarding love between women, must necessarily have differed from those now current. Secondly, such an argument assumes that a lesbian identity is of itself shameful; a view not held by lesbians now and not one which should be imputed to women in the past.

Heterosexuality has changed its form too, yet we are prepared to assume women to be heterosexual in the past who had no interest in sexual activity with men and may have endured it with total repugnance. Many nineteenth-century women, so far as we can tell, were in this position. For the married middle-class woman in the nineteenth century, a heterosexual identity based upon a positive choice of sexual activity with men, or indeed upon any concept of desire for men, would have been unintelligible. Can we include these women in the history of heterosexuality?

Heterosexuality is, of course, much more than a sexual practice. It is an institution documented by written statutes and is a cultural universe sustained by, and signified in, countless rituals, histories, art, literature, and religious and social ideology. Trying to pretend that heterosexuality or homosexuality are simply, or mainly, sexual practices, is to ignore politics entirely. There is now an enormous and growing body of published work written by feminist theorists: historians, philosophers, sociologists, literary critics and others, which explains and illustrates the ways in which society is organised to conform to heterosexual stereotypes. Heterosexuality, it becomes clear, is the organising principle of male supremacy.

Since that is so, women who won't take part drift in a limbo or form an identity for themselves which can enable them to survive with a sense of self, a culture and a social life. Lesbianism can therefore never be simply a sexual practice. The genital sexual practices currently identified by many people as characterising lesbianism have been taking place for centuries, for example between prostitutes; but in that context their function has been (and still is) to titillate and excite men. They have also been tried out by women whose commitment to the heterosexual system has never been in doubt. By contrast, lesbianism as understood by lesbian feminists is a passionate commitment to women, a culture, a political alternative to the basic institution of male supremacy, a means through which women have always gained self-respect and pursued their own goals and achievements with the support of other women. It is more than likely to include a sensual component, which may or may not take a genital form.

Whose interests does it serve to regard lesbianism solely as a sexual practice? If lesbianism is reduced to part of a list in sexological textbooks, together with bestiality and paedophilia, the emotional, cultural and political dimensions disappear. This clearly serves the status quo. Lesbianism as a sexual practice is not a threat. If it were, then it would not be the stock in trade of brothels and men's pornography. Lesbianism as an emotional universe which provides an alternative to women from slotting into the heterosexual system, on the other hand, is a threat. It is then anarchic and threatens the organising principle of male supremacy.

The Scotch Verdict

With these problems in mind, it becomes crucial to decide how to assess Faderman's second book, *The Scotch Verdict*.[6] The book treats in greater depth an incident given briefly in *Surpassing the Love of Men*. This is the case of Miss Woods and Miss Pirie against Dame Helen Cummings Gordon in Edinburgh in 1811. Dame Cummings Gordon's grandchild (the illegitimate daughter of a Scottish imperialist and an Indian woman) was a pupil at the school run by Woods and Pirie. She told her grandmother that the mistresses had sex together, and Cummings Gordon saw that all the other children were removed from the school and the teachers ruined. Woods and Pirie then brought a case against Cummings Gordon, which they won largely as a result of the inability of the judges to believe that two ladies would do such things. The book includes large chunks from the trial transcripts translated into contemporary English. These offer us tantalising glimpses of how women and girls in the period saw their relationships with each other.

Faderman chooses to rest the book on the interesting question of what Pirie and Woods were doing with each other. Were they involved in genital contact, as some witnesses in the trial suggested? Faderman is certain they were not. Her lover, Ollie, who travelled to Edinburgh with her when Faderman did her research, was just as convinced that they did. I admit to being puzzled by both their versions of events, and to being puzzled as to why the question of whether they had genital contact is a matter of such importance that it needs to be proved or disproved. I'm not sure that it's sufficient subject matter for the detective story that *The Scotch Verdict* becomes. Faderman and Ollie's versions are interspersed amongst Faderman's translations of the trial transcripts.

Faderman considers it unlikely that the two women had genital sex, for the following reasons: they lived in an era when women were likely to repress sexual feelings or at least not interpret them in a genital way; and they were unlikely to have done it (as they were accused of doing) whilst sharing beds with school students. It is quite possible to sympathise with Faderman's belief that they did not have genital sex. What is hard to accept is the energy she devotes to proving this. Here is part of her explanation:

25

Almost everything Jane Cumming and Janet Munro (school-girls) described had its counterpart in a gesture or remark that was entirely innocuous. Where there was no innocent counterpart it was because Jane Cumming invented that particular detail from a stock of misinformation and half-understood images. These she had gathered from one or two girls at Elgin school, shopkeepers' daughters who had been out in the world before they were sent to learn a trade. . . . From September to November they came to each other's beds more than a dozen times to talk. . . . Sometimes they came to argue, in subdued tones – but the strength of their emotion was so powerful that if it could not find vent through the voice, it would be expressed through the body; they might shake each other or pound the pillow or tear at the bedclothes. Sometimes they sobbed, breathing high and fast. . . . In October Miss Pirie's rheumatism would have been bad. Sometimes, when they were on good terms, Miss Woods would have gone to Miss Pirie's bed to massage her friend's back.[7]

And so on.

Ollie's version is very different. She uses a very contemporary model of lesbianism to explain for herself what these women were doing. For that reason I find it hard to accept. It does seem that she was simply transposing her own experience and definitions on to those of women in a very different time and place. Here is part of her explanation:

They became lovers – not in the romantic friendship sense, but as we would use that word today – shortly after they met, eight or nine years before the breakup of the school. . . . And there they were in bed together for over a year perhaps, maybe longer. Miss Cumming snored loudly. They had not intended to, but they found themselves making love. The long abstinence, and the necessity to be covert, the risk, all together made it more exciting than it had ever been.[8]

The strength of Faderman's determination to prove that they were not doing genital sex rang so strangely to me that I began to question her confidence in her earlier book that nineteenth-century women in passionate friendships would never have had genital sex.

I think there is a third possibility which may give credit to the fact that these women were living in a very different world with different definitions, whilst allowing some flexibility. I think it is possible that two women, engaged in passionate embraces as a usual part of a passionate friendship, might discover the interesting sensations attendant on genital friction and explore the possibility of improving on the sensations. Women do sometimes discover sex with other women in this way now, so it does not seem impossible that they would have done in the nineteenth century. I think we must be flexible and avoid transplanting on to the experience of our foresisters either a contemporary lesbian identity or a determinedly non-genital one.

What is very interesting about the book is that it shows that girls at 'nice' boarding schools in 1811 seem to have been as keenly aware of and as likely to chatter about lesbians as they are today. They talked of lesbianism with maids and nannies who all seem to have known something about it. This suggests to me that an assumption that all passionate friendships were non-genital is unwise when so many girls and women were aware of the genital possibilities of such relationships.

The Scotch Verdict is a book well worth reading in conjunction with *Surpassing the Love of Men* because it raises the question of how we are to interpret passionate friendships so acutely. Faderman's work has provided a foundation for all other lesbian–feminist history writing. She has overturned both traditional heterosexual history and more recent 'gay' interpretations. Her work helps us to enter upon the debate that is crucial to the writing of lesbian history, the debate about what lesbianism means for us now and the exploration of our differing definitions. This is a process long overdue. The subject of passionate friendships rouses passionate controversy and this suggests that it must touch on some very important political issues. Any heretical questioning of the traditional twentieth-century stereo-type of lesbianism, such as was done in 1979 in a paper later published in *Love Your Enemy*, which called on feminists to withdraw from men and define themselves as political lesbians even before they had had a love affair with a woman, leads to a storm of protest.[9]

How can we question that definition whilst protecting our identity as lesbians? If we do not question it, then lesbians will remain a tiny minority of women, defined by genital contact, fitting neatly into the category the lords and masters have assigned to us. The ramparts of heterosexuality will not be breached, and the heterosexual foundations of male supremacy will remain firm. If we do question it, then we question our own security too, inasmuch as our security and identity have been based on this definition. We need an identity that is strong, revolutionary and *lesbian*.

2

Through All Changes and Through All Chances: The relationship of Ellen Nussey and Charlotte Brontë

Elaine Miller

The idea that Charlotte Brontë, the apparent goddess of hetero-sexual romance, was in love with a woman for most of her life, in a way that would today be described as lesbian, might come as a shock, yet it is not entirely new. Most notably, E.F. Benson in his biography of Charlotte Brontë, written in 1932, described her relationship with Ellen Nussey as 'an emotional thread that for years was the vividest colour in Charlotte's life'. More directly, he assessed it as 'one of those violent homosexual attachments' and found it 'reasonable . . . to conclude that for a considerable period of her life, her emotional reactions were towards women rather than men'.[1] Even earlier, Vita Sackville-West, a lesbian herself, who kept a photograph of Charlotte Brontë on her desk, wrote in her Journal that the letters of Charlotte to Ellen were 'love-letters pure and simple' and left 'little doubt in one's mind as to what Charlotte's tendencies really were'.[2] Ernest Raymond in his book *In the Steps of the Brontës* (1948) described Charlotte's feelings for Ellen as 'a hot

29

love and exquisite passion'.[3] However, neither of the last two writers developed the idea and E.F. Benson considered that the love was finally eclipsed by Charlotte's few months of marriage at the end of her life to her father's curate Arthur Bell Nicholls, a view with which this chapter takes issue. Even Jeanette Foster, in her much respected book *Sex-Variant Women in Literature*, mistakenly saw the relationship of Ellen and Charlotte as an adolescent crush that died with the appearance of Constantin Heger, the Belgian professor whom, it is claimed, Charlotte loved.[4] Biographers who claim this do point out that Charlotte never said that she loved Heger but assert that she was just deceiving herself. Ellen Nussey denied that Charlotte ever loved Heger, a claim that has generally been disregarded.

Ellen Nussey and Charlotte Brontë loved each other almost from the time they met at school in 1831 until Charlotte's death in 1855. Long after that, it is clear that Charlotte occupied a most important place in Ellen's emotional life, despite commonly held views to the contrary. Reasons are not hard to find. They are familiar to feminist and particularly to feminist lesbian historians. Biographies written by men and by heterosexual women have had a patriarchal and heterosexist bias which tends to trivialise women's friendships and to regard lesbian love either as a perversion, or of marginal interest, or as a figment of the imagination. There is also, of course, considerable commercial advantage in emphasising the romantic heterosexual love affair which Charlotte supposedly wrote about in fictional form in *Jane Eyre* and *Villette*, confirming as it does the values of the dominant culture.

This short essay sets out to demonstrate in general terms the process by which the true nature of the relationship that existed between Ellen Nussey and Charlotte Brontë has been variously denied, misunderstood or undervalued and how and why Ellen Nussey herself has been attacked, underrated or almost filtered out of existence as a person in her own right. Several issues need to be addressed: biographers' views on contemporary attitudes towards women, on romantic love and friendship between women, and on lesbianism; how Ellen Nussey and Charlotte

30

Brontë themselves perceived their relationship; Charlotte Brontë's strong attachments to other independent, feminist and sexually ambivalent women, such as Mary Taylor and Harriet Martineau; Charlotte Brontë's frequently expressed opinion that women were the superior sex; and her resistance to marriage, despite several proposals, until a few months before her death. Relevant, too, is the feminism of her relatively neglected novel *Shirley* (despite the compromised ending) and her deep-rooted anger at a social system which gave power to men often in themselves weak and attempted to make powerless women who were in themselves strong. Writing to Ellen on 27 May 1854, Charlotte expressed the view that a 'man is indeed an amazing piece of mechanism when you see, so to speak, the full weakness of what he calls his strength. There is not a female child above the age of eight but might rebuke him for spoilt petulance of his wilful nonsense.'[5] This is mild compared with some of her other comments.

The image of Charlotte Brontë comes down to us through a triple filter, and a triple irony emerges. A woman who understood and resented systematised male power appears through the filter of patriarchy. A woman-loving woman appears through the filter of heterosexism. A woman who worried desperately about money for most of her life appears through the filter of commercialism.

Her fiction, of course, is yet another filter. Charlotte Brontë is regarded as one of the most autobiographical of novelists. She is popularly known through *Jane Eyre* in particular. This novel, and the accompanying mainstream literary criticism it has generated, is responsible for a not uncommon image of Charlotte as a woman yearning for the love of a man, falling into a deep depression because this was denied her, using her pain and frustration creatively in her fiction and finally finding happiness in marriage – or not, according to which view of Arthur Bell Nicholls is favoured. Clearly, the organic connection between her life and the novels is very complex and it is not intended here to address that complexity. What is important is that there is no essential contradiction between the type of novels she wrote and the loving relationship with a woman which was the centre of her emotional life.

My concern is with the facts of her life and relationships as revealed through her non-fiction, primarily her letters to Ellen Nussey which are by no means generally available to the common reader.[6] To read through the hundreds of letters is to read a fascinating autobiography. These letters reveal a relationship which began as a romantic adolescent friendship, developed into a passionate love as the two women lived through their twenties, and matured into a strong and deeply supportive affection, essential to the well-being of each. Writing to W.S. Williams on 3 January 1850, Charlotte described her feelings for Ellen:

Affection was at first a germ, then a sapling, then a strong tree – now, no new friend, however lofty and profound in intellect – not even Miss Martineau herself – could be to me what Ellen is. . . . She is good; she is true; she is faithful and I love her.

Like most marriages and long-term relationships, it had its jealousies, rifts and conflicts. Compared with this attachment, Charlotte's relationships with Constantin Heger and Arthur Bell Nicholls both begin to pale into relative insignificance. It is a mark of the heterosexist bias in the writing of history and literary criticism that so much time, energy and attention has been given to these two men and to Charlotte Brontë's connection with them while very little attention has been paid to Ellen in her own right and to her relationship with Charlotte. Winifred Gérin, Charlotte Brontë's best known recent biographer, even has details of the hobbies of Constantin Heger's father-in-law, who grew a particular kind of cabbage and kept wild birds. An account of Arthur Bell Nicholls' relatives in Ireland contains details of, for example, the architectural style of his uncle's house.

The importance of the Brontë–Nussey correspondence has been widely recognised but for reasons very different from the reasons given here. Winifred Gérin states that Charlotte's letters to Ellen 'form the basis of our knowledge of the outer circumstances of Charlotte's life.'[7] They are generally regarded as providing a mere framework of fact. It is not surprising then that the following letter from Charlotte to Ellen is not quoted by Winifred Gérin and is rarely even mentioned by anyone. It is a short but extremely evocative letter written on 6 December 1836 while Charlotte was teaching at Roe Head School. She was burdened by school duties and was unable to get away to see Ellen, who was living nearby:

> I wish I could come to Brookroyd for a single night but I don't like to ask Miss Wooler. She is at Dewsbury and I am alone at this moment, eleven o'clock on Tuesday night. I wish you were here. All the house is in bed but myself. I'm thinking of you, my dearest.[8]

There is little interesting information here about 'outer circumstances' but much about Charlotte's love for Ellen.

The Brontë–Nussey correspondence spans the years from 1831 to 1855. Ellen claimed that she had received 500 letters. (Some of these have been lost; others exist only in printed form with no original manuscript. Approximately 300 survive in manuscript or print.) At certain times letters flew between their respective houses, often being quite short and used much as telephone calls are today. They were in contact even more frequently than the averaging of 500 letters over 24 years suggests, since they visited each other a great deal, sometimes spending weeks at a time together, when no letter would be needed. There are also gaps in the correspondence, perhaps because of a quarrel or burnt letters. Unfortunately, only one side of the correspondence has survived, since Ellen's letters to Charlotte were destroyed. Letters are rarely destroyed for no reason. Certainly much has been made of attempts, successful or otherwise, to destroy letters written between Charlotte Brontë and Constantin Heger or letters mentioning their relationship. Little, if anything, has so far been made of the fact that not a

33

single letter written by Ellen Nussey to Charlotte Brontë survives. In a letter of July 1856, Ellen told Elizabeth Gaskell that Charlotte had informed her of her intention to destroy all former correspondence before her marriage. It is possible that some letters were destroyed later by or at the request of Arthur Bell Nicholls. Certainly he demanded after his marriage to Charlotte that Ellen destroy all Charlotte's letters to her. Ellen's reply has survived, a scathing note addressed sarcastically to 'The Magister' (The Master) from which it is clear that what Nicholls objected to was 'the passionate language' (the 'ardentia verba') of the letters.[9] There was obviously a great deal of hostility between Arthur Bell Nicholls and Ellen on account of Charlotte.

However, much can be deduced about Ellen's feelings from Charlotte's letters and also from remarks in letters to Ellen from friends such as Mary Taylor.[10] In August 1850, for example, Mary noted in a letter to Ellen that Ellen's last letter to her had been 'the most cheerful I have had from you. I suppose Charlotte was or had been with you; or was going to be.'[11] (Mary destroyed almost all Charlotte's letters to her, thinking it unsafe to keep them, an action she later regretted.)

1831–41

The correspondence begun while both young women were still at school was continued after they left, as was their custom of staying for days and weeks at a time in each other's homes. It is known that when Ellen came to stay at Haworth she and Charlotte shared a bed, a custom common at the time and therefore not, in isolation, significant. In the letters of this period, Ellen is frequently addressed as 'My Darling' and 'Dearest Ellen'. Charlotte reminds Ellen of the 'mutual promise [we] made of a regular correspondence with each other' and ends by bidding farewell to her 'dear, dear, dear Ellen.' The letters are full of romantic excitement, urgent requests for a note, fear of separation, longing to be together, embarrassment and concern that such frequent visits to each other might appear unusual to others.

Charlotte returned to Roe Head School as a teacher in 1835 which meant that she was living much nearer to Ellen, as well as to Mary Taylor. They met at weekends and on any day that Charlotte was free. Charlotte hated teaching. Only the bright thought of Ellen sustained her. In a letter of the period (1836) she wrote: 'All is bustle and confusion round me, the ladies pressing me with their sums and their lessons. . . . If you love me, *do, do, do* come on Friday: I shall watch and wait for you, and if you disappoint me, I shall weep.' She wrote of 'the thrill of delight'[12] at receiving a packet from Ellen and of being able to fight her way out of exhaustion and depression only by picturing Ellen in her mind.[13] Finding out that Ellen had to leave the district for some time, Charlotte was distraught. Her letter of 20 February 1837 is unequivocal:

What shall I do without you? How long are we likely to be separated? Why are we to be denied each other's society – I long to be with you. Why are we to be divided? Surely, Ellen, it must be because we are in danger of loving each other too well – of losing sight of the Creator in idolatry of the creature.[14]

In the midst of uncertainty and separation she wrote to Ellen: 'Through all changes and through all chances, I trust I shall love you as I do now . . .'.[15]

During this period there is mention on several occasions of the idea of Ellen and Charlotte setting up house together. Most interestingly, the letter in which this idea is expressed most clearly and unequivocally is not quoted by Mrs Gaskell and is rarely quoted anywhere. It is written from Roe Head in 1836. Charlotte was obviously feeling acute embarrassment at the strength of her feelings for Ellen but nevertheless expressed them, ending with the admission that she loved Ellen and wanted to live with Ellen, and only Ellen, for ever:

Last Saturday afternoon being in one of my sentimental humours, I sat down and wrote to you such a note as I ought to have written to none but Mary Taylor who is nearly as mad as myself; . . . I will not tell you all I think and feel about you Ellen. I will preserve unbroken that reserve which alone enables me to maintain a decent character for judgement; but for that I should long ago have been set down by all who know me as a Frenchified fool. . . . Ellen, I wish I could live with you always. I begin to cling to you more fondly than ever I did. If we had but a cottage and a competency of our own, I do think we might live and love on till Death without being dependent on any third person for happiness. . . .[16]

Several interesting points arise from the letter. Why is Charlotte so uncomfortable about expressing the extent of her passion for Ellen? She has already by this time expressed it in letters quite clearly.[17] Nor can it be simply fear of Ellen's ridicule since she is concerned about the opinions of others. And why 'Frenchified fool'? It is not inconceivable that she had in mind George Sand, for whose work and personal qualities she expressed admiration in a much later letter. George Sand was shocking Paris about this time by her very public love affairs with women such as Marie Duval, an actress, in 1833 and the publication of her novel *Lélia* in the same year. The novel contains suggestions of sexual love and desire between women. George Sand's lifestyle was a clear challenge to male power, with her habit of dressing up in men's clothes having quite a different effect on society from the romantic friendship between women who stayed looking like women. Lillian Faderman has pointed out that novels about sexual love between women began to appear in France in the late 1820s and early 1830s, coinciding with the beginnings of a feminist movement there.[18] The mention of Mary Taylor is also interesting since it was she who, with her European connections, told Ellen Nussey much later that it was worth learning French just to read one of George Sand's novels. Charlotte and Mary were close friends and Charlotte often visited the intellectual Taylor household where she could well have heard of George Sand. Was Charlotte beginning to see her feelings for Ellen as dangerous, that is, socially unacceptable? How interesting, too, that Mrs Gaskell, Charlotte's first biographer, omitted this letter. Perhaps Ellen kept the letter back to protect Charlotte. Perhaps it was Mrs Gaskell who made the decision to omit. In either case, the most likely reason was that the idea of Ellen and Charlotte setting up house together for life would, in 1836, have been seen as a lunatic and thoroughly unacceptable plan.

Since the destiny of all women was presumed to be marriage, it is hardly surprising that, early in 1839, Ellen's brother Henry proposed marriage to Charlotte. She refused him; though in a letter to Ellen she confessed that she was greatly tempted to marry Henry so that she could live with Ellen. The price, however, even for this, appears to have been too high.[19] The letter appears in Mrs Gaskell's biography but the relevant section is cut. There is no mention of Charlotte's temptation.[20] Either Mrs Gaskell or Ellen Nussey wanted to hide the fact either out of consideration for Henry or because it was unthinkable for women to consider, or even joke about, using the institution of marriage for their own purposes. There is a happy, ironical postscript to this incident. When Henry did marry in the summer of 1845, Ellen and Charlotte took the opportunity to spend some weeks together at Henry's vicarage in Hathersage, preparing the house for the arrival of the happy pair while they were on their honeymoon.

Charlotte refused a futher two and possibly three proposals of marriage and Ellen, despite various attempts by others at matchmaking, resisted marriage throughout her life, the price being that she died in so-called 'genteel poverty'.

Later the same year, in September, came the marvellous Bridlington holiday on which the two women looked back with delight, Charlotte describing it as 'one of the green spots that I look back on with real pleasure.'[21] The holiday was suggested by Ellen, a holiday alone together, just the two of them. Charlotte responded with excited enthusiasm, writing to Ellen on 26 July 1839: 'Your proposal has almost driven me clean daft. . . . The fact is, an excursion with you, anywhere, whether to Cleethorps or Canada, just by ourselves, would be to me most delightful. I should indeed like to go.' Difficulties, however, appeared thick and fast. Could Charlotte get leave of absence from her job as governess? Would there be enough money? What about transport since Haworth's only available gig for hire was in Harrogate? On top of all this, father and aunt were objecting and suggesting instead a family holiday in Liverpool. Charlotte became desperate, writing to Ellen: 'Must I give it up entirely? I feel as if I could not. I never had such a chance of enjoyment before. I do want to see you and talk to you and be with you. I must . . . I will . . . I'm set upon it . . . I'll be obstinate and bear down all opposition.'[22] It was Ellen, however, who saved the day by turning up without warning in a borrowed carriage and whisking Charlotte off while the astonished family looked on. They left the carriage at Leeds, took a train to Selby and then a stagecoach the rest of the way. An urgent message was sent by Ellen's brother, Henry Nussey, to family friends, the Hudsons, who attempted to meet them. Charlotte and Ellen, however, did not arrive at the expected time. But eventually they were found and taken for a month to the Hudsons' house near Bridlington. Ellen Nussey, always described this later in terms of a capture: they were, she said, 'entertained and detained for a month'. They were 'captive guests'. Ellen was 22 and Charlotte 23 years old. In the end, they were released for one week which they spent alone together in Bridlington. Ellen described moonlight walks on the cliffs.[23]

Accounts of this holiday in biographies are usually very short or non-existent. Winifred Gérin's unusually long one is full of facts but contains little comment. Biographers have emphasised the impact made on Charlotte by her first view of the sea, the desire of the two young women to demonstrate their independence, or Charlotte's scornful reaction to the Methodists she came across there. What always appears to go unnoticed is the eager desire of Charlotte and Ellen to be alone together. The undeniable evidence of the letters written over a period of seven years is that they loved each other and wanted to live together. A week would have been better than nothing at all.

On the evidence of the letters between 1832 and 1839, it seems inconceivable that these two young women in their twenties would not have chosen to live together as friends and lovers had they been offered different economic, social and sexual choices. They clearly knew about the limits imposed on their economic and social choices. Whether they were consciously aware of the culturally imposed limit on their sexual choices is more doubtful. As it was, they had little money, were pressurised to marry or to remain at home as dutiful, unmarried daughters, were allowed to be 'romantic friends' so long as this did not challenge accepted conventions by becoming an openly committed relationship in which their energies were withdrawn from men and given to each other.

Years later, in 1846, when Charlotte had achieved fame, she wrote Ellen a description of what life together might have been like. The domestic scene she described is based on the kind of realistic appraisal characteristic of someone who has been in a long-term close relationship. It reads like a description of a fairly successful marriage. One motive for writing this particular letter was Ellen's fear that Charlotte might forget her during a visit spent in Northamptonshire with one of her brothers. Charlotte wrote that it was

> a haunting terror lest you should imagine I forget you . . . that my regard cools with absence – nothing irritates and stings me like this. It is not in my nature to forget your nature – though I daresay I should spit fire and explode sometimes if we lived together continually and you too would be angry now and then and then we should get reconciled and jog on as before.[24]

The love of Charlotte and Ellen has been seen as an adolescent crush that died out when the two grew up. This view either completely disregards the evidence of the letters up to 1841 or considers adolescence as a somewhat protracted period continuing until the age of 25 or so. The view also takes no account of the way that, in any successful maturing relationship, passion turns into a less intense, less excited but more calm and steady love. The fact that the letters become less romantic and more supportive is evidence of the growth of the affection rather than of its decline. Whether or not the love of Ellen and Charlotte was expressed in a fully sexual way is impossible to know. It is not relevant to the argument. No one has ever suggested that Charlotte went to bed with Heger, yet this has never been regarded as weakening the argument that she loved him passionately.

1842–44

Charlotte did live away from home for two years from February 1842 until New Year's Day 1844. With financial help from her aunt and encouraged by Mary Taylor she went to Brussels to gain extra qualifications in the hope of starting a private school. Emily went with her, and Mary and Martha Taylor were also students in a Brussels school. During the months leading up to her departure, Charlotte's relationship with Ellen became very stormy. Charlotte's teaching commitments had made it difficult for them to meet and she had to walk a mile and back to post a letter. These letters are full of assurances to Ellen. On 3 March 1841 Charlotte asked her to 'contrive in some way or other to let me have sight of your face'[25] and on the 21st she begged: 'Do, do come and see me. . . . Talk no more about my forsaking you; . . . attachment . . . is too great a treasure to be ever wantonly thrown away when once secured.'[26] On 1 April Charlotte wrote to her 'Dear Nelly' with the news that she had got leave of absence for a visit. However, she finally had to break the news to Ellen of her intention to go to Brussels, news that she knew full well would distress her. Charlotte grew exasperated that they quarrelled like cat and dog and Ellen was devastated that Charlotte had not told her earlier. Ellen tried to persuade Charlotte to stay. Charlotte admitted being tempted and wrote on 20 January 1842: 'You tantalise me to death with talking of conversations by the fireside and between the blankets.'[27] Significantly, the words 'and between the blankets' were omitted from Mrs Gaskell's biography,[28] either through her own choice or at Ellen's request. It is a puzzling omission, given that it is acknowledged that Charlotte and Ellen shared a bed at Haworth and that in doing this they were merely conforming to the social norm of the time. Perhaps it was simply too direct and concrete a detail of intimacy for Victorian public taste. It is conceivable, however, that it was omitted because, even as early as 1857, such a detail might suggest a physical sexual contact between the two women which would have been a perfectly natural but socially unacceptable expression of the passion unequivocally expressed in the letters.

While Ellen was making appeals to Charlotte's love and emotional nature, Mary Taylor was addressing her intellect and common sense. Mary excited Charlotte's curiosity about the wider world and at the same time made her see the economic and hard business sense of a spell in Brussels. On this occasion, Mary won.

Discussion of Charlotte Brontë's two years in Brussels invariably revolves around her relationship with Constantin Heger, the Belgian teacher who, with his wife, ran the boarding-school for young ladies where Charlotte and Emily went to study. Charlotte, it is claimed, fell in love with Heger and this is seen by numerous biographers and critics as the major experience of her life.

What do Charlotte Brontë's feelings for Constantin Heger really add up to? There exist four letters written by Charlotte over a period of two years. It is true that she addressed them to Heger only, rather than the Hegers as a couple. It is true that they contain remarks which denote affection. She wrote, for example: 'I love French for your sake with all my heart and soul.' On the other hand, they are almost nothing compared to the passionate affection of her letters over an incomparably longer time to Ellen. Often the phrasing is similar. In 1837, for example, she had written to Ellen regarding Ellen's mother and sister, saying 'I love them for your sake.' She referred to Heger as an idol carved in rock. This is echoed in Chapter 24 of *Jane Eyre* as Jane fears that she 'could not see God for His creature, of whom I have made an idol'. On 20 February 1837, Charlotte had expressed to Ellen her fear that they were 'in danger of loving each other too well – of losing sight of the Creator in the idolatry of the creature'. It hardly needs comment that the idea of the idolised loved one is generally regarded as significant when attached to Heger but not regarded when attached to Ellen. On the evidence of language alone it is clear that any word or phrase that can be construed as expressing affection to Heger can be easily matched by similar words and phrases expressing affection to Ellen.

It is true that Charlotte was very depressed during her second year in Brussels. This is more often than not attributed to her unrequited love for Constantin Heger. On the other hand, Aunt Branwell, who had brought up Charlotte, had just died, as had Martha Taylor, the popular and well-loved sister of Mary. Mary herself had left Brussels for Germany and all Charlotte's other English friends and contacts had, by chance, left Brussels at that time too. Ellen had been unable to return with Charlotte to Brussels because of lack of money and Emily had refused point-blank to leave Haworth again. Charlotte was depressed, and with good reason. She left Brussels under a cloud but with an agreement that the Hegers would send their daughters to the Brontës' school, if and when it opened. There was also an agreement between the Hegers and Charlotte to exchange letters, and a possible return to Brussels was discussed. A letter to Ellen dated 15 November 1843 implies that there was hostility from Madame Heger but that Madame Heger's suspicions were groundless. Relations with the Hegers worsened after the publication of *Villette*. This is hardly surprising since the novel is violently anti-Catholic and contains a vicious portrait based on Madame Heger. Much has also been made of Charlotte's depression during the late 1840s and early 1850s, and Winifred Gérin, for example, explained this almost entirely in terms of Charlotte Brontë's reaction to her unrequited passion for Heger. It is more likely that it was to do with the deaths of

Branwell, Emily and Anne all between September 1848 and May 1849. In addition, her great friend Mary Taylor had left for New Zealand in 1845. Charlotte was stunned by the loss.

Commentary on the novels and particularly on *Villette* have had the effect of concentrating attention on the Brontë–Heger relationship and the novel has been regarded as evidence of Charlotte's passion for the Belgian professor. But *Villette* also contains an intriguing episode in which Lucy Snowe, called on as an understudy at the last moment, takes the part of a suitor to a young woman.[29] The part of the young woman is played by Ginevra Fanshawe, a student at the school whom Lucy knew well. Lucy adamantly refuses to dress up as a man, as the part requires, keeps her female dress, with some modifications, and goes on to play a very convincing love scene with Ginevra. The two women are completely carried away by the occasion and actually change the play as they perform, 'gilding it from top to toe', with complete spontaneity. What excites Lucy and drives her on is her determination to act to please herself and to triumph over a young man in the audience whom she knows is in love with Ginevra. Lucy is as surprised as anyone and remarks: 'What I felt that night and what I did, I no more expected to feel and do, then be lifted in a trance to seventh heaven . . . I acted to please myself . . . To me, it was not easy to sleep after such a day of excitement.' The symbolism is strong and clear. Lucy, within the framework of the play and therefore free from all the usual constraints, can spontaneously express romantic and sexual love for a woman. Predictably, conventional mainstream criticism commonly regards this episode in negative terms. Tony Tanner, for example, in his introduction to the Penguin edition of the novel, comments: 'Lucy's own ambiguous, though regretted, relish in her man's role in the play is certainly a symptom of repressed or slightly distorted elements in her character (in naming her, Charlotte Brontë intended that she be seen as a frosty and not always pleasant female).'[30]

Strong and passionate attachments between women are also evinced in *Shirley*, in the relationship between the heroines Shirley and Caroline, who conduct a conversation in a woodland

43

hollow called Nunnwood, near the ancient ruins of a nunnery.[31] Shirley and Caroline regard the place as a natural paradise into which men would be an unwelcome intrusion:

> 'We will go – you and I alone, Caroline – to that wood, early some fine summer morning, and spend a long day there . . .'
>
> '. . . Miss Keeldar, I could guide you.'
>
> 'You would be dull with me alone?'
>
> 'I should not. I think we should suit: and what third person is there whose presence would not spoil our pleasure?'
>
> 'Indeed, I know of none about our own ages – no lady at least, and as to gentlemen –'
>
> 'An excursion becomes quite a different thing when there are gentlemen of the party,' interrupted Caroline.
>
> 'I agree with you – quite a different thing to what we are proposing.'

The relationship between Shirley and Caroline (whom Ellen Nussey said was based on herself) is the one most consistently developed in this novel. But because the fiction can be used to support most, if not all, interpretations of Charlotte Brontë and her life, it is necessary to scrutinise carefully her extant letters which, not being fiction, can yield more direct evidence of which relationships really mattered to her and in what degree.

1844–53

The years in Brussels had been a difficult time for Ellen too. Possibly there had been a quarrel and an estrangement. In any event, there is a gap in the correspondence that has survived. After some initial difficulty and unease on Charlotte's return, the two women were reconciled and this period saw a maturing of the relationship into a companionable and supportive love. In 1847, however, a young woman entered Ellen Nussey's life, causing some jealousy on Charlotte's part. The young woman's name was Amelia Ringrose and, although there is a whole series of letters between the three of them which create a picture of a most interesting situation, Amelia Ringrose is mentioned only peripherally in Brontë biographies. There is very little sign of her in Winifred Gérin's long, detailed biography which contains rare factual information about, for example, those cabbages grown by Constantin Heger's father-in-law. E.F. Benson, significantly, singled her out as additional proof of what he maintained was the true nature of the affection between Charlotte and Ellen.

In 1848 Amelia made long visits to Ellen and the two became very close. At one point, Ellen's visit to Haworth had to be arranged to fit in with Amelia's plans. There is an edge to Charlotte's letters to Ellen at this time. Amelia, perhaps as a conciliatory gesture, wrote to Charlotte who flatly refused to reply, remarking when she received violets in one of Amelia's letters: 'Spring is a season which never agrees with me.' After an eloquent silence from Ellen, Charlotte gave in and wrote to Amelia. It was clear to Charlotte that Amelia adored Ellen. A letter from Charlotte dated 11 March 1848 reads:

> It was almost all about her 'dear Ellen'; a kind of enthusiasm of affection enough to make one smile and weep. Her feelings for you are half truth, half illusion. No human being could be what she supposes you to be, yet your kindness must have been very great to her to have awakened such attachment in return – whether you will miss her or not – she will indeed miss you.[32]

Eventually, however, Charlotte felt deep sympathy for Amelia because of her marriage to Joe Taylor. It puzzled Charlotte 'to know how all this affection will find repose in Joe Taylor'.[33] The marriage, in fact, occasioned one of Charlotte's most scathing and bitter outbursts against men and Victorian marriage conventions:

> After all, he [Joe Taylor] is perhaps only like the majority of men. Certainly those men who lead a gay life in their youth

and arrive at middle age with feelings blunted and passions exhausted, who have but one aim in marriage, the selfish advancement of their interest, and to think that such men take as wives, as second selves, women young, modest, sincere, pure in heart and life, with feelings all fresh, and emotions all unworn, and bind such virtue and vitality to their own withered interest, such sincerity to their hollowness, such disinterestedness to their own haggard avarice – to think this – troubles the soul to its inmost depths.[34]

The outburst exudes contempt for men, and love – possibly idealisation – of women fully consistent with her love of Ellen and her keen sense of how Victorian sexual conventions devalued both of them in the interests of what Charlotte called 'the coarser sex'.[35]

The years from 1844 to 1853 were the most creative of Charlotte's life as a novelist but included her most tragic personal losses, the deaths within nine months of her brother Branwell and her sisters Emily and Anne. Ellen supported her throughout. Towards the end of Anne's illness she accompanied Charlotte and her dying sister to Scarborough, helped with the arrangements of Anne's funeral there and stayed on by the sea with Charlotte for two weeks afterwards. Later, during the writing of *Villette* it was Ellen only who could break through Charlotte's depression and help release her creative powers. After a visit from Ellen, she found she could write again. She acknowledged Ellen's revitalising influence upon her in a letter to Elizabeth Gaskell on 25 March 1851, writing that: 'her attentions . . . her affection . . . her very presence give me a sort of new life . . . my rest at night has been calmer and more continuous since she came.'[36]

In June 1852, Charlotte felt the need to go alone to see again the district where Anne had died. She found herself thinking of Ellen and wrote: 'how sorely my heart longs for you I need not say . . .'[37] and 'Less than ever can I taste or know pleasure till this work is wound up. And yet I often sit up in bed at night, thinking of and wishing for you.'[38] At home again, in October, she was writing '. . . so let me see your dear face Ellen, just for one reviving week'.[39]

1854–5: Marriage and death

Late in 1853, Charlotte and Ellen quarrelled. They quarrelled so bitterly that Miss Wooler, their old schoolmistress and friend of more than 20 years, had to be called in to reconcile the women. The reason for the quarrel is uncertain but Arthur Bell Nicholls is a likely cause.

In 1853, Nicholls, the curate of Charlotte's father, had proposed to Charlotte and been refused. Charlotte, however, had indulged in a secret correspondence with him during the summer of 1853; not informing her father of this until January 1854, after which Mr Brontë agreed to Charlotte's marriage. In February 1854, Ellen wrote to Mary Taylor requesting her help in persuading Charlotte not to marry, a request which Mary refused.[40]

Ellen's Easter visit to Haworth was put off at the request of Nicholls. In a most moving letter of 11 April 1854 Charlotte bade farewell to Ellen, not literally but emotionally as she announced her engagement to Nicholls:

> Goodbye. There is a strange, half-sad feeling in making these announcements. The whole thing is something other than imagination paints it beforehand; cares, fears, come inextricably mixed with hopes. I trust yet to talk the matter over with you. Often last week I wished for your presence and said so to Mr Nicholls (Arthur as I now call him) but he said it was the only time and place when he could not have wished to see you.[41]

Well, he wouldn't, would he? So began a long and bitter rivalry between Ellen and Nicholls.

Why did Charlotte marry after resisting marriage for so long? It was clearly not for love. Letters written at the time are certain proof of this. In writing to Elizabeth Gaskell on 18 April 1854, she confided:

> There was much reluctance and many difficulties to be overcome. I cannot deny that I had a battle to fight; I am not sure that I have even yet conquered certain inward combatants.[42]

On 25 April, in an even more gloomy mood, Charlotte revealed to her publisher George Smith:

> My expectations however are very subdued – very different I dare say, to what yours were before you married. Care and Fear stand so close to Hope I sometimes scarcely can see her for the shadows they cast.[43]

These words echo her confession to Ellen Nussey a few days previously: 'I am still very calm, very inexpectant. What I taste of happiness is of the soberest order.'[44]

In these last two letters she also expressed what seems her primary reason for agreeing to marry Nicholls, which was to secure her father's future by enabling the aged Mr Brontë to stay on at the vicarage and have his son-in-law do all the church work for him. Writing to Margaret Wooler on 22 August 1854, two months after her marriage, she remarked: 'Each time I see Mr Nicholls put on a gown or surplice, I feel comforted to think that this marriage has secured papa good aid in his old age.'[45]

On the evening of her wedding day, 29 June 1854, Charlotte wrote a note to Ellen telling her where to write by return of post. She signed it: 'Yours faithfully and lovingly'.[46] Charlotte's letters to Ellen and to other friends shortly after the marriage indicate her regret at the step she had taken. She wrote that married women should not persuade their friends to marry, possibly a reference to advice she might have received from Elizabeth Gaskell who expressed the view that it was to Charlotte's credit that Nicholls loved her. Mrs Gaskell it was also who gave a false, fairy-tale picture of the Nicholls' married happiness in her biography. However, in August 1854, Charlotte wrote the following at the bottom of a letter which had until then been full of relatively impersonal detail. In view of what is known of Nicholls' habit of reading his wife's letters before she sent them, it is possible that Charlotte added the note after his perusal:

Dear Nell,
   During the last six weeks the colour of my thoughts is a good deal changed. I know more of the realities of life than I once did. I think many false ideas are propagated . . . Nell, it's a solemn and strange and perilous thing for a woman to become a wife. Man's lot is far, far different.[47]

A constant theme in Charlotte's letters at this time is her lack of control over her own time. Apologising to Miss Wooler for failing to reply to a letter, she explained:

My time is not my own. Somebody else wants a good portion, of it – and says you must do 'so-and-so'. We do 'so-and-so' and it generally seems the right thing – only I sometimes wish that I could have written the letter as well as taken the walk.[48]

Charlotte wrote in similar vein to Ellen:

Take warning, Ellen, the married woman can call but a very small portion of each day her own, not that I complain of this sort of monopoly as yet, and I hope I never shall incline to regard it as a misfortune, but it certainly exists.[49]

There is also a hint of unease in a later letter to Miss Wooler:

I believe it is not bad for me that his bent should be so wholly towards matters of real life and active usefulness – so little inclined to the literary and contemplative. As to his continued affection and kind attentions – it does not become me to say much of them but as yet they neither change nor diminish.[50]

These comments of Charlotte are made within the restraints of her sense of duty and loyalty as a Victorian wife and of her knowledge that her husband would read all her letters before she posted them. They suggest more restlessness than is here overtly expressed.

Writing to Ellen on 20 October 1854, Charlotte informed her of Nicholls' opinion of her correspondence:

> Arthur has just been glancing over this note . . . you must BURN it when read. Arthur says such letters as mine never ought to be kept, they are dangerous as Lucifer matches so be sure to follow the recommendation he has just given, 'fire them' or 'there will be no more,' such is his resolve . . . he is bending over the desk with his eyes full of concern. I am now desired to have done with it. . . .[51]

In October 1854 Ellen visited Charlotte and her husband. Ellen and Nicholls did not get on and the rivalry between them was obvious. Mabel Edgerley, writing in 1944, reported that during a walk on Haworth Moor, a favourite old haunt of the two women, Charlotte remarked: 'Even you (Mr Nicholls) shall not walk between us.'[52]

This visit was the last time Charlotte and Ellen saw each other alive. Visits were many times planned and then cancelled. Ellen's sister had typhoid but even when she recovered, Nicholls continued to put obstacles in the way of a meeting between the two women. On one fateful occasion, Charlotte was just sitting down to write to Ellen when she was interrupted by her husband who suggested a walk, effectively preventing a letter to Ellen that day. They were caught in a storm and Charlotte became ill. She never recovered. By March 1855 she was dead. The immediate cause was excessive morning sickness. In 'A Medical Appraisal of the Brontës' published in *Brontë Society Transactions* (1972), Philip Rhodes expressed the opinion that it was 'the neurotic vomiting of pregnancy which finally killed her'. He gave the cause of vomiting as an unconscious rejection of the child or, alternatively, general stress. He speculated that Charlotte Brontë found the sexual aspect of marriage very stressful indeed, since, in this doctor's opinion 'sexual neurosis must have been part of her overall peculiar psychology.' Perhaps she should simply have lived with Ellen.

It is interesting to trace the heterosexist bias in the presentation of Ellen Nussey in major biographies of Charlotte Brontë. Ellen herself was, of course, the person best qualified to write the first biography. In addition to her unique knowledge of Charlotte, Ellen was also a competent writer as is clear from such pieces as her account of Anne Brontë's death or of the first meeting with Charlotte at Roe Head School. Her attempt, 'The Story of the Brontës' was suppressed before publication. The situation was difficult. Ellen owned the letters themselves but Arthur Bell Nicholls owned the copyright and refused Ellen permission to use them in any publication.

In addition, as Elizabeth Gaskell pointed out, 'there [was] some little jealousy of Miss Nussey on Mr Brontë's part.' According to Elizabeth Gaskell, Mr Brontë forbade Ellen to see her finished manuscript of Charlotte's life, an order Elizabeth Gaskell to her credit disobeyed.

It was, in fact, Ellen who initiated the whole idea of an early biography shortly after Charlotte's death and it was she who, having accepted that there were too many obstacles to publication of her own version, suggested the name of Elizabeth Gaskell and persuaded Mr Brontë to make the formal request. *The Life of Charlotte Brontë* by Elizabeth Gaskell has been and continues to be extremely popular and influential. The fact that it does include extracts from some of the early letters between Charlotte and Ellen, ones which are unmistakably passionate in tone, is an indication of the general social acceptability of romantic friendship between women in 1857. However even this biography, as we have seen, omits sections of the letters in which ideas are expressed that would seem to challenge and threaten too closely the contemporary social structure.

Elizabeth Gaskell is certainly responsible for an overemphasis on the gloomy side of Charlotte's nature, as Ellen Nussey pointed out to her.[53] After all, Mrs Gaskell knew Charlotte

Brontë for only a very short time at the end of her life. Ellen had seen much more of the happy Charlotte. It is from Elizabeth Gaskell, too, that the myth of the fairy-tale happy marriage comes. The biographer was, in this instance, very much a Victorian conformist. The first biography, however well-intentioned and however influenced by the choices of Miss Nussey herself, began the trend which has marginalised Ellen and presented Arthur Bell Nicholls as far more significant in Charlotte's life.

Attacks on Ellen become more noticeable in accounts written in the first years of the twentieth century with the advent of a strong women's movement, an awareness of its subversive possibilities and the consequent stigmatising of lesbianism. In 1905, Clement Shorter accused Ellen of 'hero-worshipping to an almost morbid degree'. The word 'morbid' is a favourite word of Havelock Ellis used to describe lesbian feelings in a pejorative way in *Studies in the Psychology of Sex: Sexual Inversion* (1897). Shorter insisted, as have others after him and in similar words, on the 'limitations of the friendship'.[54] He claimed that Mrs Gaskell imbibed prejudices from Ellen; that she was boring and inferior in intelligence to Charlotte Brontë; that the friendship on Charlotte's part was based on gratitude for support given. In a letter written to him, Ellen was described as a 'poor old lady' whose 'last years had many disappointments most of them arising entirely from her warped views of life.'[55]

Subsequent biographers have made similar assessments of Ellen and admit bewilderment at Charlotte's interest in her. In *The Three Brontës* (1912) May Sinclair, having described her as 'the immortal, enchanting Nell' accused her of being a neurotic little woman who was a bad influence on Charlotte. She noted Charlotte's 'morbid excitement and introspection' and claimed that Ellen Nussey was at the bottom of it.[56] In 1941 Fanny Ratchford referred critically to Ellen's 'futile attachments to men' and described her as Charlotte's 'staid, phlegmatic and unimaginative friend'.[57]

Ellen has been most effectively devalued, however, by the biography which is the only one seriously to rival Elizabeth

Gaskell's in general popularity and influence. Winifred Gérin refers to 'Ellen's hero-worship of Charlotte'. The overall impression given is that Ellen was generally importunate and initiated everything. Gérin assumes that it might be difficult to find sufficient motive on Charlotte's side for the attachment. The vocabulary chosen to describe Ellen is revealing. She is presented as 'pressing', being 'placated', 'piously' preserving the letters which form the basis of our knowledge of 'the outer circumstances of Charlotte's life'. Gérin claims that 'Charlotte gradually succumbed to Ellen's proffered love';[58] that 'her knowledge of Charlotte had never penetrated beyond the domestic personal limits of an old school friendship.'[59] She implies that Ellen was deluded with self-importance, always seeing herself in Charlotte Brontë's novels.

Even more recently, Margaret Lane has referred to Charlotte's short friendship with Elizabeth Gaskell as '*the* fruitful friendship' claiming that Charlotte found a far more seductive, or rather, receptive confidante in her than in Ellen Nussey.[60] Even a feminist writer like Helen Moglen wrote in 1984 that Ellen and Charlotte had 'a relationship which seems so strange because of the inequality of the parties'.[61]

Rebecca Fraser, in her recent biography of Charlotte Brontë,[62] admits that Ellen and Charlotte '. . . had had after all the sort of relationship which in some ways was close to a marriage',[63] yet persists in refusing to recognise the love between them, even at its highest, as anything but second best; '. . . It had been full of intimacy and emotion which both parties had not been able to find elsewhere.'[64]

But Ms Fraser then follows the tradition of deprecating Ellen. Describing Ellen's reaction to the forthcoming marriage of Charlotte and Nicholls, she considers that 'Ellen clothed her sense of betrayal in highflown Victorian maidenly talk, wallowing in the cult of self-sacrifice . . . .'.[65]

Ms Fraser asserts that for Ellen 'passion was a closed book'. Admitting the ardent quality of the early love letters (circa 1835–7) and noting that 'some biographers' have seen these as 'indicative of a lesbian tendency in Charlotte',[66] Ms Fraser then goes on to state categorically that 'the notion of a physical relationship must be dismissed.'[67] This is to state as a certain truth something which can never now be verified. It is clear that some nineteenth-century women knew about lesbian sex and experienced sexual contact with each other. See, for example, *The Diaries of Anne Lister.* Anne Lister lived in West Yorkshire, the same county as Charlotte and Ellen. [68] Conceding that 'Perhaps Charlotte was a little in love with Ellen',[69] Ms Fraser proceeds immediately to devalue their relationship:

> Certainly, she used her friendship with Ellen as an outlet for her increasingly violent emotions, which had no other respite, except in her writings – and these frequently reveal how she lived a vicarious life of heterosexual love through the Duke of Zamorna's adventures.[70]

Charlotte's fiction is again being used as firm biographical material to deny the primacy of her love for Ellen Nussey. This is despite the fact that women known to be lesbians can write and have written convincingly about heterosexual love.[71]

Ellen, then, continues to be seen as an unhealthy influence, an importunate nuisance, a foolish gossip, a boring acquaintance, a poor substitute for the man Charlotte could not find or, at best, a close friend. She has been most effectively marginalised so that heterosexist fantasies can be freely woven around Charlotte to transform her into a romantic heroine who never truly recovered from the rejection by the great love of her life, the Belgian professor. Charlotte's view of Ellen was quite different. She wrote of the relationship with her 'dearest Ellen' as one destined to be an exception to the general rule.[72] As for Ellen, she was quite sure what Charlotte meant to her:

> 'She told me things she never told anyone else. I have hundreds of her letters and I had her heart.'[73]

3

Edith Simcox and Heterosexism in Biography: a lesbian-feminist exploration

Pam Johnson

'I should like to know how many women there are who have honestly no story to tell.' This entry for 17 October 1887 written in Edith Simcox's small, often difficult to decipher, hand in her *Autobiography of a Shirt Maker* has a telling irony.[1] For were it not for the fact that the 'love passion'[2] of her life was for the novelist George Eliot (Mary Ann or Marian Evans) and the happy chance that the diary in which she recorded and analysed that passion is preserved in the Bodleian Library, Oxford, it is doubtful whether anyone today would have heard of Edith Simcox. As it is, anyone who has an interest in George Eliot is likely to have come across some reference to Simcox in biographies of the novelist. But all too often these accounts are marred by the sexism and heterosexism of their authors. This is sadly true of our major source of information on Simcox – K.A. McKenzie's *Edith Simcox and George Eliot* (Oxford University Press, 1961).

Feminists such as Elizabeth Sarah have drawn attention to the difficulties of interpreting the political viewpoints and achievements of individual women when the framework within which historical judgments are made is subtly as well as overtly biased.[3] The way in which McKenzie treats Simcox's life is a good example of this point for, despite the fact that he gives us much evidence of Simcox's political activity and quotes generously from the *Autobiography*, the overwhelming impression left by his book is of a pathetic, neurotic creature marginalised from society. It is not that McKenzie is hostile to Simcox – indeed he treats her with friendly condescension – but that the two prerequisites necessary to make sense of her life – an understanding of nineteenth-century feminism and an awareness of the emotional significance which friendships with members of their own sex had for *many* nineteenth-century women – are totally absent from his work.

I shall look, first, at Simcox's life, together with some of McKenzie's distortions. Next, it is important to consider how McKenzie and other Eliot biographers have treated the relationship between Simcox and Eliot, in the light of the significant amount of work published over the last decade on nineteenth-century women's friendships.

Even if Edith Simcox had never met George Eliot, she would still have great interest for lesbian–feminist historians as an example of what Martha Vicinus has described as a small group of middle-class woman who from the middle of the nineteenth century 'could afford to live, however poorly, on their own earnings outside heterosexual domesticity or church governance'.[4]

Born on 21 August 1844 into a middle-class family, Simcox was at various times in her adult life engaged in a wide range of political and intellectual activities. She was a writer and journalist who contributed to the major Victorian journals the *Academy*, *Nineteenth Century* and the *Fortnightly Review* as well as to *Co-operative News*, *Women's Union Journal* and *Labour Tribune*. With Mary Hamilton she founded a shirt-making co-operative –

Hamilton & Co. in Dean Street Soho in 1875 – and continued to be involved in it for the next seven years. She was active in the Shirt and Collar Makers' Union, also founded in 1875, and she and Emma Paterson became the first women to be admitted as delegates to a Trades Union Congress in 1875. In 1883 she attended the International Workmen's Conference in Paris. From December 1879 to November 1882 when she withdrew she was active in the Westminster District of the London School Board and also organised a lodgers' league in Stepney and lectured to working men's clubs.

The activities in which Simcox was involved were similar to those in which many middle-class nineteenth-century women, whom, while recognising the broadness and flexibility of the term, we would now refer to as feminists, also participated. However McKenzie, whose priorities are perhaps indicated by the fact that his chapter on Simcox's early life begins with four pages about her father and brothers,[5] resolutely refuses to accept feminism as a serious issue: 'To speak of the "Women's Movement" is rather misleading for the term implies a programme and co-ordinated advance under a single leader or group of leaders towards a predetermined goal.'[6] Despite the fact that McKenzie gives plenty of examples of Simcox's feminist activity, his reluctance to admit the term distorts the view of Simcox and other nineteenth-century women mentioned in his book. Of Barbara Leigh-Smith (later Bodichon) for example, he writes that she used her father's legacy to 'support many *liberal* causes, such as giving to married women the rights to own property, the granting of women's suffrage' (my emphasis). While McKenzie does concede that Simcox 'defended women's capacity and gave support to exclusively feminist causes', he insists that her 'main social interest was in improving the lot of the toiling masses of mankind in general'.[8] His steadfast refusal to acknowledge the autonomy of women's politics leads McKenzie into statements of breathtaking banality: 'If her [Simcox's] sympathies were sometimes more with women than with men, it was because women were worse paid, and more of them were unemployed than men.'[9] It could be argued that McKenzie was writing in a period before the second wave of feminism, beginning in the late 1960s, prompted detailed research into nineteenth-century women's politics. Nevertheless, books such as Ray Strachey's *The Cause: a short history of the women's movement in Britain*, first published in 1928, and Sylvia Pankhurst's *The Suffragette Movement* (1931) would have been available to him and would have provided ample evidence that a Victorian 'Women's Movement' existed and was documented and recognised.

If we abandon McKenzie's attempt to belittle Simcox's feminism and turn to her *Autobiography* itself, it becomes clear that Simcox's political analysis is often very acute. She saw clearly the limitations of philanthropy:

> Ladies who 'work among the poor' think it right to save their money for charity, and buy cheap costumes, made far off by the same sisterhood (tailoresses living in slums): and who can tell the ladies that their so called charity is a theft, and they themselves parties to more oppression than the district-visiting of a lifetime can atone.[10]

She realised that many working-class women would not support protective factory legislation when a reduction of their working hours was accompanied by a reduction in their wages.[11] At the Bristol Trades Union Congress she advocated that female inspectors should be used in workshops where only women were employed.[12] Her commitment to international trades unionism included the belief that 'the workmen's party in all countries should pledge itself to promote trade organisation among the workers of both sexes.'[13]

In common with many other nineteenth-century women she resented keenly the fact that inadequate formal education had retarded her ability to develop and focus her life. She regretted that she had not met George Eliot and been exposed to her intellectual influence earlier: 'I shouldn't have been handicapped with the leaden weight of wasted years. It is urgent in more ways than one to help the young – especially young women – to harness their finest impulses & enthusiasms.'[14] The *Auto-*

biography, too, with its many references to anxiety over money and to penny-pinching economies, such as walking rather than taking public transport, shows up the financial insecurity of middle-class nineteenth-century women living independent lives. The entry for 4 October 1880 remarks that she consulted 'Mrs Anderson about a trifling ailment and was told that its usual subjects were half-starved slave driven maids of all work!',[15] suggesting the world of genteel penury described in George Gissing's *The Odd Women* (1893), which was based on the personal experiences of friends of Gissing, some of whom may even have known Edith Simcox.

Much of the 170,000 words of Simcox's *Autobiography* is concerned with expressing her feelings for George Eliot. The diary was begun on 10 May 1876 and its final entry is 29 January 1900, but two thirds of the entries cover the years 1876–81. The interest of the diary for a modern lesbian–feminist is the relentless intensity with which Simcox probes, celebrates, grieves over and attempts to define her love for Eliot, but the actual 'facts' of their relationship can be briefly summarised. Edith Simcox first met George Eliot on 9 December 1872. McKenzie suggests that Simcox had probably written to Eliot as an admirer of her work, asking to meet her.[16] At the time of their first meeting Simcox was 28 and Eliot 53. They continued to meet, often at the Sunday afternoon gatherings which Eliot and George Henry Lewes, with whom she lived, held at their house, The Priory, 21 North Bank, Regent's Park. They also corresponded, though the only letter which survives is one that Simcox did not send, tucked into the final, blank pages of the *Autobiography*. It is clear that Eliot controlled the frequency of their meetings and that for several months of the year while Eliot and Lewes were out of London on holiday Simcox did not see her. In November 1878 Lewes died and Eliot saw only a few close associates in the next few months. Simcox did not see her again until April 1879. On 7 May 1880 Eliot married a younger man, Johnny Cross, and went abroad on honeymoon. On 19 December 1880 Simcox saw Eliot for the last time: on 23 December Eliot died.

Just as McKenzie's sexism prevents him from fully understanding Simcox's political commitment, his heterosexism
renders him sometimes patronising, sometimes embarrassed
about her love for Eliot. McKenzie's book is given the academic
endorsement of an introduction by Gordon S. Haight, one of
Eliot's principal biographers, in which Haight reveals a limited
and confused set of criteria for assessing the significance of the
Simcox–Eliot relationship. By an astonishing sleight of pen
Haight informs us that we must be cautious about interpreting
pre-Freudian relationships as 'what the school girl today labels
Lesbianism'.[17] Yet he himself uses the very vocabulary he warns
us against when he refers to Simcox's love for Eliot as a 'pathological obsession'.[18] Haight is almost proprietorially defensive of
Eliot, admonishing the reader that one 'must always remember
that George Eliot never reciprocated her [Simcox's] feeling'.[19]
Haight has to acknowledge that Eliot drew a circle of younger
women around her, but his final desperate defence is that she
attracted more men than women.[20] How does he know?

McKenzie is scarcely less crude in his analysis. He defines
the pathology indicated by Haight by suggesting that Simcox
'belonged to the type which psychiatrists call leptosomatic, and
that she tended towards schizophrenia'.[21] He goes further than
Haight in acknowledging the possibility of lesbianism, but
appears to subscribe to the pathology/sin model when he writes
'at least the more innocent elements of Lesbianism appear in the
fondling and caressing so often described'.[22] Clearly a kind-
hearted man, McKenzie tries to view Simcox sympathetically,
but sometimes it all becomes a little too much for him. For
example, after quoting from Simcox's *one* preserved letter to
Eliot which, as I shall show, is a very valuable revelation of the
way she viewed their relationship, he comments: 'Perhaps it is
well that no more of this rather wordy sentimentality has been
preserved'.[23] Sometimes a little joke helps to relieve his
embarrassment. After quoting a passage in which Simcox writes
of having spent the day visiting schools, going to meetings and
preparing a lecture, McKenzie comments: 'It is almost comical
to find her adding immediately after this stiff list: "All this with

perhaps a dim idea of earning the right to go and see her today".'[24]

Biographical writing on Simcox and Eliot through the sixties and early seventies usually exhibits the same muddle. With the kind of confidence that can only come from ignorance the word 'lesbian' is frequently used as a magical absolute without any attempt to place it within a nineteenth-century context. Thus Walter Allen asserts that Simcox 'was without question a lesbian'[25] and Marghanita Laski tells us that she was 'undoubtedly an emotional lesbian'.[26] Lesbianism is often conflated with masculinity. When discussing Eliot's relationships with women, in his introduction to McKenzie's book, Haight comments that 'despite her rather heavy features there was nothing masculine about George Eliot',[27] revealing his assumption that lesbians are pseudo-men. His confusion about whether femininity is inborn or acquired is illustrated by this remark in Eliot's biography where he suggests that femininity is not related to facial bone structure but to clothes-consciousness: 'In their [Eliot's and Lewes'] days of poverty Marian seemed utterly indifferent to clothes; now she began to show quite a normal feminine interest in them.'[28] Of course, this sort of nonsense has its roots in the era in which it was written, when a post-Kinsey consciousness promoted a false sophistication and a liberal tolerance of non-heterosexual sexual practice, but left gender roles unanalysed and the primacy of the heterosexual couple unchallenged. Marghanita Laski perfectly demonstrates this heterosexist viewpoint when she writes: 'among the most devotedly attached to her [Eliot] there is usually a lack of normal emotional satisfactions.'[29] It is a great relief to turn to Ruby V. Redinger's biography of Eliot (1975), to which I will refer later, and find her discussing Eliot's relationships with Simcox and other women without recourse to spurious notions of normality.

If pop psychology and kindly avuncular obtuseness are inadequate analytical tools for understanding Simcox within the context of her times, does more recent work on nineteenth-century women's friendships help us to make a more informed appraisal of Simcox's feelings for Eliot?

Since the publication of Carroll Smith-Rosenburg's 'The Female World of Love and Ritual' and Lillian Faderman's *Surpassing the Love of Men* it has become clear that large numbers of middle-class women in eighteenth-century Britain and America enjoyed 'romantic friendships'.[30] These friendships could involve passionate avowals of love, kissing and embracing, and were either tolerated or actively encouraged by contemporary society. Between then and now, however, the perniciously influential theories of the sexologists were published and promoted, so that it becomes very important to our understanding of the original relationships to examine how they are interpreted by historians now. For example, Jeffrey Weeks, a gay historian, comments about the relationship between Charlotte Brontë and Ellen Nussey:

> It is almost meaningless to attempt to analyse this along the modern polarity of lesbian/heterosexual, because for very few women up till the present century was such a polarity even conceivable. . . . Many of the close relations might have become 'physical' in a modern sense: others did not. To say more than this would be to push modern definitions on to an alien scene.[31]

This seems to suggest that because romantic friendships do not conform to twentieth-century definitions of lesbianism, they must therefore be left unanalysed. If his argument is taken to its logical and depressing conclusion, there can have been no lesbianism before the twentieth century.

Faderman's more flexible definition, discussed by Sheila Jeffreys in Chapter 1 of this book, allows the inclusion of romantic friendships. As Jeffreys points out, it is more useful – and probably more accurate – to assert that many of the relationships enjoyed within the conventions of romantic friendship have some relationship to lesbianism, rather than to insist upon definitions that either specifically include, or specifically exclude, genital sexual expression.

I think it is clear that Simcox's feeling for Eliot bore 'some relationship to lesbianism', although it apparently never achieved genital sexual expression or emotional requital. Indeed the fact that Simcox used the *Autobiography* in order to cope better with Eliot's rejection, by expressing and dissecting her feelings, is what makes it such a valuable document. I think that both Simcox and Eliot realised that Simcox's feelings could not be contained by the rather watered-down version of romantic friendship current in Eliot's circle. It is clear, too, that in parts of the *Autobiography* Simcox comes very close to defining her feeling for Eliot as sexual. This is all the more remarkable since these parts were mostly written in the 1880s, several years before Edward Carpenter's *Love's Coming of Age: a series of papers on the relations of the sexes* (1896), Havelock Ellis' and John Addington Symonds' *Sexual Inversion* (1897) and the writings of Magnus Hirschfield, which did not begin to appear until the 1890s. Thus Simcox did not have the benefit of a clear 'homosexual' identity, but neither did she have the burden of having to define her own emotional nature as 'pathological'.

At this point it is relevant to look briefly at the importance of female friendship in Eliot's life. As a young woman she had enjoyed close friendships with other women. In 1828 at the age of nine she met Maria Lewis, then aged 28, the head governess of Mrs Wallington's school in Nuneaton, where the young Mary Ann was a boarder. The women's friendship continued after Eliot's schooldays and they corresponded regularly. In 1840 and 1841 the letters become more intense in tone and use flower nicknames – Maria is Veronica; Mary Ann is Clematis.[32] An even deeper friendship was formed with Sara Hennell, seven years her senior. From September 1843 Eliot is writing to Sara as 'Beloved Spouse'.[33] In April 1849 she wrote to Sara:

> I have given you a sad excuse for flirtation [exactly what is meant is not known], but I have not been beyond seas long enough to make it lawful for you to take a new husband – therefore I come back to you with all a husband's privileges

63

and command you to love me . . . I sometimes talk to you in
my soul as lovingly as Solomon's Song.[34]

After Eliot began her relationship with Lewes in 1854 the tenor
of her friendships with women gradually changed. In the latter
years of her life Eliot had a number of friendships with younger
married women. Mrs Burne Jones (Georgina Macdonald) and
Mrs Mark Pattison were both born in 1840 and were thus 21
years younger than Eliot. Mrs Elma Stuart (Elvorinda Eliza
Maria Fraser) was born in 1837 and began her friendship with
Eliot in 1872.

Although there is nothing unusual in a middle-class Victorian
woman having the types of relationship outlined above, it is
worth remembering that Eliot was by no means a 'typical'
middle-class Victorian woman. Social disgrace, intellectual and
cultural prestige gave her both vulnerability and exceptional
power. Prurient rumours circulated about her: it was said that
she had had a son by her publisher, John Chapman, and that she
and Lewes had never had a sexual relationship.[35] Solicitude for
her reputation made her husband, J.W. Cross, very careful in his
selection of material for his *George Eliot's Life as Related in Her
Letters and Journals*, published in 1885. Redinger states that
Cross 'silently deleted' such passages as the one above in which
Eliot writes of being a husband to Sara Hennell.[36] The difficulty
of ascertaining how Eliot felt about her women friends is com-
pounded when we learn that many of the letters she wrote to the
women concerned are not extant. None of Eliot's letters to
Simcox are available (Haight thinks that Simcox had them
cremated with her)[37] and Eliot's letters to another woman
friend, Maria Congreve, were destroyed by Mrs Congreve's
nieces after 1960.[38] Thus Haight's 'definitive' edition of Eliot's
letters has significant omissions; as Redinger perceptively points
out: 'One can read even the Gordon Haight *Letters* without
realising that Edith was more than a slight acquaintance who
occasionally made formal calls at the Priory.'[39]

Why were some of Eliot's letters destroyed or suppressed?
While it is possible that her letters to Mrs Congreve were

destroyed because they suggested lesbian feeling, we cannot assume that Cross, working 80 years before, saw the letters that he censored in the same light. As Redinger shows, Cross attempted 'to secure George Eliot against the charge of masculinity' and she quotes from his life of Eliot:

> But it was one of the most distinctly marked traits in her character that she particularly disliked everything generally associated with the idea of a 'masculine woman'. She was, and as a woman, wished to be, above all things feminine. . . .[40]

We can see here the origins of Haight's insistence on Eliot's femininity discussed earlier, but whereas Haight confuses lesbianism with masculinity I do not think that Cross does so. I think it is likely that what Cross objected to in the letter to Sara Hennell, previously quoted, was not the emotional address to another woman but that its energetic and commanding tone directly conflicts with the aura of femininity in which he was anxious to envelop Eliot. The relationships with women which Eliot conducted in the later years of her life seem to have been based on a mother/daughter model and their social acceptability is indicated by the fact that they were encouraged by Lewes and were a source of pride to their younger participants. The change in focus from 'husband' to 'mother' is significant. While one woman acting as a husband to another certainly suggests masculinity, an older, childless woman who 'mothers' younger women has her femininity enhanced, rather than diminished. It is clear from the *Autobiography*, however, that Simcox's relationship with Eliot did not fit smoothly into this pattern and it is useful to analyse the ways in which Simcox's feeling overstepped the boundaries of the Eliot version of women's friendship.

Paradoxically, it is not the extravagant avowals of love, which strike a modern ear as going beyond the limits of heterosexuality, which distinguish Simcox's passion from the norm of romantic friendship. Discussing friendships between women in nineteenth-century women's colleges, Martha Vicinus writes:

Although a religious or spiritual vocabulary frequently masked personal desires, women consistently spoke of their love in terms which replicated heterosexual love. Quite unselfconsciously women referred to their relationships as marriages, complete with the exchange of rings and promises of lifelong fidelity.[41]

Simcox takes religious terminology to the extreme of elevating Eliot to the status of a deity. Even in 1879, before Eliot's death, Simcox writes that at the beginning and end of each day 'the first thing and the last thing is always to kneel in thought of her', and: 'It is strange, I never wanted or sought a religion and it has come to me of itself as the supreme blessing of one's life.'[42] In the same year she writes of being in a sort of spiritual competition with Elma Stuart:

> Of old it used to make me unhappy to imagine that Elma was a disciple more advanced than I, better skilled in the teaching of our Lord. Now it saddens me to see that after all I am in the main the better scholar; how can one who has learnt from her fall away.[43]

References to 'the perfect Union I have always longed for'[44] (though what is meant by this is never made clear), passionate kisses and jealousy of rivals were also acceptable within the terms of the relationship. Simcox's jealousy of Johnny Cross becomes a subject of light-hearted banter between Simcox, Eliot and Lewes:

> they had laughed at the fatality of my crossing with Johnny last week: I said I knew I should poison his shirts some day, and she hoped I wouldn't, he saved them a great deal of trouble about money affairs besides being the best of sons and brothers – I said of course that was just why: I was jealous.[45]

Lewes, too, was willing to encourage Simcox's physical expressions of feeling:

He was affectionate, and when I said I wanted to kiss her feet he said he would let me do it as much as I liked – or – correcting himself – as much as she liked. He could enter into the desire though she couldn't. I did in spite of her protests lie down before the fire and for one short moment give the passionate kisses that filled my eyes with tears – and for the rest of the evening her feet avoided the footstool where I found them.[46]

Though Eliot does not welcome the kisses there is no indication in this passage that Simcox's behaviour is seen as eccentric. Indeed, a passage in the *Autobiography* written after the death of Lewes which marks Eliot's explicit rejection of any 'perfect Union' with Simcox, ends with an exchange of kisses: 'I asked her to kiss me – let a trembling lover tell of the intense consciousness of the first deliberate touch of the dear one's lips, I returned the kiss to the lips that gave it and started to go – she waved me a farewell.'[47]

Significantly it is the privileges which Eliot refuses to allow Simcox and the areas of emotion which Simcox wishes to keep secret which indicate that Simcox's feelings did challenge the primacy of heterosexuality. It is interesting that Eliot did not like Simcox to call her 'Sweet Mother', despite the fact that she signed most of her letters to Elma Stuart 'Mother' and Stuart is described on her tombstone as 'one who for eight and a half blessed years George Eliot called by the sweet name of Daughter'.[48] In her *Autobiography* entry for 26 December 1879. Simcox writes:

She did not like for me to call her 'Mother' . . . she knew it was her fault, she had begun, she was apt to be rash and commit herself in one mood to what was irksome to her in another. Not with her own Mother, but her associations otherwise with the name were as of a task, and it was a fact that her feeling for me was not at all a mother's – any other name she didn't mind: she had much more 'respect and admiration' for me now than when she knew me first, but etc.

– she hoped I was not hurt.[49]

This passage suggests that Eliot was aware that Simcox's feelings for her would not fit comfortably into the mother/daughter pattern of relationships prevalent in her circle. It also conveys a fairly urgent need in Eliot to distance Simcox from her, which is evident particularly after the death of Lewes. Redinger goes as far as to state that emotional pressure from Simcox 'may also unwittingly have helped George Eliot toward her decision to marry Cross'.[50] Though the term 'mother' seems relatively innocuous, the fact that it was withheld from Simcox's use suggests that Eliot was unwilling to give Simcox any endorsement of the relationship, however mild.

The first entry in the *Autobiography* for 10 May 1876 strikes a valedictory note. She begins by quoting from Browning's *The Last Ride Together*:

> Since nothing all my love avails,
> Since all my life seemed meant for fails,
> Since that was written and needs must be

and continues, 'behoves one to realise and accept the fact with everything involved in it'. Later in the same entry she writes: 'I don't see how I can possibly be mistaken in the interpretation of her letter.'[51] The letter which Simcox refers to was written in March 1876 and referred to in an entry of 16 May as 'that painful letter', and Simcox never discloses what it contained.[52] It seems likely that it involved some kind of rebuke or rejection, yet despite the finality of the first *Autobiography* entry, Simcox's hopes revive at many points as the diary continues. On 16 November 1878, for example, she writes: 'I dream of new ways of wooing her – if I could feel that she was learning to know and love me more!'[53]

This reticence in a diary which seems so generally frank is puzzling as well as frustrating. Yet Simcox does show a reluctance to be explicit not only about her own feelings, but about

68

those of another woman. After the death of Eliot, Simcox visited Maria Congreve:

> Went yesterday to see Mrs Congreve. Learnt with a rush of pleasure that she had loved my Darling lover-wise too – too much to repeat much of her words, but she told me how on seeing her again after an interval, her heart was palpitating so violently that to avoid a painful breaking down she forced herself into a calm that seemed cold.[54]

Simcox found a way of expressing her feelings in a series of vignettes published in 1882 under the title *Episodes in the Lives of Men, Women and Lovers*. The book consists of a series of stories supposedly contributed by various friends staying on an island. Each tells a tale based on her or his own experience, which is then written down in a large book, and each episode features a love story between a man and a woman. Simcox obviously found the discipline of channelling her emotion into a literary form helpful, but she is concerned that no one should guess the real subject of her book – her own reaction to the turbulent time when Lewes died and Eliot retreated into grief, before emerging to marry Johnny Cross. Even before she began the book she worried that her own family might divine its personal significance: 'I should not like my own people to guess quite how much autobiography there might be in it.'[56] She also worried about Eliot's reaction: 'Am a little anxious about "Vignettes" lest I should anywhere let slip what might be too plain a confession to her, if she saw it.'[57] After *Episodes* was published she comments in her *Autobiography* on her identification with her male characters: 'I don't choose to say, or wish it guessed but I am Arnold, I am Reuben.'[58]

I do not think that Simcox wished to conceal her love for Eliot for, as we have seen, she was willing to express and discuss her feelings, up to a certain point, in the presence of both Eliot and Lewes. I do, however, think that Simcox was aware and in some parts of her diary makes explicit, that her feeling for Eliot is not what Victorian society, despite its sympathy with romantic friendship, thought women should feel for other women. In many places in the *Autobiography* Simcox analyses her love for Eliot. She acknowledges that Eliot's attraction was partly physical. In the long entry of 17 October 1887 she writes: 'I did not fall in love with her person but with her qualities,' but then puts an asterisk and writes at the side of the page: 'nay: this is not quite exact. I did fall in love with her person so as to care infinitely more for her qualities & all than I could care for any qualities and Human ambitions.'[59] In her unsent letter to Eliot of 28 March 1880, Simcox draws a distinction between what she feels and friendship:

> Do you see darling that I can only love you three lawful ways, idolatrously as Frater the Virgin Mary, in romance-wise as Petrarch, Laura, or with a child's fondness for the mother one leans on not withstanding the irreverence of one's longing to pet and take care of her. Sober friendship seems to make the ugliest claims to a kind of equality: friendship is a precious thing indeed but between friends I think if there is love at all it must be equal, and whichever way we take it, our relation is between unequals.[60]

It is significant that Simcox acknowledges that the complex emotions she feels for Eliot cannot be subsumed in simple friendship.

In a very suggestive entry in the *Autobiography* Simcox compares herself with Maggie Tulliver, the heroine of Eliot's *The Mill on the Floss* who is ostracised because a strong sexual attraction causes her to run away with her cousin's fiancé, Stephen Guest:

> My love for her has made her understand such temptations as Maggie's. . . . I felt always that it was by no choice of mine that I was doomed to woo her only by trying ah how vainly! to be good! I must – I do try to be thankful for what I have had, to think of that rather than of what I never wanted. It *is* a blessing that what was abnormal in my passion caused no pain

or grief to her – bore nothing worse than mere denial for me.[61]

The reference to Maggie Tulliver and the word 'abnormal' (at which I looked long and carefully in the manuscript to make sure that I had not misread it) indicate that at some level of consciousness Simcox was aware of a sexual element in her feelings. This feeling of guilty deviance seems to have been shared by some other late-Victorian women who became aware that their intense emotional feelings for other women were also sexual. In 1878 Minnie Benson, wife of the Archbishop of Canterbury, called upon God to bestow chastity upon her relationship with Lucy Tait:

> Once more and with shame O Lord, grant that all carnal affection may die in me, and that all things belonging to the spirit may live and grow in me. Lord, look down on Lucy and me, and bring to pass the Union we have both so blindly, each in our own region of mistake, continually desired.[62]

Simcox frequently refers to ways in which she manages to live with Eliot's rejection of her. At times she suggests that she sublimated her feelings in political and intellectual activity:

> It is something known, lived through and unalterable, that my life has flung itself at her feet – and not been picked up – only told to rise and make itself a serviceable place elsewhere – So be it – so it is, I have said, I have sworn to myself, again and again, I do not, I will not complain, I will take the life she points to, lose myself in it and leave a few impersonal footprints.[63]

At other times she expresses anger:

> Is it my fault that every wholesome, natural, reasonable passion I have felt from the young ambition of the tomboy to the fierce worship of Her lover – is it my fault that all without

71

exception have been choked off by a churlish fate and I hauled back upon the one inexhaustible gospel of Renunciation?[64]

The reference to 'tomboy' in the above passage is interesting, for at several points in the *Autobiography* Simcox examines her own development, her lack of interest in marriage and her awareness that she does not fit the Victorian ideal of woman. Because she is writing in a pre-Freudian and 'pre-pathological' period she is able to deal with these points frankly and as matters of interest rather than guilty signs of perversion. But at the same time she lacks a vocabulary with which to analyse them fully and a conceptual framework in which to place them. In the long introspective entry of 17 October 1887 she records that she has 'a want of sympathy with girls' games and talk – I didn't care for dolls or dress or any sort of needlework'. She goes on to recall that she was 'passionately and spoonily fond of my mother, and easily attached myself to older girls or women, if, as at school, intimacy was achieved in spite of my shyness'. In particular there was 'one big, plain Mademoiselle Legrand about whom I used to hang or romp caressingly at times'. She continues by saying that she never felt any inclination towards young men and jokingly remarks that only a J.S. Mill or a Garibaldi would have tempted her to marriage.[65]

Yet Simcox was a Victorian woman exposed to marriage propaganda and notions of ideal womanhood so that it would be surprising if she managed to survive with her self-respect completely unscathed. Sometimes she complains at the narrow range of options open to Victorian women. She says that it is humiliating to 'be told again and again that the association called up by my name is always that of a woman who might find a husband if she would take a little more pains with her dress and drawing room conversation'.[66] The subject of whether they were more committed to men or women came up fairly often in Simcox's conversations with Eliot. One conversation was sparked off by a reference to an Italian officer who had helped Simcox when her train was snowed up beyond Foggia:

She said unlike most people she believed I should have thought more of the adventure if a woman had been kind to me. I said I might have if I had had the opportunity of being kind to a woman, but that I had no prejudice whatever against man. He and she said . . . they have [noticed] before that among chance acquaintances men are more appreciative and courteous to her than women. I said that I found women kinder than men, which she was 'glad to hear', as showing they could be kind to each other – and I didn't explain either that I had always taken their kindness as a sign that I was half a man – and they knew it; or that I thought it rather hard she visit as a fault my constitutional want of charm for men.[67]

Notice Simcox's secrecy – doubts about her womanhood are not to be voiced before Eliot and Lewes, and the only way in which she can express to herself her incompatibility with ideal Victorian femininity is to describe herself in masculine terms.

Eliot's references to men and women become rather more defensive when Lewes is not present. Simcox records that Eliot said 'she herself even now had a difficulty sometimes in realising that I was not feeling supercilious towards her. She said perhaps one reason was that I "did not like men" – against which I protested as usual – perhaps as usual in vain. . . .'[68]

After Lewes' death, in the conversation in which Eliot rejects a more intimate relationship with Simcox, Eliot makes clear that her primary commitment is to men:

Then she said – perhaps it would shock me – she had never in all her life cared very much for women – it must seem monstrous to me – I said I had always known it. She went on to say, what I also knew, that she cared for the womanly ideal, sympathised with women and liked for them to come to her in their troubles, but while feeling near to them in one way, she felt far off in another – the friendship and intimacy of men was more to her.[69]

While Lewes was alive Simcox's love for Eliot could be

contained and expressed in ways which could benefit Lewes as well as Eliot. Not only was Lewes willing to intercede with Eliot on Simcox's behalf, but he also tried to gain kisses for himself:

> There was something very innocently boyish about Mr Lewes and it did not seem to me unnatural that he should expect to be kissed or petted a little when he was ill, but when he was well, in the Palace of Truth, I think I should have betrayed an impression that he was rather too hairy for the purpose. But since he thought it appropriate to our relationship as brother worshippers at one dear shrine, I had nothing against it.[70]

The entries in the *Autobiography* which give accounts of conversations when all three were present illustrate very clearly how, given the appropriate conditions, friendships between women, far from threatening the institution of heterosexuality, can help to shore it up – Simcox was obliged to keep her emotional suffering to herself and both Eliot and Lewes could use her as a kind of animated looking-glass, reflecting their interest and delight in themselves and each other. That a heterosexual viewpoint completely misses this interpretation is illustrated by Walter Allen's comment that Lewes 'made what could have been a difficult relation cosy'.[71] Cosy for whom? It is noteworthy that during her period of semi-seclusion after Lewes' death Eliot did see other women friends such as Mrs Congreve, Mrs Burne-Jones and Elma Stuart, but not Simcox. I think it is probable that the combination of Simcox's emotional intensity and her unmarried status made Eliot wary of too close an involvement with her and that she preferred the more conventionally acceptable younger married women of her acquaintance who could be safely transformed into surrogate daughters.

After Eliot's death, Simcox grieved. The *Autobiography* provided her with one safe place in which she could try to analyse their relationship. She summed up the achievements of her life so far and attributed them to Eliot's inspiration: 'I begin to wonder how I shall find as much as that to fill the next decade – For you see, all this came from Her influence.'[72] She settled down to live at a 'lower level of expectation'.[73] She continued with her journalism and political work and in 1894 published, as the culmination of many years' work, *Primitive Civilisations, or outlines of the history of ownership in Archaic communities*. After 1882 entries in the *Autobiography* become less frequent, but Eliot is still the emotional centre of her life. In 1898, not long before her own death, she wrote: 'I am widowed when not far past the prime of modern life.'[74] She died on 15 September 1901, after a long illness.

Clearly, Simcox's love for Eliot did have some 'relationship to lesbianism' – the difficulty is delineating the exact nature of that relationship. Simcox writes about her early interest in girls and women, asserts that she had never been attracted to marriage or men, hints at sexual frustration (she has 'no practical doubts that the melancholia which darkened many years of my life was due to what I may call the emotional inanition of spinsterhood'),[75] yet never draws what to the modern lesbian feminist is the obvious conclusion – that what she really needs is a sexual relationship with a woman. On the other hand, despite her lack of access to modern definitions of lesbianism, her reticence in parts of the diary, the distinction she makes between those women who loved Eliot 'loverwise' and the rest of her circle, and passages such as the one in which she compares herself to Maggie Tulliver, all point to an awareness of sexual feeling.

By acknowledging that she had fallen in love with Eliot's 'person' and by pursuing the object of her love, Simcox was offending against two major tenets of late Victorian femininity – that women should not be sexual and that they should be passive. For the same reason Minnie Benson agonised over her sexual feelings for Lucy Tait, and from the 1850s women such as Elizabeth Sewell were expressing concern about masturbation in girls' schools.[76] I would argue that it was not Simcox's love for a woman which gave her a feeling of deviance in late nineteenth-century society, but the way in which she experienced this love – to worship as a deity or adore as a mother figure was acceptable, to desire and to make emotional demands was not. Simcox's emotional state was further complicated by the fact that Eliot would not grant her the conventional privileges of romantic friendship, nor would she allow Simcox to call her 'Mother'.

Edith Simcox's diary reveals her profound uneasiness with the sexual/emotional options open to her and an acute sense of dislocation from the heterosexual conventions of nineteenth-century society. *Autobiography of a Shirt Maker* is a valuable document to anyone interested in women's sexuality and the history of women's relationships with each other. Simcox deserves more sensitive and intelligent treatment than she has achieved at the hands of K.A. McKenzie, and the very richness and ambiguity of her diary indicates the complexity of women's relationships with each other in the nineteenth century and the impossibility of making them fit neat, schematic definitions.

4

By Their Friends We Shall Know Them: The lives and networks of some women in North Lambeth 1880 – 1940

Rosemary Auchmuty

North Lambeth – that part of central London which lies to the south of Westminster across the river Thames, encompassing Kennington, Waterloo and part of Vauxhall as well as North Lambeth proper – is rich in associations with women and communities of women. In that it is by no means unique: my special interest in the area lies in the fact that when I wrote this chapter, I lived there. My home overlooked the site of Doulton's Lambeth Studio, where from the 1870s to the 1950s skilled local artists, most of them women, turned out the handsome salt-glazed pottery – each piece individually painted and signed – which is so collectable today. Further up the embankment stands St Thomas' Hospital, which Florence Nightingale helped to design in the 1860s and where she established the first training school for nurses. But the women I have chosen to discuss here are those concerned with the setting up and formative years of the Lady Margaret Hall Settlement in Kennington, the Old Vic, and Morley College. These three institutions were all founded towards the end of the nineteenth century within a radius of about half a mile of each other. They all played an important role in social work, education and the arts in the area. It is hardly surprising, therefore, that the women involved in them knew each other, or that their paths crossed those of so many other well-known women in London and elsewhere. Yet these associations and networks have largely been ignored or glossed over by historians and biographers who, following the priorities of patriarchal scholarship, have concentrated on their female subjects as *famous individuals*, and on their relationships with *men*.

Why women's friendships are important

Biographies traditionally deal with people's public lives: their work and achievements, the things that made them important. In this sense we can call biography a masculine craft, for public life traditionally belongs to men. In the conventional division of labour, men's sphere is that of work and action, politics and war – the subject-matter of history books – while women's sphere is home and family, passivity and peace-making – the private areas, into which the scholar should not delve. Women's biography is therefore a hybrid product: an attempt to study a female subject using techniques designed for the male. The majority of women who have biographies written about them are themselves anomalies, for they have stepped out of their sphere and achieved something worthy of note in the masculine, public world. But since they are still women, biographers must also consider their private, domestic role. An investigation into women's private lives is in any case obligatory in a society which defines women in sexual terms. Indeed the tension between a famous woman's public and private life, and social responses to a person who tries to cross sex-role boundaries, constitute intriguing themes for biographers of women to explore. The very expression 'famous woman' is a paradox, a contradiction in terms, and a source of endless fascination to writers and readers – especially men.

I do not propose here to deal with all the characteristics of women's biography and the role they play in socialising readers. I want to concentrate on one aspect of particular significance to lesbian historians as well as to feminists generally: the treatment of women's friendships. Consider, for example, Edna Healey's biography of the Victorian banking heiress and philanthropist Angela Burdett-Coutts. Coutts' relationships to all the men in her life (father, Prime Minister, Great Novelist, husband) are described in detail; but Hannah Brown, with whom she lived for 52 years, is dismissed almost with contempt. Whatever the nature of this friendship ('The pursuit of this theme . . . is best left to the psychoanalysts,' Healey comments; 'Of such ideas Miss Coutts and Mrs Brown, like Queen Victoria, were happily unaware'),[1] it was obviously the central one in Coutts' life – she married only after Brown's death – and deserves appropriate prominence and analysis in the biography. Coutts' other women friends are dealt with even more superficially, if at all.

Feminist historians are now beginning to realise the importance of friendships in women's lives. In the masculine academic tradition there are fixed ideas about what is historically important: party politics, property, paid employment and war matter, the family, feminism and friendships do not. For women, however, friendships with other women have always been significant, though we have suffered (and still do) from a conflict between the value we personally place on our women friends and the value society places on them. When we re-examine historical evidence that has been discarded, distorted or suppressed, it becomes clear that many women have always spent the major parts of their lives with other women; that they have always confided in each other, sought and received sympathy and help from each other, supported and been supported by each other. The North Lambeth network is just one story of women who preferred women's company to men, and of what historians and biographers have done to them.

79

The Lady Margaret Hall Settlement[2]

The Lady Margaret Hall Settlement in Kennington owed its creation on the one hand to the movement to open university education to women and on the other to late-Victorian philanthropy. One significant pioneer in the latter field was Octavia Hill, who was primarily involved in the management of slum housing, but also took an interest in 'settlement work'. This was an early form of social work in poor areas undertaken by university students and ex-students. The first settlement was Toynbee Hall in the East End, founded in 1884. This was run by men; but in 1885, inspired by their example, Octavia Hill acquired four houses in Nelson Square, near Blackfriars Bridge, for a University Women's Settlement. Situated in one of the poorest slum areas in London, it was to be supported by all the existing women's colleges at Oxford and Cambridge.

Octavia Hill is of considerable interest to lesbian historians. She never married, though she had a very brief engagement, broken off within 24 hours; her main relationships were with women. A passionate affair with the pioneer doctor Sophia Jex-Blake, when both were in their early twenties, was ended by the intervention of Hill's mother. Hill lived for the last 35 years of her life with Harriot Yorke, and they are buried together in the churchyard at Crockham Hill, near Edenbridge, Kent.[3]

Among the earliest workers at the University Women's Settlement were several ex-students of Lady Margaret Hall at Oxford, including Nelly and Maggie Benson and Edith Langridge. The Benson girls knew Octavia Hill through their father, the Archbishop of Canterbury, who had sought her advice on the management of some church property in Lambeth. They had gone to Lady Margaret Hall because its first principal was a family friend, Elizabeth Wordsworth, daughter of the Bishop of Lincoln. The Benson family is a splendid source of information about women's friendships because they left on record such a mass of detail about their lives. One of the brothers, E.F. (Fred) Benson, published a biography of his mother, while another brother, A.C. Benson, wrote a memoir of each of the two sisters. All are refreshingly frank about where the women's primary affections lay. Certainly Minnie Benson, the mother (known to her intimates as 'Ben'), did not hide the fact that she fell in love with Elizabeth Wordsworth when they first met in 1869. At the time Minnie was 30, a headmaster's wife and mother of five; Elizabeth was a year older, and a spinster. Elizabeth never married, and her relationship with the Bensons was (as her biographer noted) 'the deepest friendship of her life'.[4] For Minnie Benson it was one of a number of close attachments to women which culminated, after her husband's death, in her setting up home with Lucy Tait, daughter of the previous Archbishop of Canterbury.[5]

Women like Octavia Hill, Minnie Benson and Elizabeth Wordsworth are important to a study of women's networks because in their respective roles they met and inspired so many other women. The influence of Minnie Benson on her own children is quite clear: she gave them a model for same-sex relationships which every one of them followed. But such women had a much wider sphere of influence than their immediate family, and we come across their names time and time again in accounts of their women contemporaries.[6]

Nelly (Eleanor) Benson, the elder daughter, was an intimate friend of the lesbian composer Ethel Smyth, who wrote movingly in one of her autobiographical volumes about Nelly's early death in 1890 from diphtheria.[7] Nelly had done social work in Vauxhall, alerting her sister and friends to the needs of that district. They determined to set up a settlement there supported solely by Lady Margaret Hall graduates and closely linked with the Anglican church. By a piece of good fortune, the rector of St Mary's Lambeth (the parish church next door to the Bensons' London home, Lambeth Palace) was one of the trustees of the Walcot Estate which had a vacant house in a Georgian terrace in Kennington Road. (He was also a relative of Elizabeth Wordsworth.) In 1897 the Lady Margaret Hall Settlement opened at 129 Kennington Road, with Edith Langridge as its first head.

They were soon immersed in social work in North Lambeth,

starting up children's clubs at the Salamanca Mission; Sunday Schools at St Anselm's, St Mary's Lambeth and St Peter's Kennington; charitable work with elderly and sick people; and classes for ill and disabled children. Octavia Hill maintained an interest in both the Lady Margaret Hall and the University Women's Settlements: one of her rent collectors, already working in the area, joined the former, while other women including Mary Sheepshanks, later Vice-Principal of Morley College, worked at the latter.

In 1902 Edith Langridge resigned to undertake missionary work in India. Her place was taken by Edith Pearson, who had been one of the earliest students at Lady Margaret Hall and – after a period as a mistress at Wimbledon High School – Vice-Principal of St Hugh's (another Oxford women's college founded by Elizabeth Wordsworth) and then of Lady Margaret Hall. She too was a friend of Maggie Benson. She was keen to give support and training to pupil teachers and apprentices in Kennington, and was on the Board of both the Kennington Girls' High School (now part of Lilian Baylis School) and the Beaufoy Institute. Another early settlement worker was Dorothy Kempe, who took up charity organisation social work in Lambeth after coming down from Lady Margaret Hall. She was acting head of the settlement from 1909 to 1911, a lecturer at Morley College and Vice-President of the Lambeth branch of the Workers' Educational Association, then in its infancy. Later she married the Reverend Gage Gardiner, rector of St Mary's, and wrote a history of Lambeth Palace.

The story of the Lady Margaret Hall Settlement has not been written in detail, though there are pamphlets and reminiscences. But enough has been said to demonstrate the importance of friendship networks in the lives of the women associated with it, and the way in which the personnel of the various educational and charitable bodies, both locally and throughout London, and indeed throughout Britain, overlapped and co-operated. These connections continued. In the 1930s we read of Lilian Baylis, manager of the Old Vic, attending a party at the settlement on the theme of 'Vauxhall Revisited' – an attempt to capture, in the back garden at Kennington, the atmosphere of the great pleasure gardens which had flourished nearby up to the mid-nineteenth century.[8] There were associations with women working in other local institutions too: teachers at nearby schools, for instance, and nurses and social workers at St Thomas' Hospital.

When Morley College was bombed in October 1940, some settlement workers were among the dead. The settlement itself, though damaged, served as an evacuation centre and shelter for nearby residents. The later history of the Lady Margaret Hall Settlement broke with the early traditions: in 1963 they accepted male workers (long before Lady Margaret Hall itself accepted male students, though this did happen in the 1970s) and in 1980 they moved away from Kennington into freehold premises in Wandsworth Road. Thus did one important network for single women in Lambeth come to an end.

The Old Vic

Emma Cons (1838–1912), founder of the Old Vic and Morley College, had been a close friend of Octavia Hill in her youth. They met in the 1850s, when the 14-year-old Emma, obliged by the illness of her father to earn her own living, joined the Ladies' Co-operative Guild set up by Octavia's mother. Emma Cons was an artist, and worked successively as an illuminator, a watch engraver and in stained glass. In all these trades she was opposed and finally forced out by men resentful of female competition. From 1864 she helped Octavia Hill as a rent collector in some of her workers' properties off Oxford Street. When they eventually fell out, years later, it was over the way they dealt with difficult tenants: Hill got rid of them and gave their places to the more deserving, while Cons tried to win them over. Out of such experiences grew the idea of the temperance music hall which became the Old Vic.

The Hill sisters made a priority of the need to bring beauty as well as material comforts into the lives of the poor. Octavia Hill was one of the founders of the National Trust; her sister

83

Miranda set up the Kyrle Society, which took concerts into the slums and hospitals; another sister, Emily, married Frederick Denison Maurice, founder of the Working Men's College and Queen's College for women. Emma Cons shared this vision. Her tenants were given teetotal clubs and outings to the country. She helped to found Swanley Horticultural College, and took a leading part in the campaign to buy Vauxhall Park as a public open space.

It was in 1875 that she first turned her attention to South London, when she was asked to take over the management of some model dwellings in Lambeth. She decided to concentrate her efforts in this area, and to that end bought the house and grounds of the late James Wyatt, JP for Lambeth, at the corner of Kennington Road and Lambeth Road. Here she built a block of workers' dwellings which she called Surrey Lodge.[9] Close by was the Cut, an area famous in the nineteenth century for its market and music halls, but notorious for crime and poverty. Dickens, Sala and Mayhew had all written of its Cockney charms – and its horrors. There was an obvious need for decent housing. Emma Cons' Surrey Lodge comprised four sides around a central space, two of tenement flats and two of cottages. She and her sister Ellen Cons lived in two of the cottages knocked together. 'We used to say that Emmie was like the strong husband and Ellen the devoted wife', wrote their niece Lilian Baylis, who as a child spent her Sundays helping to entertain the residents of Surrey Lodge. Baylis also remarked that her aunt Emma was 'a bit of a tomboy . . . I know, for instance, that she always carried a knife and a piece of string in her pocket, even when she was wearing evening dress'.[10]

A strict teetotaller, Emma Cons was convinced that drink was the cause of much despair and degradation among the working class. For this reason she decided to open a music hall for her tenants where no alcohol would be served, only coffee. Nineteenth-century music halls depended largely on bar sales for their profits, but she intended to make variety shows, ballad concerts, temperance meetings and the occasional lecture available to the people of North Lambeth at a price they could afford.

She sought the backing of rich benefactors like the millionaire textile manufacturer Samuel Morley MP and the Duke of Westminster to found the Coffee House Music Halls Company in 1879 and to purchase the lease of the Old Victoria Theatre in Waterloo Road. The Old Vic had started life in 1818 as the Royal Coburg Theatre and was lying empty when she took it over. It re-opened on Boxing Day 1880 as the Royal Victoria Coffee Hall and, despite financial crises in the early years, was well established as a home for the entertainment and education of the working class by the time the Charity Commissioners bought the freehold in 1888.

Beatrice Webb wrote in *My Apprenticeship* (1929) that Emma Cons was 'one of the most saintly as well as one of the most far-sighted of Victorian women philanthropists'.[11] Yet there has been no biography of her apart from Lilian Baylis' chapter in Cicely Hamilton's book *The Old Vic* (Cape, 1926), from which most of the material about her in this chapter has been taken. All later accounts of her life, such as those in Richard Findlater's biography of Lilian Baylis and Denis Richards' history of Morley College (see later in this chapter), seem to be based on this. For 19 years she was commemorated by a blue plaque at 6 Morton Place, Lambeth, the home she shared with Lilian Baylis until her death; this was pulled down in 1971. A shabby open space opposite the Old Vic, formerly owned by the Greater London Council, was called Emma Cons Gardens; there is a bronze plaque in the stalls bar of the Old Vic (formerly, more appropriately, the pit entrance), and a photograph at the entrance of the auditorium named after her in Morley College. There was also a portrait in County Hall, the one reproduced in books. Emma Cons was one of the first three women members elected to the London County Council. When Beresford Hope, an arch-opponent of women's rights, successfully challenged the women off the council on the ground that the law permitted them to elect members, but not to stand for election, Emma Cons continued to attend, though unable to vote.[12]

Her commitment to women was evident in all she did. She set up some of the first hostels for girls, creches and clinics for her tenants, and a Home for 'Feeble-Minded' Girls at Bodmin. She was active in the Women's Liberal Federation, and a Vice-President of the London Society for Women's Suffrage. Her closest friends were two wealthy spinsters who were very generous to her schemes: Caroline Martineau (d.1902), who lived with her in Surrey Lodge and became Principal of Morley College, and Ethel Everest (d.1916), daughter of the soldier–surveyor after whom the mountain is named, at whose country home (Chippens Bank, Hever) she spent most of her weekends. Old Vic employees and, later, Morley students often accompanied them. One student recalled:

> we slept on hay in the barn, and I can remember, though it's nearly sixty years ago, Miss Everest and Miss Cons visiting us in the middle of the night with storm lanterns to see if all was well.[13]

After Emma Cons' death her ashes were scattered by Lilian Baylis in the daffodil wood at Chippens Bank. Ethel Everest bequeathed the house and garden to the National Trust for use as a home of rest for men and women, in memory of Emma Cons. The National Trust – whose founder, Octavia Hill, died in the same year as Emma Cons – refused the bequest for practical reasons.

Morley College

Morley College grew out of the lectures which Emma Cons had organised in the very early days of the Old Vic. Two members of the audience so enjoyed a scientific talk in 1884 that they requested follow-up classes. The times were sympathetic to adult education: in 1887 the Charity Commissioners decided to use some obsolete legacies to endow institutions for popular education and recreation, as they put it. They were inspired by the success of F.D. Maurice's Working Men's College, founded in 1854, where Octavia Hill had taught for a while, and its successor the Working Women's College. Incidentally it is interesting to note that the Working Women's College split in 1874 over the issue of mixed or women-only classes. The majority group, which favoured admitting men, remained in the original building in Queen Square under the new name of the College for Working Men and Women. The minority took premises in Fitzroy Street as the College for Working Women, later the Frances Martin College. The former closed down in 1901 but the latter survived, though physically within the Working Men's College, for over half a century more.[14]

In 1888 Emma Cons applied to the Charity Commissioners, with a supporting deputation and petition from potential students, for funds to establish the Morley Memorial College for Working Men and Women. The college was named after the Old Vic's benefactor Samuel Morley, who died in 1886. Funds were forthcoming, and Morley College opened on 29 September 1889 in the dressing-rooms behind the stage of the Old Vic, where it remained for 35 years. From a slow start the classes, in basic academic subjects, began to attract more and more students, so that by 1890 there were 1270 on the roll. Most were under 30 and most were men. There were also gym groups, not counted as classes; these were sex-segregated, though the classes were mixed. The Extra-Mural Department of the University of London provided tutors in more advanced studies, and later the Workers' Educational Association was also involved. Cultural clubs as well as classes developed out of the informal association with the Old Vic, where Morley students could get tickets at half price.

In 1921 the London County Council told Lilian Baylis that her dramatic licence would not be renewed unless there were major structural alterations to the Old Vic. This meant, in effect, that Morley College had to go. New premises were opened at 61 Westminster Bridge Road on a site once occupied by the Magdalene Hospital for the Reception of Penitent Prostitutes. These were almost completely destroyed by a bomb in the second world war; the present buildings stand on the same site.

In 1888 it was unusual for the charter of an adult education institute to have written into it that women were equally eligible to study there and to insist that a certain number of the council must be women. Moreover, although men made up the majority of staff and students, the first principal was a woman, as were all but one of her successors up to 1950.[15] Emma Cons, Caroline Martineau and Ethel Everest were members of the first council, and the first principal was Miss Goold, ex-principal of the Working Women's College. When she retired in 1891, Caroline Martineau took over as unpaid acting principal until her death in 1902.

Like Emma Cons, Caroline Martineau had trained as one of Octavia Hill's assistants. We know very little about her, but she seems to have been a feminist of a sort: once, apropos of Shaw's play *Mrs Warren's Profession*, she remarked to an unmarried woman colleague:

> I don't like any *spoken* protest against the position of women; you and I are far more effectual protests than any mere speaking can be. When people see that we will not marry while the position of women is so unsatisfactory, they will begin to take action.[16]

These views were in a tradition exemplified by Florence Nightingale and other Victorian spinster feminists, and later expounded by Cicely Hamilton in *Marriage as a Trade* (1909, reissued by The Women's Press in 1981).

This aspect of Caroline Martineau's character was not put forward by Denis Richards in his history of Morley College, *Offspring of the Vic* (1958). Rather, he describes her in this way:

> A large but quiet and self-effacing woman of notably generous and unselfish disposition, an ardent scientist and convinced Unitarian as befitted the niece of the great Dr James Martineau, she was admirably fitted for her task [Principal of Morley College].[17]

This description raises some of the points already noted about the ways in which historians treat women's lives. 'A large but quiet and self-effacing woman . . .': what does her size have to do with Caroline Martineau's ability? Would Denis Richards, himself a former principal of Morley College, care to be depicted as (for instance) 'a small but loud and bumptious man . . .'? Men cannot resist the temptation to judge women by their appearance! Then we learn that she was an *ardent* scientist, as if her scientific work were a hobby rather than a serious professional study; and that her religious convictions derived not from her own deliberations but from the influence of a man, 'the great Dr James Martineau'. Note, moreover, that James' somewhat greater sister Harriet, the economist, Caroline's aunt, goes unmentioned in this account; yet she must have been significant, if only because she shared (and perhaps influenced) her niece's attitudes to education and marriage.

Richards further illustrates the different standards by which men and women are judged by his comment: 'If Caroline Martineau had one deficiency, it was perhaps that her solid virtues were not accompanied by an equal measure of feminine vivacity and charm.'[18] One senses a laborious pun in the use of the word 'solid', but as for the absence of feminine qualities, why should these be thought necessary for the post of college administrator? Would Denis Richards expect to be censured for an absence of 'masculine' qualities in his job?

Richards also perpetrates an even less fortunate image of Emma Cons. Setting the scene for Morley's foundation in 'the 1880s, when a large part of the neighbourhood was hungry, and another part drunk', he writes graphically that 'a middle-aged woman named Emma Cons was bringing the College to birth in the dressing-rooms of the Old Vic'.[19] There is something voyeuristic and obscene about this image of a woman who, though childless and past child-bearing age, is described in inappropriately physical terms.

In 1899 Mary Sheepshanks became vice-principal of Morley College. She was the daughter of the Bishop of Norwich, and had been a worker at the University Women's Settlement at Blackfriars. Shortly after she came to Morley Caroline Martineau became ill, and then died; her (male) successor was very active in politics, so Mary Sheepshanks ended up acting as principal (though without the pay and status) for 14 years. Though only 27 when this period began, she was an outstanding woman with strong social and political commitments, and went on to have a long career in international movements for women's rights and for peace.

Mary Sheepshanks' story has been told in Sybil Oldfield's *Spinsters of this Parish* (Virago, 1984). The author rightly emphasises that she had a special interest in the women students and did her best to build their physical and intellectual confidence with appropriate studies at Morley College. Thus, she encouraged the gymnastic as well as the cultural classes, and tried to keep the college accessible to everyone by forbidding the wearing of evening dress which many could not afford.

The biography is nevertheless marred by an excessive and inappropriate emphasis on Mary Sheepshanks' relationships with men – few as they were. She is supposed to have loved but one, Theodore Llewelyn Davies. He died, possibly by suicide, and she never married. She had, by contrast, many female friends. There was Theodore's sister, Margaret Llewelyn Davies, General Secretary of the Women's Co-operative Guild, and the latter's colleague and lifelong companion Lilian Harris. Margaret Llewelyn Davies lent Mary Sheepshanks her cottage near Reigate for the use of Morley students for summer holidays. Davies' friend Virginia Woolf, who supported her work in the Women's Co-operative Guild, also taught at Morley College from 1904 to 1908. Then there was another of Virginia Woolf's friends, the aforementioned Ethel Smyth, composer and suffragette, who Mary Sheepshanks said was the most dynamic being she had ever met. Mary Sheepshanks lived for some time with the daughter of Smyth's closest male friend, Harry Brewster, and later with 'a succession of other interesting young women' including many prominent professional women and suffragists.[20]

In 1913 she became secretary of the International Women's Suffrage Alliance; and as a pacifist during the first world war she shared a political perspective with Margaret Llewelyn Davies and Virginia Woolf. She died in 1948. Of Mary Sheepshanks it could truly be said, she put women first. Yet this biography plays down the importance of her relationships with other strong independent women. Its author, though a woman, has followed the principles of male, heterosexist scholarship.

During Sheepshanks' time in charge at Morley, Christabel Pankhurst and Margaret Bondfield addressed the students on women's suffrage, along with Amber Reeves, the woman upon whom H.G. Wells based his feminist heroine Ann Veronica in the novel of that name (1909). Amber Reeves' mother Maud Pember Reeves wrote the Fabian survey of poverty in Vauxhall, *Round About a Pound a Week* (1909, reissued by Virago in 1979). Many years later, in 1949–50, Amber Reeves – by this time Mrs Blanco White – was acting principal of Morley College.

One more women's network must be mentioned in connection with Morley College. In 1906 Ralph Vaughan Williams and Cecil Sharp gave lecture recitals on English folk songs and dances, then enjoying a renaissance. Later Vaughan Williams and Gustav Holst taught at Morley for many years. During their time the first country dance class was set up, in 1912; its tutor, Miss Walsh, was secretary of Cecil Sharp's newly-formed English Folk Dance Society. Readers of Elsie Oxenham's 'Abbey School' books for girls will recognise the importance of women's friendship networks in the country dancing world.[21] It became the second most popular subject at Morley between the wars, and the Folk Dance Club won many prizes at competitions.

Many of Elsie Oxenham's characters were based on real officers of the English Folk Dance Society; and it is interesting to note that one of this circle, Clemence Housman, sister of A.E. and Laurence, had lived in Kennington in the 1880s while a student at the City and Guilds School of Art in Kennington Park Road. Perhaps she knew some of the Old Vic and Morley women or her neighbours from the Lady Margaret Hall Settlement. Later as a suffragette – she designed the banners for the Women's Social and Political Union – she certainly knew Cicely Hamilton, Ethel Smyth and their friends; and in the twenties she must have known Elsie Oxenham's folk-dancing circle. Like the Benson family, all three of the Housmans were primarily interested in relationships with those of their own sex.[22]

Lilian Baylis

Lilian Baylis (1874–1937) is the best-known of our North Lambeth women. She appears in *Who's Who* and the *Dictionary of National Biography*. She has been the subject of one full-length biography, and the main character in half a dozen studies of the Old Vic and Sadler's Wells, the two theatres she managed and in a sense created. There is a portrait of her in each theatre. But justice has not been done; she still needs a sympathetic biography by a feminist who will not claim, as 'Richard Findlater' (pen name of Kenneth Bruce Findlater Bain) did, that because she had no male lover she had no private life. Her work, wrote Findlater, was her life. Since he admitted that she left few personal records and seemed to have covered her tracks pretty thoroughly, one wonders at the grounds for this assertion.[23] When women destroy all evidence of their personal lives, this should immediately alert us. The fact that so many women in the 1930s did this – for instance, Baylis' friend Cicely Hamilton – suggests that the lesbian witch-hunt which followed the trial of Radclyffe Hall's novel *The Well of Loneliness* in 1928 may have forced them underground. It was simply not safe even to be suspected of lesbianism in the 1930s; and all single women, especially those with close women friends, were under suspicion. None of this concerned Richard Findlater, who simply wrote that 'Lilian Mary Baylis has sometimes been romanticised as a Cockney Cinderella who achieved a throne without a prince'.[24]

Lilian Baylis was the eldest of the five surviving children of two musicians, her mother being a sister of Emma Cons. From childhood the whole family were professional performers: Lilian played the piano, violin, mandolin and guitar; she sang and gave music lessons, and at the age of 15, after a very interrupted schooling (she regretted her lack of education all her life), she became a full-time teacher. She was a frequent entertainer at her aunt's Victoria Music Hall. But in 1890 the Baylis family emigrated to South Africa, where they toured giving musical shows. Lilian Baylis organised a ladies' orchestra and gave lessons in Johannesburg. In South Africa, aged 19, she became engaged to a gold prospector. When after three years she broke it off he disappeared into the middle of Africa and was never seen again.

In 1898 Emma Cons asked her niece to come back to England to take over the management of the Old Vic. It was Lilian Baylis' opportunity; she widened the theatre's repertoire to include symphony concerts, films and excerpts from opera. During the first world war, now licensed to produce plays, the Old Vic became established as the national home for Shakespeare; in the years between 1914 and 1923 all his plays were performed there, frequently with women playing male roles. Baylis' other main venture was the refurbishment of Sadler's Wells Theatre in Islington, which re-opened in 1931 as the Old Vic of North London. As the Old Vic developed into the National Theatre, Sadler's Wells concentrated on opera and ballet and led the way to the English National Opera and the Royal Ballet.

So much for Lilian Baylis' public life; what about the private? While both her aunts lived, she shared a house with them in Moreton Place, Lambeth, now demolished. After Emma Cons' death Ellen Cons and her niece moved to 27 Stockwell Park Road. Ellen Cons died in 1920 and Lilian Baylis in 1937. Here is Richard Findlater on Baylis' relationship with Emma Cons:

> Lilian and Emmie were not only bound by ties of family affection. They were, in some ways, much alike – not least in the settled celibacy of their private lives (though they both enjoyed working with men), and their dependence on and, at the same time, empire over a circle of faithful female friends and disciples.[25]

(Note the patronising use of first names, often found in biographies of women, never in those of men.) According to the dictionary 'celibacy' means the unmarried state, though we tend today to associate it with lack of sexual activity: here (of course) heterosexual activity is assumed. But Findlater treats the women's friendships with other women not as equal but as simultaneously dependent and tyrannical. Indeed, he represents Baylis' sexual energies as sublimated in both work and power relationships which took the form of intense hatreds and extreme crushes, the latter on men, though women (he said) often had crushes on her. Note this choice of language, which would not have been used in the case of a man: 'She attracted lesbians, although there seems to be no question of her having had any overt homosexual inclinations herself, and indeed she was slow to recognize them in others.'[26] We have no proof that Lilian Baylis engaged in genital contact with other women; it is hard to imagine what sort of proof would be available. But we have enough evidence of the social milieu in which she moved to cast some doubt on this assertion by Findlater. Who were Baylis' closest friends? He says her best friend was Louie Davey, who accompanied her on a world cruise in 1910. Other intimates included her ex-fiancé's sister, Harriet Webster; Katie Moss, composer of songs including the 'Floral Dance'; the more famous composer Ethel Smyth, already mentioned; Winifred Holtby, novelist and journalist; and Cicely Hamilton, actress, dramatic and feminist, who wrote the first history of the Old Vic. Baylis bought a hut near Cicely Hamilton's converted tram in Surrey as a holiday home, and they spent a lot of time together. Through Hamilton she joined the women's professional organisation, the Soroptomists; she also knew, and was advised on financial matters by the founder of the Business and Professional Women's Association in Britain, Miss Gordon Holmes, a stockbroker. These, together with the administrators and actresses who worked at the Old Vic and Sadler's Wells, were Lilian Baylis' female circle.

Now who were *their* other friends? Ethel Smyth knew just about everyone – certainly many women whom we now judge to have been lesbians. Both Minnie and Nelly Benson were close friends of hers, and so was Virginia Woolf. Smyth was particularly friendly with a network of women active in the arts and the suffrage movement. These included Edith Craig, actress–producer daughter of Ellen Terry, and her companions Christabel Marshall, who called herself Christopher St John and wrote, among other things, a biography of Ethel Smyth, and the painter Clare (known as Tony) Atwood. These three women lived in a ménage-à-trois at Smallhythe in Kent where they were regularly visited by other friends including Radclyffe Hall and Una Troubridge, Virginia Woolf and Vita Sackville-West. Cicely Hamilton was also a close friend of the Smallhythe trio.[27] It is inconceivable that Lilian Baylis could have mixed happily with such women without realising and accepting that many of them were emotionally and sexually involved with women.

It is true that she refused to employ Edith Craig (though she had employed her mother) at the Old Vic, saying 'We don't want another woman here. And anyway we don't want Edy. She would upset the staff.'[28] But this is unlikely to be a reference to Craig's sexual preferences, since many lesbian actresses had appeared at the Old Vic. Indeed, according to Richard Findlater, it had a reputation for being a 'lesbian stronghold', and Lilian Baylis was often assumed to be a lesbian, partly because she was

> a dominating unmarried woman whose closest friends and colleagues (monks and clergymen aside) were mostly women (most of them unmarried); and because those who did not know her believed her, quite wrongly, to be mannish and butch. Lilian was, in fact, for all her brusqueness and bossiness, a very feminine woman.[29]

(Observe the stereotyped image of the lesbian here which, for all its contradictions and confusions, the author does not feel it necessary to explain.) Chaste, Lilian Baylis may have been – or she may not – but a biography which dwells on her relationships with a rejected (and dead) fiancé and a priest–confessor, but not on her friendships with some of the most prominent women of the day, can hardly be said to present an adequate picture of the person.

Gordon Holmes devoted a chapter to Lilian Baylis in her autobiography *In Love With Life*. The niece of Baylis' deceased ex-fiancé, Holmes had as a child visited Lilian Baylis and Emma Cons in Lambeth and been to the Old Vic. But her mother disapproved of the association, and so they did not meet again for 30 years, when they came across each other at a women's club. (Women's clubs proliferated between the wars, and must have been wonderful places for networking.) 'From then onwards till her death I admired and deeply cared about her,' wrote Holmes.[30] The nice thing about Gordon Holmes is that she never prevaricates about her love for women. She always knew she would never marry, and described her friendship with Dr Helen Boyle, to whom her autobiography is dedicated, as 'above all other things in all my fortunate life, the fortunate thing I have been most profoundly grateful for'.[31] Dr Boyle founded the first British psychiatric hospital for women in Brighton in 1905, where a congenial feminist network of medical women and their supporters soon gathered. It was in Brighton in 1921 that Dr Louisa Martindale helped set up the New Sussex Hospital for women, whose subscribers included Elizabeth Robins, actress, writer and former suffragette, and Viscountess Rhondda, the proprietor of *Time and Tide* for whom not only Elizabeth Robins wrote but also Cicely Hamilton and Winifred Holtby (also a friend of Gordon Holmes). How did they know each other, one wonders? Martindale (who lived with a woman companion, the Hon. Ismay Fitzgerald, and whose widowed mother had been a close friend of Minnie Benson) met Hamilton during the first world war when both were serving in the hospital at Royaumont in France,[32] together with a number of other women including Louisa Aldrich-Blake, Dean of the London School of Medicine for Women, who became consulting surgeon at the New Sussex. Aldrich-Blake lived with Rosamond Wigram.[33] Both Robins and Rhondda were divorcees; the former lived with Octavia Wilberforce, who was Virginia Woolf's doctor, and the latter with Theodora Bosanquet, another journalist, and biographer of Harriet Martineau.[34]

If these paragraphs read like a confusion of repeated names and overlapping circles, this is to make the point that the women's networks of the interwar years did intersect in some quite remarkable ways. It cannot be an accident that two very different groups such as the women doctors and the theatrical–feminist set knew each other. *They must have had something in common.* Lilian Baylis is interesting as an example of a woman whose circles of friends spread outwards from the local connections in North Lambeth through the London theatrical and professional women's scene into a wider national network of – what? Of unmarried, woman-centred women, many of whom were lesbians.

Conclusion

In response to modern feminism, historians have begun to tackle the task of writing women back into history. This endeavour, though essential, is not by itself enough. We need also to reconsider and revise the biographies of women who have *not* been forgotten, those who have been claimed as 'famous' by men. That very act of co-opting should put us on our guard: what purpose do these women serve? How have their stories been distorted to fit a patriarchal ideology? What lessons can we learn from the reality of their lives and their subsequent fate at the hands of historians?

One aspect of women's biography that deserves close attention is that of friendship. Patriarchal history decrees that the only woman worthy of notice is the one who has danced upon men's stage, to a script prepared and directed by men, in company with other men. Women are rarely permitted to be seen acting in concert with other women or by themselves. In this perversion of history, men whose roles were really minor are allowed to dominate the stage while the vital female members of the cast are crowded off.

The reality is that women have women friends and women

lovers and that these are central, not peripheral relationships, however much society tells us that our lives should revolve around men. All the women in this chapter had extensive circles of female friends who gave them professional, social, emotional and domestic support, and whose significance, and even existence, has been ignored, distorted or denied by biographers and historians. The reason for this is plain. In a heterosexist world women are judged by their relationships with men, can only indeed be *seen* in relationships with men; women without men are invisible, or must be made invisible. There is always the fear that other women might be tempted to follow their example – an intolerable threat to male supremacy.

5
'Embittered, Sexless or Homosexual': Attacks on spinster teachers 1918 – 39

Alison Oram

An earlier version of this piece appeared in Arina Angerman et al., Current Issues in Women's History, *Routledge, 1989.*

During the interwar years in Britain, the perceived image of the spinster teacher suffered an increasingly negative change, resulting in the stereotype of an embittered, thwarted, sexually frustrated or deviant woman.

This can be seen in the substance and tone of the many attacks which were made on single women teachers by the press, by anti-feminist men teachers, and sometimes by the local authorities which employed them. I shall examine the terms of this increased hostility and suggest some reasons for it, and then go on to look at the response made by women teachers in the context of interwar feminism.

My interest in spinster teachers and how they were portrayed stemmed in the first place from my wider research into the position of women teachers between the wars, and especially their response to the marriage bar.[1] The teachers I discuss worked in the state sector of education in England and Wales.

They were mostly elementary (i.e. primary) school teachers although some reference is made to state secondary school teachers. School teaching was the only profession in which large numbers of women could earn a salary which was much above subsistence level, although they still received only four fifths of men's pay. Schoolteaching was a public role; women teachers were visible, and indeed important figures in their local communities. They also, of course, had authority and influence over the children in their schools.

During the 1920s and 1930s most women teachers were spinsters. This was due to the fact that in the early 1920s the majority of local education authorities introduced regulations requiring women teachers to resign on marriage. The censuses of 1921 and 1931 show that around 85 per cent of all women teachers (in all types of school) were unmarried. Separate figures for elementary schools confirm this pattern, while for secondary schools the figure was probably higher. The actual number of spinster teachers working in state schools was about 150,000 throughout the period.

The large number of single women teachers at this time could also be explained by demographic factors. There had been more women than men in the population since the mid-nineteenth century, when it was first seen as a problem, and the high rates of mortality suffered by men during the first world war exacerbated the pattern. This situation obviously had an impact on a generation of women teachers, although throughout the interwar period the balance between the sexes steadily became more equal and the marriage rate rose.[2] While the demographic facts showing women's reduced chances of marriage cannot be questioned, they do obscure the possibility that some women may have *chosen* not to marry, and that teaching may have been a route to secure this goal. None the less, the predominance of spinster teachers could be explained by circumstances beyond their control: the loss of men in the war and the marriage bar. Why, then, should women teachers be abused as spinsters?

My investigation into this contradiction was further prompted by my involvement in the Lesbian History Group in London, and by the general questions which were emerging as important ones to ask about lesbian history and how the definition and control of women's sexuality had implications for all women.

One major set of questions has concentrated on the effects of the newly developed science of sex – or sexology – at the turn of the century. While it identified women's capacity for sexual enjoyment, sexology privileged heterosexuality as the only acceptable type of sexual expression and created a particular definition of 'lesbian'.[3] I wanted to examine how far these ideas, which increasingly stigmatised celibate women too, applied to a particular group of unmarried women – teachers – in the period from 1918 to 1939. Did their treatment by colleagues and by the popular press, reflect this wider change?

There has also been an important debate about the definition and use of the word 'lesbian' (see Chapter 1).[4] Lesbian feminist historians today wish to reject an entirely sexual definition of themselves. That is how male sexologists have defined and controlled lesbians. While stressing sexual love between women as the primary significance of lesbianism, a feminist approach has also emphasised the position of lesbians as women outside heterosexuality who by their very existence challenge the myth of its inevitability. If heterosexuality is one of the ways in which men's power over women is maintained, then lesbianism is or can be a threat to that power. This aspect of resistance involves all women outside heterosexuality, including celibate or unmarried women. Like lesbians, they are all women who are not subject to men's social and sexual power through a personal relationship. Thus although attacks were made on unmarried women teachers primarily as *spinsters*, rather than as lesbians, it is probable that they were maligned for being outside heterosexuality. The use of lesbianism as a stigma is a tactic for controlling all women. While individual spinsters may well have felt that they had 'missed out' on marriage, they none the less could be seen as a threat because they were outside conventional womanhood. Some spinster teachers were undoubtedly 'lesbians', whatever definition we take, but all were affected, and their status attacked, by accusations that they were warped, repressed and deviant.

However I don't want to offer an explanation entirely dependent on changing ideas about women's sexuality. The particular kind of heterosexuality which was encouraged in this period assumed women's financial dependence on their husbands. Men also feared economically independent married women, hence the marriage bar, the regulation which in many areas required women teachers to resign on marriage. There were also economic reasons for these attacks on spinster teachers. It is important to look at women teachers' feminist politics and their position within the profession *vis-à-vis* men. Women teachers had a particularly high profile in this period because of their battles for equal opportunities in the profession. The most important issues were equal pay, equal promotion prospects and the marriage bar. A great deal of antagonism was created between women and men teachers as a result, and the National Union of Teachers (NUT) was split. Just after the first world war, some women teachers broke away to form the feminist National Union of Women Teachers (NUWT), and at much the same time a group of anti-feminist men teachers left to set up the National Association of Schoolmasters. Thus women teachers posed a feminist challenge to their male colleagues.[5]

One of my main sources for remarks about and attacks on spinster teachers in this period was the *Times Educational Supplement*. This weekly paper reflected informed opinion in the educational world and also reported speeches made at teachers' conferences and in local government debates. In contrast the popular press presented more sensationalised attacks on spinster teachers. To gauge the NUWT's response I used their reported speeches, together with articles in their journal *The Woman Teacher*, which reflected their unified public face. But since the union avoided discussing the issue of sexuality openly, more revealing material was found in personal correspondence in their archive.

Although I hope to show that unmarried women teachers were attacked as spinsters in a very negative way and with increasingly sexualised overtones, I have continued to use the loaded term spinster rather than the more neutral word 'single' in describing them. This is what they called themselves, and some of them were clearly trying to show that they were not ashamed of being spinsters.

Sexology and spinsters

Abuse of and contempt for spinsters was not of course a new development of the 1920s. In the Victorian period popular prejudice had labelled spinsters redundant, superfluous women, and scorned them as old maids who had failed in the marriage market:

> For what else do women come into the world but to be good wives? . . . Poor profitless, forlorn creatures they are, when they live single and get to be old; unless indeed they are rich enough to keep up an establishment, with a parcel of dogs and cats and parrots.[6]

Women's sexuality in the interwar period, as in the nineteenth century, was still to a large extent conflated with maternal instinct.[7] For women teachers this had particular relevance. Maternal feeling sometimes seemed to be as much part of the job description for women teachers as intellectual capacity. As one educational writer put it: 'Indeed, this very mother-love is the most characteristic feature of the born teacher of "babies" – the hall-mark of her high calling.'[8] This commonplace observation was applied not only to infant teachers but right up to secondary school level. Teaching was seen as a substitute for actual motherhood, for those women who were unfortunate enough not to be able to find a real husband and children. 'Teaching was the greatest profession open to women, except motherhood itself.'[9]

It was rather a contradiction then, that single women teachers were increasingly criticised for not being actual mothers themselves, despite the fact that they would have lost their jobs on marriage in most areas. The pressure on women to marry and produce children had become more intense and overt by the 1930s, in the context of alarm over the falling birth-rate. There was a renewed emphasis on teaching mothercraft and domestic subjects in schools in the 1920s and 1930s. Women who were childless were seen as unfulfilled and abnormal, and this prescription of women's role as mothers had a particular edge for teachers.

Single women teachers just could not win. On the one hand they were necessarily using their maternal qualities in their work. But on the other hand they were wasting their eugenic qualities as 'the cream of British womanhood'. Spinster teachers' lack of participation in motherhood was not only inauspicious for the future of the state and of the race but, if they didn't watch out, it could also be psychologically harmful to themselves.

Abuse of spinster teachers as old maids who lacked the social and sexual qualities to find a husband was not new, but it acquired a new edge during the 1920s and 1930s. This was a period when the notion of marriage as a psychological as well as social necessity for women was introduced. Popular sexology texts proclaimed that sexual relations with men was the only way to psychological health and fulfilment for women. They characterised women without male sexual partners as frustrated, a prey to complexes and neuroses.

By the 1930s, women teachers who failed to marry were subjected to warnings with ominous psychological overtones. In an address to the 1933 conference, the president of the Association of Assistant Mistresses declared that most women desired marriage, but if it didn't happen then women teachers should use their energy in their work and avoid becoming abnormal and bitter. The answer to this newly discovered problem was 'great power of sublimation on the part of the unmarried teacher'.[10] Psychological theories would have carried particular weight in the world of education where psychology was becoming fashionable. Both education policy and teachers themselves were influenced by it during the interwar years; for instance there was

104

a plethora of books on child development written for the teacher.

Attacks on women teachers' professional capacity gained force if they were couched in sexual terms, and especially when they came from the medical world. This began to happen in the 1930s. 'A warning of the danger of rearing a generation of "spinsters' sons", by allowing boys in elementary schools to be taught only by women, was uttered by Dr H. Crichton-Miller . . . They were likely to be warped in their development.'[11] This accusation was part of a debate over whether boys should only be taught by men teachers.[12] But neither were spinster teachers necessarily welcome in girls' schools, for different reasons.

The growing sexology literature suggested that single women and female friendships were potentially perverted. Thus as well as supposedly suffering heterosexual frustration and its consequences, spinster teachers were also at times depicted as more sinister. During the 1920s and 1930s there was a widening public awareness of lesbianism, or rather, lesbianism as defined by the sexologists, and by the 1930s spinster teachers were subject to much more aggressive attacks in sexual terms. In 1935 this report of an educational conference appeared in a national newspaper:

Dr Williams had dealt with the effect on the temperament of the ductless glands, and said that games such as hockey and lacrosse develop that part of the suprarenal gland which presides over the combative element of a person's character. 'You cannot confine the desire and aptitude for combat to cricket and football,' he said. 'They inevitably appear in the whole character, and what was originally a gentle, feminine girl becomes harsh and bellicose in all relations to life. The women who have the responsibility of teaching these girls are, many of them themselves embittered, sexless or homosexual hoydens who try to mould the girls into their own pattern. And far too often they succeed.' Dr Williams declared that girls who have no desire to play combative games are cajoled and coerced into taking part by 'these thin-lipped, flat-chested, sadistic creatures.'[13]

This kind of accusation was fairly extreme; most did not go so far. What is interesting about this particularly outrageous example is that by the 1930s it was possible for attacks of this type to be made, and to be backed up by supposedly serious medical evidence. This one echoes the sexologists' definition of real lesbians as being masculine creatures who were a danger to normal women, especially if, as teachers, they had influence over young girls.[14]

The date of this attack is significant. Media interest in lesbians began during and after the first world war. In a scandal which hit the headlines in 1918, the dancer Maude Allan failed in her libel action to counter the charge that she was a lesbian. Radclyffe Hall won an action for slander in 1920 which was also reported in the press. In 1921 lesbianism was discussed in Parliament, but the attempt to bring it within the scope of the criminal law in the same way as male homosexuality was defeated.[15] But it was the prosecution in 1928 of Radclyffe Hall's novel in defence of lesbianism, *The Well of Loneliness*, which really marks a watershed in public awareness of lesbianism. This obscenity trial aroused a huge amount of publicity that identified the existence of lesbianism, and led to suspicion being cast on single women, a suspicion which could be extended to spinster teachers. This harsher condemnation of women's friendships as perverse after 1928 has been identified by other writers.[16]

These new ideas and awareness about sexuality were frequently used to attack feminism. It has been argued that the sex reform movement of the 1920s and 1930s directly challenged militant feminism. The newly invented notion of the frigid woman became a problem of major concern, and a term applied to spinster feminists who had rejected marriage, allegedly on the grounds of 'man-hating'. One sex reformer suggested the harm that could be done by spinster teachers:

As a teacher, the frigide wields considerable power over the unformed mind of her pupils. She rarely takes pains to examine the justice of her indictment of man, and her bias is obvious to those whom she instructs. Her prudery is often imitated by the girls she is able to influence.[17]

The insinuation that spinster teachers were lesbians was also used when attacking them as feminists. Throughout the nineteenth and twentieth centuries feminists have been attacked in terms of their sexual status; as spinsters who, it was implied, could not get a man and were therefore against men. They were unfeminine, power-hungry, and wanted to be men themselves. At the 1924 conference of the National Association of Schoolmasters it was said, 'The claim of the teacher feminist was no longer for equal rights, but for the canonisation of the spinster'.[18] By 1939 women teachers were accused by the NAS of wanting to be men. 'There is in the teaching profession a small politically minded minority of advanced feminists who curse their Maker that He did not allow them to enter this world wearing trousers.'[19]

Anti-feminism and economics

The sexual threat that spinster teachers were seen to pose cannot be disentangled from the economic threat that they presented to men. They were attacked as sexually independent spinsters and as feminists, but also as economically powerful women who challenged men's authority by demanding equal opportunities in the profession. The stigmatisation of spinster teachers wasn't solely a result of sexology but also part of a postwar climate which was hostile to women's economic and political power.

During and just after the first world war, women extended their sphere in 'male' areas of work and won the vote for women over 30.[20] Many groups of men feared and opposed the emancipation of women. In the slump just after the war women workers were accused of stealing men's jobs and were told to 'go back to the home'. Women's work was considered to be marriage and the home, not outside employment, and domestic values were re-emphasised. Men's anxiety focused on the greater opportunities and higher wages for women that war had opened up. Having experienced a greater degree of economic independence, women might have less incentive to provide domestic services in marriage for men and children, and might even be able to avoid marriage altogether. This fear was at times quite explicitly expressed.

Women teachers were in the forefront of the economic challenge to patriarchal power relations. They had a high profile in feminist campaigns generally and were very involved in various battles concerning their own profession throughout the period. During the first world war, women teachers obtained better representation within the NUT and got equal pay accepted as union policy. Marriage bars were relaxed in most areas until the early 1920s and more women became teachers in boys' schools. Women teachers obtained a higher proportion of men's pay than before although they did not win equal pay. The cuts in education spending caused by the recession of the early 1920s (and again in the 1930s) destroyed some of the women teachers' gains and also increased men teachers' anxiety to safeguard their jobs.

Equal pay was one focus of discontent. Antagonism towards women teachers' economic position was frequently expressed by the National Association of Schoolmasters (NAS), or by men teachers with similar views. Male control of the NUT hierarchy ensured that the union quietly ignored their equal-pay policy throughout the interwar years. It is likely that many of the men teachers in the NUT privately agreed with NAS policies, but didn't want to lose the benefits of belonging to the largest union.

In fact national pay awards in the interwar period fixed women teachers' pay at four fifths of the male rate. The NAS argued that the differentiation should be even greater. For example at the union's 1937 conference a Mr Rice:

said they had no desire to deprive women teachers of anything and they were not anti-women, but they were concerned about their own existence. What was an adequate wage for the spinster teacher was entirely inadequate for the family man.[21]

The battle over equal pay versus the family wage (i.e. an income sufficient to support a wife and children) continued intermittently throughout the period. Concern and hostility was expressed about women teachers' standard of living in relation to men's. It was frequently alleged by the NAS that even with unequal salaries single women teachers could afford to take holidays abroad and run cars, while men had to take on additional work such as evening classes in order to fulfil their family responsibilities.

Women teachers were seen as being paid too highly as women workers, irrespective of the work they were performing. It was quite a commonly held view that men teachers should get more money, not just for economic reasons – their assumed family responsibilities – but on the grounds of sex superiority alone. They were paying

> too much money to bachelor women. . . . It must be obvious to anyone that in starting a young man at £172 10s., scale 2, and a girl of the same age and same scale with £160 was grossly unfair in the social system of the country. It was productive of late marriages, and was inclined to elevate the bachelor girl to a position in this country that she should not attain.[22]

An article in the *Times Educational Supplement* in 1932 commented that 'they can usually earn a steady wage, higher than their fathers' or brothers'; and if the teacher happens to be a slip of a girl this is not pleasant'.[23] Clearly, women weren't supposed to earn enough to be able to live comfortably and independently.

Nor were they supposed to be in positions of power and authority over male colleagues. Continuing concern by both women and men teachers that the other sex was gaining a disproportionate number of headships also led to acrimony.

'Nearly 4,000 women were teaching purely boys' classes. Only a nation heading for the madhouse would force on men, many married with families, such a position as service under spinster headmistresses.'[24] Thus increased hostility towards spinster teachers in the interwar period was part of a postwar backlash against women and against feminism in particular, a backlash which was strengthened by sexology and which reflected economic issues.

The feminist response

How did spinster teachers respond to this stigmatisation? Of considerable interest is their reaction to the hostility that had been expressed in sexual terms. One significant development was the establishing of the National Union of Women Teachers (NUWT), the small feminist teachers' union which split from the National Union of Teachers in 1920. The majority of the most active feminists left the NUT to work within the NUWT at this point, and the women who remained in the NUT were not at all vocal about any women's issue which might be seen as divisive.

The evidence shows that feminist teachers in the NUWT themselves took on to some extent the negative attitudes towards spinsters, especially when arguing for a married woman's right to work. They ignored or deflected attacks which used sexological ideas about frustrated spinsters or lesbian teachers. Altogether they were on the defensive, having lost a feminist political analysis of sexuality which had existed before the first world war.

Other historians have shown that many feminists, during the years before the first world war, argued that remaining unmarried was a personally and politically important decision for women to make.[25] For them, celibacy plus the freedom of a career or work within the women's movement was a more rewarding life than the subordination of marriage, and slavery to men's sexual demands. If women remained unmarried, this would improve the position of the spinster and indeed all women, give women a real choice between marriage and spinsterhood, and would eventually improve the conditions of marriage for women. Among prominent feminists who promoted celibacy in this period were Christabel Pankhurst and Cicely Hamilton, in her book *Marriage as a Trade*, published in 1909.[26] Celibacy may even have been used as a label by turn-of-the-century feminists to indicate that they prioritised women in their lives.

Just before the first world war however, a different attitude was developing among some other feminists, which was to become more influential between the wars. These feminists were influenced by sexology, especially the writings of Havelock Ellis. They supported 'free unions', divorce law reform and the use of birth control to separate sex from reproduction. These women, including Stella Browne, Dora Russell and Marie Stopes, demanded that women had a right to sexual pleasure, in heterosexual sex. But at the same time – in accordance with the growing sex reform movement which stressed the necessity of heterosexual intercourse for women and the dangers of sexual repression – they also attacked lesbians and spinsters who remained outside heterosexuality.[27]

This changing politics of spinsterhood had some parallels with general changes within feminism. During the interwar period a divergence developed within the women's movement between old-style equal rights feminism on the one hand, and the new feminism or welfare feminism on the other, with the latter predominating by the 1930s. The equal-rights feminists, having won the franchise for women, were concerned with equality under the law and with obtaining 'a fair field and no favour' for women in employment. New feminism, associated with Eleanor Rathbone and the National Union of Societies for Equal Citizenship, stressed reforms which took account of the different nature and circumstances of women's lives compared to men's, such as demands for family allowances, birth control and other benefits for women as mothers.

While the equal-rights feminists at any rate continued to concern themselves with spinsters' rights, this was mainly in the fields of employment and housing. They did not continue to assert the political value of celibacy, although lone voices like Winifred Holtby did challenge the increasingly prevalent view of the frustrated and neurotic spinster.[28] Interwar feminists did criticise marriage, demanding more rights for wives, divorce law reform and so on, but they did not advocate avoiding it, as earlier feminists had done. The increasingly influential new feminism only rarely questioned men's power in marriage and heterosexuality and did not generally include any positive vision of the spinster's role in feminist action. By 1930 the feminist and Labour MP Ellen Wilkinson – herself unmarried – could write (about spinster teachers):

> The Suffragettes were hungry for life and for freedom. They fought to open the great storehouses of learning to women, that they might make a big thing of life. Has that vision become blurred, till all it means is the right to a bed-sitting room and a pensioned old age? It is not good enough. There is something wrong when thousands of women spend the best years of life discontented, lonely and thwarted.[29]

In arguing for a full life for women including the right to personal relationships, Wilkinson suggested that there was no longer a coherent and exciting politics of spinsterhood which included a further option – that of women's communities.

So, where did the National Union of Women Teachers fit into the world of interwar feminism? Clearly its emphasis and campaigning focused on employment rights of women teachers, especially the fight for equal pay, and this put it firmly in the 'equal-rights' camp. The union worked closely with other equal-rights feminist groups, but it did also have links with some of the more welfare orientated groups.

The women in the NUWT had formerly worked as a feminist pressure group within the National Union of Teachers, but had broken away from the main union to form a separate organisation at the end of the first world war, believing that they would never be able to fight unhindered for feminist aims such as equal pay within a mixed organisation. They were a strongly feminist group of women teachers, a group which numbered between 5000 and 10,000, with branches all over the country. Practically all its members were single women – as were the NUT's – because of the marriage bar. Many NUWT members had formerly been active in the campaign for women's suffrage. Two of its official organisers had been among the leadership of the Women's Social and Political Union, the Pankhursts' militant suffragette organisation, and several of its leading figures had been involved in the Women's Freedom League, another militant group before the first world war. As feminists of this generation it is likely that some of the older spinster teachers in the NUWT had remained single as a political decision. But by the 1930s it was evident that a generation gap was emerging between these women and the younger post-suffrage women teachers, and in 1938 a Youth Conference was organised 'to give the younger members some knowledge of the significance of the women's movement.'[30]

This generation gap and its associated political differences over spinster identity within the NUWT was interestingly revealed in its response to the attacks on spinster teachers as sexually frustrated or deviant women. Generally the union seems to have tried to ignore or remain aloof from negative references to spinster teachers. In 1920 it attempted to brush off an attack on the NUWT as being composed of 'jaundiced spinsters'. Their accuser, a man teacher, quoted from a marriage manual to argue that the permanently unmarried were living abnormal lives:

'Those who can marry and do not are thus deliberately disregarding their biological duty to the race to which they belong. Those who would marry but cannot are supremely unfortunate. Both of them are a menace to the society in which they live . . .'. Now I submit that the N.F.W.T. [i.e. the NUWT] is dominated by such as are here described, and that the unrest exhibited by that organisation is not caused by inadequate salaries, but by the morbid condition of its mili-

113

tant members.

The union's journal *The Woman Teacher* published this letter but refused to comment on this accusation as it was in such 'bad taste'. 'It is so unspeakable that we refrain from commenting on [these] points.'[31]

But sometimes the attacks were so outrageous that the NUWT felt compelled to respond, as they did to the attack made by Dr Williams in 1935 that: 'The women who have the responsibility of teaching these girls are, many of them themselves embittered, sexless or homosexual hoydens who try to mould the girls into their own pattern.' His accusation was angrily repudiated by the NUWT but, very interestingly, in terms of women's sexual impulses being *maternal* ones: 'he should know that in the vast majority of cases a woman teacher's work is a complete outlet for her maternal instincts. Her womanly impulses are sublimated and diverted, but splendidly employed.'[32] The NUWT was resorting to an earlier idea of women's sexuality in order to deflect the attack on spinsters.

A tendency for the union to ignore spinsters' rights was first identified by some members in 1934.

I . . . suggest that the problem of the woman worker and also the status of women as a whole will be easier solved if a little more decent attention is paid to the bachelor woman and her welfare and dignity as a worker. . . . This preoccupation with the rights and desires of the married woman has reached such proportions and the statements publicly made and circulated have become at times so disparaging both to the house-keeping family woman and to the wage-earning spinster . . .[33]

The major clash within the union occurred in the context of the NUWT's campaign against the marriage bar. The NUWT was concerned to get the bar lifted, and part of their case involved arguing that the experience of marriage and motherhood enhanced women's teaching skills. The implication of this, however, was that single women were less competent. Feminists might also fall into displaying negative attitudes towards spinsters if they were arguing that the marriage bar limited women's choices in life.

In May 1935, an NUWT official, Elsie Fisher, wrote an article for a popular newspaper on the marriage bar, with the headline 'Where Are My Children? Spinsterhood Forced on the Teacher'. This argued that the marriage bar forced young women teachers into clandestine marriages and illicit unions with men, and ended:

> Young teachers all over the country refuse to remain celibate, refuse to see their lives thwarted, refuse to deny themselves the love and companionship that means a fuller, deeper, richer life. Why indeed should they be sterilised by the order of town councillors?[34]

Note how she portrays spinsterhood as so negative – as thwarted, denied and sterilised. One older NUWT member, Miss Morrison, took exception to the article, especially the suggestion that many young women teachers lived with men. She wrote to Ethel Froud, the General Secretary of the union to complain that this was a serious libel on the habits and ethics of young women teachers. In the correspondence on this matter between Elsie Fisher and Ethel Froud, it emerged that Miss Fisher, rather than deploring free love, as she does in the article, in fact privately endorsed it. 'As you probably know I personally believe profoundly in companionate marriage and the freedom of the Russian system with regard to this relationship [meaning free love], but I carefully avoided committing the Union to this . . .'. Elsie Fisher, then, presents herself as a good example of the postwar sex-reform type of feminist thinking on sexuality. In her letter to Miss Froud she goes on to say, 'I am really more concerned with your criticism than with that of the writer of the letter, because I hadn't realised how deep a division of opinion could exist *inside* the women's movement on this question'.[35] She underestimated the strength of Miss Morrison's convictions as 'an old campaigner in the fight for Votes for Women', and, for that matter, Miss Froud's, who belonged to the same political generation.[36]

Two months later, in July 1935, came the debate in the London County Council over the raising of the marriage bar in London. This was the fruition of the NUWT's long campaign over this issue. The report of the council's Education Committee stated that 'the duties of both doctor and teacher call for certain personal qualities which may be thought to be enriched by marriage . . .'. The *Times Educational Supplement* also commented that a staff composed of celibate women teachers tended to create an over-academic, cloistral atmosphere in schools, too much divorced from the normal home life to which the pupils were accustomed. In the debate itself one London councillor 'agreed that they should not face with equanimity the prospect of the teaching service being entirely filled by spinsters'.[37]

Miss Agnes Dawson, a London councillor sponsored by the NUWT, also argued this line. The *Times Educational Supplement* reported her as saying:

given a good teacher, marriage must bring fresh experience and more human understanding. To debar married teachers the opportunity to serve was to do a disservice to education. Men would not send their boys to schools where all the male teachers were celibates. They would consider it an unhealthy atmosphere. She claimed the same for the girls.[38]

At this, Miss Morrison wrote again to the union to deplore the line that married women were better than single women teachers. She said that it was unfortunate that progressive women should still, in 1935, consider a woman incomplete unless linked with a man:

That 'wives give best work' or are 'enriched by marriage' (especially modern marriage) or are given 'better understanding' or are in any way superior to a celibate woman I absolutely challenge; and a Union largely composed of devoted celibate teachers, giving their creative energy unstinted to

116

their profession, that allows this attitude and these statements to go unchallenged is no good to me . . .

In her reply, Miss Ethel Froud (the General Secretary) blamed the statement on the distortion of the male press, repeated the union line that married women should be as free as single women to follow their profession, but added, 'No, we can't have it said that we celibates are only some fraction of a human being.' Miss Morrison continued to press her point, saying that women are not improved, or their intelligence augmented by intimate physical contact with a member of the male sex. Also that the union must not imply that spinsters are unhappy, or go back to considering them less fortunate. Ethel Froud replied that to a large extent she shared her feelings.[39]

These fundamentally different attitudes towards spinsterhood among women in the NUWT reflect the changing position of mainstream feminism towards sexuality in the interwar period. Miss Morrison was expressing her very positive political identity as a spinster in 1935, 20 years or so after it would have ceased to have a resonance for feminists generally. Now, views like Elsie Fisher's – of spinsterhood as a thwarted, negative state – were in the ascendancy in the women's movement, as well as in the wider world.

Conclusion

Hostility towards spinster teachers in the interwar period focused on their failure to marry and produce children, on their unhealthy influence as celibates or lesbians in the schools, on their earning power and on their feminist politics. The popularisation of sexology explains some of these attacks. It underscored heterosexuality as normal, and so any woman outside such a relationship was vulnerable to being labelled as frustrated, unfeminine or lesbian. But the economic context is also important. Postwar unemployment and cuts in public spending led to increasing restrictions on women's work generally, and a back-

117

lash against feminism. Women teachers were strongly union-ised, relatively highly paid, and spoke out as feminists for equal opportunities in their profession. Thus spinster teachers could be seen – and sometimes feared – as a group of economically independent women, not sexually subordinate to men, politically organised and with social power in their communities.

Sexology and the sex reform movement can also be blamed for the feeble response from spinster teachers. Without a firm critique of male-defined heterosexuality, they no longer had a feminist politics of sexuality to make sense of this stigmatising of spinsters. The women's movement itself in this period increas-ingly emphasised motherhood and incorporated sex reform ideas at the expense of spinsters.[40]

6
You're a Dyke, Angela!
Elsie J. Oxenham and the rise and fall of the schoolgirl story[1]

Rosemary Auchmuty

> Jen's eager eyes widened in delight when Rhoda returned, followed up the drive by a tall, sunny-faced girl in khaki tunic and breeches and big boots, a shady hat covering her yellow hair, which was tied in a bunch of curls behind. Rena was tanned and healthy and straight, strong with a year's work in the moorland garden at Rocklands, and very pleasant to look at. Her gardening outfit was neat and useful, and suited her, and she looked ready for tramping the heather, digging, mowing, tennis, or morris dancing at a moment's notice.
>
> She touched her hat in a boyish salute, as she came up to the couch. Jen stretched out her hands with an eager cry . . .[2]

Friendships have always provided women with vital social, emotional, professional and political support. They are also important in any examination of the construction of sexuality. Tolerated – even encouraged – when perceived to keep women content and not meddling in men's affairs, they become profoundly threatening whenever women seem to be banding together to plot against men's power, either publicly (like the suffragettes) or privately (as lesbians, for instance). Because schoolgirl stories are fundamentally about female strength and bonding, they provide an interesting example of a phenomenon which was at first tolerated and even encouraged, but which came to be seen as a threat of such magnitude it had to be exterminated.

The rise of the schoolgirl story

School stories were a Victorian creation, product of the middle class that emerged in Britain after the Industrial Revolution and rose to cultural domination in the nineteenth century. The long haul up the social ladder was accomplished by means of education. New public schools like Marlborough and Rugby, set up for middle-class boys, were copied later by the pioneers of girls' education at Cheltenham, St Leonard's, Wycombe Abbey and Roedean. Lacking an alternative model for a genuinely equal girls' schooling, feminists like Emily Davies campaigned for a structure and curriculum identical with boys', given the odd concession to feminine accomplishments. They argued that men would never take women seriously unless they could be seen to succeed in the same system. Middle-class girls' schools thus acquired the familiar characteristics of boys' schools – examinations, compulsory games, school uniforms, prefects, a moral code based on honour, loyalty and playing the game – and, of course, they were single-sex institutions. These ideas were taken over in turn by the girls' high schools and passed on, after the Education Acts of 1870 and 1880, to board-school children by ex-students who went into teaching. Hence, although the schoolgirl culture and the books which described it were the privilege of a small proportion of the population, compulsory education created a large new reading public steeped in middle-class ideals and aspirations, who were to become the main market for the schoolgirl story.

The credit for writing the first Victorian school story belongs not to Thomas Hughes for his famed *Tom Brown's School-Days* (1857), but to the feminist and economist Harriet Martineau, whose novel *The Crofton Boys* appeared in 1841. Girls' school stories were a later development. Though authors like L.T. Meade (Mrs Elizabeth Thomasina Smith) produced some amongst a larger output of girls' fiction, the real founder of the genre must be Angela Brazil (1869–1947), who published her first school story in 1906 and went on to write nearly fifty more. The 1920s and 1930s were the heyday of the formula. Its popularity was enhanced by the evolution of the *series* where the same characters featured in a number of books as they traversed the path from schooldays through marriage and motherhood to their daughters' schooldays. For the readers who eagerly awaited each new instalment, a real-life drama seemed to unfold. Angela Brazil did not write series, but popular authors like Elsie J. Oxenham, Dorita Fairlie Bruce and Elinor M. Brent-Dyer were among its most successful exponents.

It is easy to be critical of schoolgirl stories. Most of them had the common faults of popular fiction, were marred by banality, simplism and absurdity, not to speak of values which readers then as well as now must sometimes have found hard to swallow. These issues have been much discussed by literary critics and I do not propose to consider them here. My interest is in school-girl stories as *a source for the history of attitudes to women's friendships*; for as Gillian Avery remarked of one favourite series:

In England in the 1920s and 1930s Elsie J. Oxenham carried this world of intense female relationships even further with her novels of the Abbey Girls. The husbands, if there are any, count for little beside the support that the closely-knit circle of girls give to each other. They suffer each other's griefs acutely and rejoice in their triumphs, and much emotion is expended on the suffering that characters must endure when female friends are torn from them in marriage. . . . *The great popularity of these romances without any masculine element shows that there was a large public who wanted just that.* (my emphasis)[3]

A world of their own

The typical successful writer of schoolgirl stories was female, middle-aged and unmarried. Apart from this, we know little about her; there are few biographies, and the literary critics are notoriously uninterested in these 'inferior' writers. But among those on whom we have some information, one significant common factor emerges: in real life as well as in their writing they devoted their energies to girls and women. Angela Brazil organised parties for local schoolgirls. Elsie Oxenham was an enthusiastic member of the English Folk Dance Society and a Camp Fire Guardian. Elinor M. Brent-Dyer, as well as teaching girls, was interested in folk dancing and the Girl Guides. Dorita Fairlie Bruce was involved in a similar organisation, the Girls' Guildry. To judge by the dedications in their books (dedications are very revealing), their chief friends were women. Indeed, Bruce, Oxenham and Brent-Dyer all dedicated books to one another.

What was their purpose in writing schoolgirl stories? Most wrote for a living. Brent-Dyer, it is true, ran a girls' school for ten years, but she gave it up (her biographer tells us) because she found the reality of school life more troublesome than the fantasy.[4] Most were emphatic that they wrote out of love for their subject and their audience, which were of course the same: 'I confess I am still an absolute schoolgirl in my sympathies,' wrote Angela Brazil.[5] In *The Abbey Girls Go Back to School* (1922), Cicely promises Madam and the Pixie that 'Some day, when I have time, I'll write a book and put you in, and tell you just what we think of you' (p. 308). The in-joke is that Cicely is a thinly-veiled Elsie Oxenham and Madam and the Pixie represent the two members of the English Folk Dance Society to whom the book is dedicated.

Implicit in these remarks is a third motive. Schoolgirl story writers wrote for themselves. Brent-Dyer's biographer suggests that her imaginative world was in part a kind of wish-fulfilment, depicting the life she would have liked for herself. Several writers tried to reconstruct their own reality into a more artistic image, for instance by changing their name (not just for writing purposes). Elinor M. Brent-Dyer grew up as Gladys May Dyer and went through various changes of nomenclature before she settled on the cumbersome final version. Elsie Oxenham's surname was really Dunkerley, but when her father – a minor religious writer – changed his name to Oxenham, she followed suit. Angela Brazil altered the pronunciation of hers: when all the rest of the family pronounced it like the country, she placed the stress on the first syllable. They were also inclined to change details of their lives – date of birth, for example – and to conceal any piece of information which might spoil their image. Just as Enid Blyton in her autobiography omitted to mention a failed first marriage,[6] so Elinor Brent-Dyer preferred to refer to her mother as widowed, not deserted by her husband, and Angela Brazil's errant older brother disappeared from view. This desire to improve upon reality goes beyond simple vanity. It reveals a wish for an image which conforms to a social ideal: the one presented in the novels.

According to Raymond Williams, a major impetus behind the cheap publishing that began in the Victorian era was the desire to control and mould public opinion.[7] Popular literature was designed to show readers the roles they should play in a rapidly changing and socially self-conscious era. By presenting them with an idealised version of the world they knew, it ensured they both identified with it and aspired to it. Popular fiction is therefore both evidence of and propaganda for a particular world view. It posits certain institutions, ideals and moral values as the unquestioned and unquestionable norm. These institutions (for instance, marriage and the family), ideals (romantic love, chivalry), and values (respect for authority, the team spirit) help to ensure a docile, submissive population. Within this framework, storybook characters appear to live happily and successfully. They face no serious moral or practical problems, and find the kind of fulfilment that is rare in real life. Control is consolidated when the poor reader, having internalised the message and endeavoured to follow it, experiences discord between the idea and her reality. Perhaps for her, marriage is not a bed of roses; perhaps she misses out on marriage altogether. Perhaps real dilemmas (divorce, abortion, lesbian attraction) rear their ugly heads. Inevitably she feels that *she* is to blame; if the ideal or the institution works for everyone else, then the individual must be at fault. She is a social failure; and as a failure, she is effectively disabled from challenging the system.

Popular fiction therefore has a special significance because it sheds light on the value system of its era. Schoolgirl stories functioned as a form of control of female opinion and behaviour. In some ways the writers of schoolgirl stories were as much victims of the dominant ideology as their readers. In order to have any stake in the system they were obliged to abide by its rules. That readers still managed to take from their books a message of positive strong individuals and alliances is a measure of women's ability to subvert a system which is weighted against them.

Escape to the Abbey

Both women and girls read schoolgirl stories. Older correspondents to the *Chalet Club Newsletter* were among Elinor Brent-Dyer's most enthusiastic fans, confessing that they read the Chalet School books because they were 'more interesting' than anything else, and describing the characters as 'almost real – one knows them as friends'.[8] More than once the publishers were asked for a prospectus for the school, and readers made a pilgrimage to the Austrian lake where it had supposedly originated. These adult readers were often educated women, as Jill Paton Walsh observed. 'We have all, I expect, met them; – they come forward eagerly to talk to us, bringing their children as excuse and disguise.'[9] Psychologists suggest that juvenile fiction offers grown-ups a retreat out of the often complicated and disappointing adult world into the imagined security, order and hope of childhood. In this respect schoolgirl stories resemble other forms of popular fiction like romances, the reading of which (according to Q.D. Leavis) 'for many people is a means of easing a desolating sense of isolation and compensates for the poverty of their emotional lives'.[10]

That children also read for escapism is not denied, but critics take the didactic purpose of juvenile literature much more seriously. Books are supposed to form children's 'character', providing them with role models and explaining their place in the world. Hence the popularity of the school story with the less privileged but newly educated schoolgirl and her advisers between the wars. This was an era of social unrest and conservative reaction. Then, as now, a return to the old ideals of discipline, family life, hard work and deference to authority was seen as the answer to insecurity. These were all values promoted by the school story. But it offered little practical guidance for dealing with the real dilemmas of the age. By and large authors ignored the passing of time and major political and social events (though Brent-Dyer and Bruce made good capital out of the second world war), replacing them with the elements of escapism that the school story shared with its cultural contemporary, the movie: exotic settings, beautiful and well-to-do heroines and improbable plots.

Schoolgirl stories therefore enjoyed conservative support because they represented, or at least did not challenge, conventional values. Their commercial success was not, however, solely due to the Establishment; these books were bought by many whose outlook was progressive, not to say feminist. The right to education had been one of the great battles fought by the Victorian women's movement, and their victory was still fresh in their beneficiaries' minds. As Sara Burstall, former Headmistress of Manchester Girls' High School, wrote in 1933:

For generations men have felt loyalty and gratitude to their schools: emotion which has found its way into song not only at Eton and Harrow and Clifton. Stirring and beautiful as these songs are, they do not express more than is felt by women who, under the new era, have gained from their schools opportunity, knowledge, discipline, fellowship, and who look back in loyalty and affection to those who taught them.[11]

School stories also offered hope in the face of a strong social reaction against feminism in the years after the first world war. This was a profoundly repressive era for women. The general opinion in the twenties was that women had become too independent as a result of the political and economic gains of the Victorian women's movement, their war work, and the granting of the vote in 1918. Now they were forced back into the home, with marriage and motherhood presented as the only acceptable female goals. As women's opportunities shrank, the timeless apolitical character of schoolgirl stories played a liberating role. Books where the heroine never grew up left readers 'free to entertain the possibility of an alternative to conventional womanhood', as Bobbie Ann Mason noted in her study of popular American girls' fiction.[12] In series where the heroines did grow up and marry, they always managed to preserve an independent spirit as well as close links with the girlfriends of their schooldays.

The other significant characteristic of the schoolgirl heroines was that, in contrast to the domestic and heterosexual tenor of the times, they inhabited a female world. All authority figures as well as colleagues and comrades were women. The action was carried on by women, and all decisions were made by women. Women rose to the challenges presented by ideals such as honour, loyalty and team spirit. All emotional and social energies were directed towards women, and women's friendships were presented as positive, not destructive or competitive, and sufficient in themselves. In later years this was one of the main criticisms levelled against them. Schoolgirl stories were dismissed as 'irrelevant' because they did not deal with the *real* world, with relationships between girls and boys, and women and men.

126

The Abbey girls in love

The Abbey books of Elsie Jeanette Oxenham (1885–1960) are probably the richest source of information about female friendship in schoolgirl stories. About 40 books in the series appeared between 1914 and 1959. While clearly intended for the female juvenile market, many of them are only loosely linked to the school which the girls attended and its customs (in particular, country-dancing and the annual crowning of a May Queen). They really focus on the relations between the various women characters, even after they have left school.

To dip into these early volumes is to be transported into a world where women's love for women is openly and unselfconsciously avowed on almost every page. Joy, a young heiress, lives in a large country house with her cousin Joan and former schoolfriend Jen, then after their marriages with her devoted secretary Mary, and her two adopted daughters Rosamund and Maidlin. Though nearly all the characters eventually fall in love with men and marry, these events are seen not as ends in themselves but in terms of their effect upon their women friends. A necessary lesson the women must learn is that if they really love their friends, they must take second place to male suitors and husbands.

> 'She's up against a tragedy, if she really hadn't realised that Lady Marchwood's marriage would make a difference. I don't mean necessarily a difference in her feeling for Maidie; it probably won't. But a husband must come first. If Maidie is expecting still to be first with Lady Marchwood, she'll break her heart.'[13]

Friendship is presented as mutual support and selfless giving way to the 'real thing': heterosexual love and marriage.

> A fortnight ago, Joy had not known she loved Andrew Marchwood; now he was her man, and she was ready to go across the world with him. And her friends who had seen her since her engagement knew that restless Joy was satisfied at last;

she had found something for want of which her life had till now been incomplete . . .[14]

Theoretically, then, the books profess to prioritise heterosexual romance and marriage over mere friendship. Yet when we read them, somehow we get a different message. This is partly because Oxenham was never very convincing in her attempts to portray men or heterosexual love. Perhaps more significantly, she was extremely acute at describing a whole range of emotions between women. These books are concerned with women's struggles to relate to each other in a mature, loving and non-possessive way –

Maidlin: 'Is Ros going to like these girls better than us?'
Joy: 'We shall really keep Ros more closely if she goes, feeling we're backing her up, than if we keep her here unwillingly.'[15]

to come to terms with faults and disappointments in a beloved –

Mary: 'I had loved Joy Shirley so, for a year. She had been so good to me. I'd thought her perfect. . . . That night, and for some days afterwards, I felt as if I'd lost her. . . . I found after a while that I was wrong. All I had lost was my picture of her. I still loved the real Joy, although she had faults.'[16]

and to want what was best for her – 'Jen: "You care more that Joy should love you as you wish than that Joy should be happy and have what is best for herself." '[17]

In the 1920s women's loyalty to other women was sufficiently important a subject to absorb Oxenham's sympathetic pen through page after agonising page. When Mary lets Jen down in *The Abbey Girls Win Through* (1928), she reflects:

'I ought to be thinking about Jen. I've been sorry for her all through, and I've wanted to help her; but I've been thinking about myself, what *I* wanted, how *I* felt. Ann forgot all about herself, and thought only of helping Jen. But almost from the

128

first I was thinking how I'd failed her and how awful it was; and it made me still less able to help. . . . I was hardly any use; I just collapsed like a baby – and it was because I was so much upset because she turned from me to Ann.' etc., etc. (p. 73)

The real thing

To all the major characters except Mary, an older woman drawn into the Abbey circle through folk-dancing, the prize of marriage is granted. Mary, however, like Oxenham herself a writer of schoolgirl stories, is made to understand the nature and pitfalls of friendship better, perhaps, than any of the other Abbey girls. She exemplifies above all the maxim that true friendship means self-denial. Mary's love for Jen and Joy constitutes the principal subject-matter of three or four books, but her timely intervention secures the marriage of both; and when Kenneth asks for her help in his courtship of Jen, Oxenham comments without intending irony, 'How was she to give advice on love affairs, she who had dreamt of knights and heroes but had never known love in real life?'[18]

This *is* ironic, for Mary's experience of love comes across far more truthfully and memorably than Oxenham's feeble attempts at depicting heterosexual emotion. Mary has been rescued from a dull and potentially dangerous life of office work and unhealthy daydreams by the glamorous Joy and Jen, who introduce her to the healing art of country-dancing. Joy and Jen become vitally important to her, so much so that when Jen announces that she won't be in London all spring, Mary is devastated.

'Not – in London?' Mary looked at her with such blank dismay in her face that Jen's heart smote her suddenly. She had never realised till that moment how much she had counted for in Mary's new life. . . . [Mary], too, had not

129

realised how much she depended on Jen's help, on her visits, on the constant sight of her at classes. . . . It was as if Hyde Park or St Paul's had suddenly announced it was leaving London. The centre of everything would be gone if Jen were not in town.[19]

Some extracts from an early volume in the series, *The Abbey Girls Go Back to School* (1922), illustrate Oxenham's struggle to balance the two types of love. At a vacation school of the English Folk Dance Society the Abbey girls meet 'Madam', of whom Cicely remarks: '*Like* her! There *isn't* anybody else! . . . If she looked ill, I'd feel there was something wrong in the universe' (p. 187).

But this hero-worship must give way to the greater claims of heterosexual love; Cicely is engaged to be married by the end of the book, after an extraordinarily brief courtship mercifully concealed from the reader. We are given an insight into the conflict of interests when 'Miss Newcastle' warns the Abbey girls that if they tease Cicely or interfere in her blossoming romance, they will risk losing her friendship:

'Look here, Newcastle,' Joy protests, 'we can't have the President falling in love with any old man! We won't allow it! She belongs to us!'

'Well, I'm warning you that she won't belong to you any longer if you try to butt in now,' Miss Newcastle tells her. 'You can't help some things happening; you've just got to stand aside and let 'em go, and then make the best of them afterwards.'[!]

'Then you really think –' Joan began, a wistful note in her voice. 'It would change everything, Newcastle!'

But she pulls herself together: 'The one thing that matters is to go on being friends. That can last, whatever happens, even if – well, if outside people have to be allowed to come in! The awful thing would be if something happened to our friendship, after all these years. None of us could bear that' (pp. 235–7).

130

By the last week of the vacation school, Cicely has got her emotions sorted out. When Madam returns to teach them, 'Cicely's face had grown radiant at sight of her the moment she entered the classroom, but she had not made straight for her as she would have done three weeks ago' (p. 267). No, Madam's place has now been more appropriately filled by 'Dick'.

Husbands are quite rightly resented by the unmarried women for taking their friends away. When Joy marries, in *Queen of the Abbey Girls* (1926), Jen moans: 'I daren't face the thought that we've really lost Joy; it doesn't bear thinking about' (p. 129). And when Joy returns from her honeymoon leaving her husband game-shooting in Africa, Rosamund declares: 'It's ripping to have Joy come back alone. We like Andrew, of course; but I'm quite content to have him in East Africa.'[20] So, clearly, is Oxenham, who contrives to have him murdered on safari by some 'wild natives' so that Joy may be left free to bring up twin daughters unencumbered by a man, with the help of her women friends.

Another clue to Oxenham's real feelings on the subject of love lies in her unselfconscious descriptions of individuals and groups of women, which often in these early books reveal a sensuous pleasure in women's bodies. Consider, for instance, the quotation at the start of this chapter, as well as Joan's appreciation of Madam's 'perfect poise and balance' in *The Abbey Girls Go Back to School* (1922): 'her eyes followed Madam, when presently she came down from her perch to demonstrate a movement, with hungry eager delight' (p. 110). 'Hungry' and 'eager' are favourite words of Oxenham in this sort of context.

Sisterhood

These books were written in the years of Oxenham's close involvement with the English Folk Dance Society, which provided models for a number of her characters and almost certainly (to judge from the way she wrote about them) a significant focus for her emotional energies at that time.

Through the eyes of Cicely she described her feelings at a vacation school run by the Society:

> for the first time she saw the whole school together and began to sense its atmosphere, of eagerness and excitement, of friendship and good fellowship, of keen artistic joy in beautiful sights and sounds. . . . The majority of the students were girls, though there were many men [Oxenham was not interested in the men, so she tells us more about the women] . . . many of the girls had brilliant jumpers over their tunics and looked more boy-like than ever, with almost no skirt at all showing – especially those who had bobbed their hair, and there were many of them. Keenly interested in everything and everybody, Cicely wondered again how many of these girls were teachers; how many had come because they had found in this folk-art the widening and uplift of which Miss Newcastle had spoken; and if it would be possible to make friends with many outside their own immediate circle.[21]

The importance of such movements, which brought large numbers of women together in the years after the first world war, is captured here with lengthy descriptions of the 1920s equivalent of 'sisterhood', in a social world far more woman-centred than today. In *The New Abbey Girls* (1923) several pages are devoted to a typical country-dance evening in London at which the women students, who refer to each other by their surnames, are booking partners for a forthcoming party. 'What are you going to do with me at the party, Morgan?' 'Anything you like, old sport' (p. 108). One senses the excitement with which Oxenham entered into the activities of the Folk Dance Society, to whose women members she dedicated so many of her 'Abbey' books. It is possible that a minor character called 'The Writing Person' who appears at this period may stand for Oxenham herself, for she is described as an older woman who only took up dancing a few years before. Herself a poor dancer, she would 'go anywhere' to watch Madam (who is based on a real officer of the English Folk Dance Society, Helen Kennedy North), and finds dancing an inspiration for her work as a writer of schoolgirl stories. 'Really, I consider folk-dancing responsible for most of the work I've done in the last two years,' she declares – which, if she *does* represent Oxenham, is all the Abbey books to date! 'It's a most valuable stimulant! And such a healthy one! I'm better in every way.'[22]

It is the Writing Person who reveals to Jen and Joy that

'there is one very interesting thing about nearly all these people! If you talk to them for long, you find they have "girls" in the background. . . . Sometimes it's the children in their day-school classes; most of them are teachers, of course. But very often it's big girls, Guides, or a club, or Guildry, girls to whom they're teaching folk-dancing in the evenings, mostly just for the love of it.'[23]

The death of romantic friendship

The 1930s brought a change. When the eleventh book in the series, *The Abbey Girls Play Up*, appeared in 1930, the characters had moved on a few years. The focus was now very much more domestic – Joan, Joy and Jen all have young families – and a new and even less convincing approach to heterosexual romance is in evidence. Jen introduces Maribel to her husband's cousin, and a relationship develops which seems to be entirely based upon meaningful looks. 'Mike Marchwood's eyes had been saying something very emphatic, which he might not put into words' (p. 163). Maribel discusses the phenomenon of love with her chum, but the subject embarrasses them: 'Oh, I say, Bel, don't let's be idiots! Come and play tennis, and forget all this tosh!' (p. 166). Would that they did! But Maribel is engaged by the end of the book.

Already in *The Abbey Girls at Home* (1929) there are signs of the different approach. Like its predecessors, this book is mainly about love between women: there is plenty of kissing and pages of discussion about feelings: 'I never knew how much I cared about you till I thought you cared more for Betty than for me,' Joy (now widowed) tells Jen (now married) (p. 103). But in this book, first Joy and then Mary and Jen realise they are no longer so obsessed with folk-dancing. 'At present I feel I've come up against real things too sharply ever to go back to a play thing like country-dancing,' declares Joy (p. 191).

Mary takes up the metaphor: 'The dancing is all right. It's beautiful, and the music is jolly; the figures are fascinating, and it's a splendidly healthy recreation, and one must have some recreation, some way to let oneself go. . . . But it *is* play. And there are more important things, *real* things' (p. 234). Jen agrees: 'I used to think country-dancing came first of everything. You've shown me its right place. . . . I think perhaps there are adventures ahead of me that are worth while!' (p. 238; she is expecting her first baby).

Perhaps it is far-fetched, but I wonder if we can read 'country-dancing' as a symbol for women's friendships? I suggest this because it is quite clear that the members and activities of the English Folk Dance Society were of central importance to Oxenham in the early and mid-1920s. If by the late 1920s she had come to feel that her attitude to them was no longer appropriate, she might well use such a metaphor (even unconsciously) to stand for a more personal relationship. And is it too much of a coincidence to observe that this altered stance occurs in a book she was writing in 1928 – the year of the trial of *The Well of Loneliness?*

Lesbians at the Abbey

Feminist scholars assign the beginning of systematic repression of women's friendships to the 1920s, and there is much evidence to support this view.[24] By the 1920s the writings of Havelock Ellis, Krafft-Ebing and Hirschfeld on normal and deviant sexuality were well known in intellectual circles in Britain. But the attempt in 1921 to bring lesbian acts within the Criminal Law was defeated because of a consensus that silence was a better deterrent. Lesbianism was therefore slow to enter the public consciousness. Then came the successful prosecution for obscenity of Radclyffe Hall's novel *The Well of Loneliness*. This, as one male critic put it, had 'all the character of a bursting dam. A dam of ignorance, of complete unsuspiciousness was breached only by a book that no one could fail to read as lesbian.'[25] The press coverage of this scandal was probably the most significant factor in creating a public image of lesbianism, as defined by sexologists and psychiatrists. Though Radclyffe Hall's novel was banned, there could hardly be a reader in the country who did not know what it was all about. Elsie Oxenham and her sister-writers must have realised that the behaviour of their characters was now open to 'misinterpretation'.

Take, for example, the ingenuous introduction to Norah and Con in *The Abbey Girls Win Through* (1928):

> They were a recognised couple. Con, who sold gloves in a big West-End establishment, was the wife and home-maker; Norah, the typist, was the husband, who planned little pleasure trips and kept the accounts and took Con to the pictures. (p. 9)

Descriptions such as these caused critics great amusement in the 1950s and afterwards. How could the author have been so naive – or so explicit? Remember, however, that she wrote these words before the *Well of Loneliness* trial, before the lesbian scare had made women in couples into objects of suspicion and disgust. I would argue that Oxenham was simply describing a phenomenon which she and her readers were familiar with, which they saw all about them in the male-depleted generation after the first world war, and thought nothing of. In *The Abbey Girls Win Through* Ann observes that 'Perhaps Miss Devine [Mary] remembers that girls often live in twos. She used to be in the office herself; she'll know girls don't like to go and leave their other half alone' (p. 12).

Elsie Oxenham distinguished between 'healthy' and 'unhealthy' relationships between women, but in the 1920s

135

books the distinction was not the one that psychiatrists would have made. In *Queen of the Abbey Girls* (1926), Amy has a crush on Mary which is not reciprocated. After Mary leaves London to live at the Abbey, she receives a letter from Amy in which, Mary tells Jen: 'She said a lot about how much she missed me in the office, and a lot of nonsense that I hardly liked to read; it made me hot all over to think of any one giving herself away in a letter like that, and saying such absurd things to me' (p. 185).

Jen's response is to observe: 'I've heard the girls at school talk like that about certain mistresses, but I didn't know grown people in business kept it up' (p. 186). Then she adds:

'Of course it's a sign there's something wrong with the girl. Not that she should like you; I admire her good sense, and quite agree with her. But that she should let her liking run away with her, as if she were a schoolgirl. That's wrong. It's uncontrolled; want of balance' (p. 187).

And that is the sum of her analysis: the relationship is wrong because it's *uncontrolled*. Not because it's unnatural or perverted. To make matters perfectly clear, Jen sums up: 'It's unhealthy, of course, and silly; but it isn't vicious' (p. 194).

The triumph of heterosexuality

From this point on there is an ever declining ration of expressed love between women, and the books make much more of a feature of heterosexual romance, marriage and motherhood. Possibly because it was now clear that only young women could safely be open about their feelings for one another, Oxenham made the interesting decision in 1938 to revert to the pre-marriage years of her original characters. She produced seven stories which filled in gaps in the first sequence. The title of the first of these – *Schooldays at the Abbey* – is revealing of the switch: though the books continued to be about women's friendships, the relationships described were reduced to the level of schoolgirl passions. Meanwhile, heterosexual love was idealised beyond belief. Here is Joan, aged about 18, in *Schooldays* (1938): 'It must be a wonderful thing. I don't suppose it will ever happen to me, but it must be the happiest thing in the world' (p. 116). (Contrast Jen in *The Abbey Girls in Town* (1925): 'It's that man. Being in love's a fearful disease. I hope I never catch it' (p. 299).) In *Tomboys at the Abbey* (1957), which though written nearly 20 years after *Schooldays* depicts Joan as only a year older, she expands upon the theme:

'I don't know anything about being in love; I've had no experience. But – I've always imagined that it was a feeling for which one would give up everything and be glad to do it. That if I fell in love, for instance, I'd be willing to go away with – him! – and leave Mother to Joy's tender mercies, and leave my Abbey, that I love so much. . . . And that if I wasn't willing to leave everything, I shouldn't be really in love and it wouldn't be worth while getting married' (p. 125).

(Contrast Jen in *The Abbey Girls Go Back to School* (1922): 'Isn't this awful? Are Joan and Cicely going to think about these men all the time?' (p. 216). Or Joy, after Joan is married, in *The Abbey Girls Again* (1924): 'I say it must be such a nuisance having a man round all the time' (p. 106).)

The second-generation novels, written alternately with the retrospective ones after 1938, are frankly dreadful. *Song of the Abbey* (1954) resuscitates Carry Carter, Joy's antagonist in the very first book in the series, now 'about thirty-seven, unmarried [!], smart and lively', who spends her life at bridge-parties, dances, and the theatre (p. 14). To avenge herself upon the school, which 20 years before chose Joy instead of her as May Queen, she leads the new Queen astray by taking her to the ballet against her aunt's wishes. (Where now is sisterhood, one wonders?)

If the early Abbey books were about women's friendships, the later ones are about marriage pure and simple. Nanta has scarcely left school before her thoughts turn to it: 'But now

137

she was nineteen, and at Kentisbury and at the Abbey she had seen many happily married couples; her mind had grown and broadened and she thought more deeply' (p. 143). Needless to state, there are no unhappily married couples in the Abbey books! Even Mary, the only spinster among the principal characters, and the one who earlier stood for Oxenham's own experience and aspirations, becomes a mouthpiece for the 1950s party-line. World-famous ballerina Damaris gives up her career to marry. 'Other people can dance, but only Damaris can marry Brian,' says Mary, incredibly. 'Other people don't dance as she does,' Nanta objects. 'You do think she ought to give it up, Mary-Dorothy?' 'To be married – yes, Nanta, I do.' (p. 172)

Two Queens at the Abbey (1959), the last in the series, is yet more preposterous. With a sense, perhaps, that she had to tie off all loose ends before she died, Oxenham launched every character into frenzied heterosexual activity. Nanta, aged 19, marries and falls pregnant. Littlejan, aged 19, marries and has a baby. Rosamund has her seventh, Jen her ninth. Jansy, Joan's daughter, talks of marrying Dickon, Cicely's son; both are aged 16. Lindy gets engaged to Donald, one of Maidlin's rejects. When good old understanding Mary prepares supper for Littlejan (Queen Marigold), whose husband has just gone off to the Antarctic, she remarks, apparently without innuendo, that 'Marigold is hungry for more than sandwiches to-night' (p. 65). In 1924 Mary had been hungry for a sight of Jen!

The death of the schoolgirl story

As a source for attitudes to women's friendships over forty years, the Abbey books are remarkable. They show how in the 1920s schoolgirl story writers had a unique freedom to explore all the dimensions of women's love for women. As the years passed this freedom was progressively curtailed, with writers becoming more and more confused and restricted by the new heterosexual demands and the negative image of lesbianism. In later decades critics looked back and sneered at their naïvety, or amused themselves by exposing (or denying) the homosexual tendencies of schoolgirl heroines and their creators. A.O.J. Cockshut, for example, takes up 'The Lesbian Theme', commenting that 'an inferior writer like Elsie Oxenham might in her innocent unawareness use language seeming to imply a lesbian relationship, while meaning no such thing'. He noted, however, that the public showed a 'calm acceptance' of her 'puerilities'. 'Lesbianism simply did not enter into most people's calculations.'[26]

Of course it didn't. This was because during the period in which the schoolgirl story flourished, lesbianism was progressively redefined. From a deviant sexuality caused by abnormal genetic or social development it was extended to encompass all intimate relationships between women, whether explicitly sexual or not (in which case they were categorised as 'latent' or 'unconscious'). This was represented as a newly discovered scientific *fact*, not the man-made invention that it was. A new equation sank into the public mind: close friendships between women = lesbianism = sexual perversion.

Among those who swallowed this version of women's psychology were Mary Cadogan and Patricia Craig, authors of the immensely readable but often unsympathetic study of girls' fiction, *You're a Brick, Angela!* (1976). They dismiss Madam in *The Abbey Girls Go Back to School* as a 'stop-gap love object' for Cicely, for whom 'a more potentially satisfying relationship' in the person of her future husband is subsequently provided. They seize upon the many instances in which Oxenham's heroines share a bed as evidence that the women's intimacy is (however unconsciously) *not* 'healthy' or 'normal'.[27]

In the 1960s sleeping together became a synonym for sexual activity, but it is a misreading of history to impose this idea on the social mores of the 1920s. For Elsie Oxenham and her public, sharing a bed with a girlfriend was but one way of showing affection, and a perfectly acceptable one at that. In *The New Abbey Girls* (1923) Jen (aged 18) establishes this point when she suggests to Joy (aged 21) how she could make shy 14-year-old Maidlin feel she is welcome in the Abbey household:

> 'Why don't you have her to sleep with you, at Jack's? [Jack is Jacqueline, a former school chum of Jen's, whom she refers to as 'husband'.] You know Jacky-boy said she'd get a bed ready for the heiress! You could tell her not to, and Maidlin could go in with you, and I'd tuck in with my husband. You know she always wants me to!' (p. 175).

What this reveals is not unconscious perversion but a very conscious love for women which in 1923 was fine and after 1928 became abnormal and unhealthy, representing a level of intimacy which was too threatening to be allowed to continue. Censorship was inevitable. From the late 1950s to the early 1970s a handful of Abbey books were reprinted in cheap condensed editions. Oxenham's often tautologous prose can take a bit of blue-pencilling, but it is significant that the portions excised were frequently the passionate and to post-Freudian eyes sexually suggestive scenes between women. In the bowdlerised version of *The New Abbey Girls* (1959), for instance, Jen no longer suggests that Joy sleep with Maidlin.

Elsie Oxenham died in 1960. By the mid-1970s her Abbey books, along with virtually all schoolgirl stories, had disappeared from the publishers' lists. Readers were told there was 'no demand'. The truth was that the critics had condemned them to death, the later books ostensibly for being appallingly written (which they were), the early ones for the lack of 'relevance' and 'social realism'. What this meant was that *they were not heterosexual enough*, or rather, they were too positive about women's friendships and love for each other. The destruction of the schoolgirl story is a major piece of evidence for the imposition of compulsory heterosexuality in twentieth-century Britain.

7

'The Best Friend Whom Life Has Given Me.' Does Winifred Holtby have a place in lesbian history?

Pam Johnson

Attempting to write about the life of Winifred Holtby from a lesbian-feminist perspective provides an almost perfect case study of the difficulties of uncovering lesbian history. Despite the fact that Holtby died in 1935, recently enough to be within living memory, and that two biographies and two selections of her letters were published within a few years of her death she remains enigmatic. In part this illustrates the general heterosexism which often bedevils discussions of the personal lives of women who do not follow the pattern of marriage/affairs with men and motherhood. (It is useful to compare Holtby with Rebecca West, her almost exact contemporary, whose relationship with H.G. Wells, by whom she had a son, is well documented.) More precisely, Holtby's case is complicated by the fact that her principal biographer, Vera Brittain, was also the most important friend of her life. Brittain's biography of Holtby, *Testament of Friendship*, shows evidence of extreme defensiveness about lesbianism and of a very careful and self-conscious presentation of her relationship with Holtby. Subsequent commentators have accepted uncritically Brittain's version of the relationship and have, if anything, exaggerated Brittain's carefully constructed account. Before examining *Testament of Friendship* and its successors, I shall give a brief account of Holtby's life and achievements and discuss her friendships with women, particularly Vera Brittain.

Winifred Holtby was born in Rudston, Yorkshire in 1898 into a middle-class farming family. In 1917 she went to Somerville College Oxford, but left after one year to join the Women's Auxiliary Army Corps. She went to France where she met Jean McWilliam, with whom she continued a friendship after the war was over. Returning to Somerville in 1919 to read history, she met Vera Brittain. After graduating, Winifred and Vera shared flats in London until Vera's marriage in 1925. From 1925 until her death in 1935 from Bright's Disease, Winifred had her permanent home in London with Vera and Vera's husband, George Catlin, who spent part of each year teaching in America.

While marvelling at the pace of Winifred's life in the twelve years or so before her death, we should remember that her private income and the fact that she and Vera had domestic help from very early in their life together gave her a measure of freedom from mundane concerns. Winifred lectured for the WEA and the League of Nations and contributed to a number of papers including the *Manchester Guardian* and the *Yorkshire Post*. Significantly, after a series of rejections she became a regular contributor to the feminist journal *Time and Tide* and in 1926 became one of its directors. As well as her commitment to women's rights and the peace movement she increasingly became involved in anti-racist work after a visit to South Africa in 1926, and in opposition to fascism during the 1930s. Vera Brittain sees Holtby's life as dominated by the 'conflict between the claims of art and the demands of social service'.[1] And certainly in addition to her other activities she was a prolific novelist, publishing five other novels between her first, *Anderby Wold* (1923), and her last, *South Riding*, which appeared posthumously in 1936.

In her position at *Time and Tide* Winifred Holtby was influential in both forming and reflecting feminist ideas during the twenties and thirties. Rosalind Delmar places Holtby in the context of the debate between 'old' and 'new' feminism in the 1920s. The 'new feminists', for whom Eleanor Rathbone, President of the National Union of Societies for Equal Citizenship (NUSEC) was a powerful spokeswoman, argued that the emphasis of feminism should shift from demanding rights which men had but women were without, to campaigning for women's specific needs.[2] Holtby, in a 1926 article, emphasises the humanistic side of her own 'old' feminism and presents the struggle for equality as a necessary inconvenience:

> I want to be about the work in which my real interests lie, the study of inter-race relationships, the writing of novels and so forth. But while the inequality exists, while injustice is done and opportunity denied to the great majority of women, I shall have to be a feminist with the motto 'Equality First'.[3]

Nevertheless I think it would be a mistake to see Holtby as simply an equal-rights feminist who wanted nothing more than changes in legislation. Dale Spender suggests that Holtby's feminism toughened towards the end of her life,[4] and this is borne out by *Women and a Changing Civilisation*, published in 1934, which contains some incisive analysis of anti-feminist ideology.

Many of the arguments in *Women* are directly relevant to feminism in the 1980s. Holtby sees girls' education and ambitions to be thwarted by the amount of unacknowledged work they undertake in the home, and by the lack of female role models. She comments on women's general lack of property and material resources. She deals with the 1930s version of 'all she needs is a good screw' by demolishing the myth of the 'frustrated spinster'. While being careful to emphasise that spinsterhood and celibacy are not synonymous, Holtby points out that a spinster doctor, teacher or political organiser is likely to experience much more fulfilment than an unoccupied middle-class

143

wife. She neatly exposes the spinster/bachelor double standard by remarking that: 'I have not yet seen the newspaper which refers to those eminent bachelors, Noel Coward, Colonel T.E. Lawrence, Herr Hitler and the Prince of Wales as "this distressing type" – the words which Sir Oswald Mosley in the *Fascist Week* recently applied to unmarried women.'[5]

The reference to Mosley is significant, for it is her critique of fascist ideology and its implications for women which is, I think, the most impressive aspect of *Women*. Vera Brittain tells us that Holtby's experience in South Africa had made her aware of the parallels between female and Black oppression.[6] In *Women* she comments on the way in which women and Black people have both been labelled infantile, lacking in social responsibility and inferior, relating this to the subordination of reason to emotion which she sees as basic to fascism. By juxtaposing a particularly unpleasant passage from Lawrence's *Aaron's Rod* with a pronouncement on leadership by Goering, she illustrates how pervasive the cult of the virile leader had become and warns her readers to beware of 'lauding of the instincts and the emphasis of "biological", "natural" or "traditional" values.'[7]

Holtby criticises the popularisation of Freudian theory in the thirties for pressurising women into (hetero)sexual activity and polarising male and female roles so that Mosley's slogan 'We want men who are men and women who are women' was given a spurious intellectual credibility. At the end of *Women* she rejects the fascist restriction of women and men to sharply segregated spheres, and argues that both sexes should

> release their richness of variety. We still are greatly ignorant of our own natures. We do not know how much of what we usually describe as 'feminine characteristics' are really 'masculine' and how much 'masculinity' is common to both sexes. . . . We do not even know – though we theorise and penalise with ferocious confidence – whether the 'normal' sexual relationship is homo- or bi- or heterosexual.[8]

Such a questioning of common assumptions about gender and

sexuality implies a modern feminist position, which recognises gender and sexual identity to be socially constructed rather than biologically predetermined. *Women* is a popular rather than an academic work, a book which seeks to disseminate rather than to develop ideas, but from the acuity with which Holtby identifies the patriarchal links between Freud, Lawrence and Mosley and the vehemence with which she denounces their influence, I think it is possible to argue that, had she lived, her feminism would have become increasingly radical.

Letters to a Friend (1937), Winifred's side of her correspondence with Jean McWilliam, is edited by both Jean McWilliam and Winifred's mother, Alice Holtby. The book shows signs of careful presentation but, significantly, words and phrases which would now be regarded as compromising are not deleted, indicating a considerable shift in linguistic mores between the 1930s and the present day. The two women corresponded using nicknames derived from Shakespeare's *As You Like It*. Jean was Rosalind and Winifred Celia and many of Winifred's letters end with 'I love you'. A light-hearted reference to 'innocent' homosexuality is even included. On a ship going to South Africa in 1926 Winifred met a Miss Graham who had been taught by Jean. The two women held 'pleasant communion on the nature of our loves – as did those charming youths in the Platonic dialogue whose name I forget, but which is staged in a gymnasium, with nice little boys cooling themselves after the games, and blushing at the mention of their lovers' names'.[9]

Evelyne White was editor of *The Schoolmistress*, to which Holtby was a regular contributor, and her memoir *Winifred Holtby As I Knew Her* (1938) is little more than a record of professional meetings with Holtby. Perhaps White was inhibited by her knowledge that Vera Brittain had yet to publish the definitive biography. Certainly references to Brittain are few and formal: 'In June she [Holtby] acted as bridesmaid to her friend Vera Brittain, who was married to D.K.G. Catlin, at St James's Church, Spanish Place London.'[10] There are two oblique references to lesbianism in the book, but as in the case of *Letters to a Friend*, they are droll and unrevealing. White records that in

145

1933 she and Holtby discussed two plays which dealt with lesbianism in a school setting, *Regiment of Women* and *Mädchen in Uniform*, and that Winifred said 'the first headmistress of her school kissed all the girls every Saturday evening, and she suggested humorously that it must have been a terrible ordeal for her as there were about two hundred in the school.'[11] Holtby also interviewed the flamboyant lesbian composer and suffragist Dame Ethel Smyth 'but the interview was reversed and Winifred was catechised on the women's question'.[12]

Most accounts of Winifred Holtby emphasise her friendliness and popularity and it is clear that she had a wide range of women friends and acquaintances in the educated, professional and feminist circles of her day. She soon developed a close friendship with Lady Rhondda, founder of *Time and Tide*, who lived for many years with another contributor to the journal, Theodora Bosanquet, and was also on good terms with another *Time and Tide* contributor, Cicely Hamilton, author of a scathing critique of heterosexuality's major institution, *Marriage as a Trade*. Other friends included Violet Scott-James, Hilda Reid, novelists Stella Benson and Phyllis Bentley and teacher Dorothy McCalman, who like Winifred died tragically young. Brittain records that she became a friend of Ethel Smyth to whom, with Cicely Hamilton, *Women and a Changing Civilisation* is dedicated. Holtby is also mentioned in the autobiography of single, successful businesswoman Beatrice Gordon Holmes, *In Love with Life* (1944).

Holtby's friendship with Vera Brittain, however, stands out as a major relationship in both women's lives. After an initial misunderstanding, Vera, strained and nervous after her experiences of nursing in the first world war, quickly became close to Winifred, five and a half years her junior. The exclusiveness of the relationship was remarked upon. Paediatrician Dr Cecily Williams, who as an undergraduate was a close friend of Holtby, said that Vera 'gobbled up Winifred'.[13] Later many people commented upon the strength of their friendship and some, like feminist Monica Whately, believed it to be a lesbian relationship.[14] In the Prologue to *Testament of Friendship* Brittain explains that she did not write Holtby's biography earlier for a variety of reasons – grief; the wish to attain a sense of perspective; and the difficulty of giving an account of Holtby's relationships with other people. I think it is also likely that Brittain needed time in order to develop a strategy for both celebrating 'the best friend whom life has given me'[15] and squashing the lesbian rumours.

There are three major elements in Brittain's presentation of her relationship with Holtby: a rehabilitation of friendship between women; an amused denial of the lesbian rumours; and the creation for Holtby of a heterosexual love interest. Brittain's defensive stance is clear from the Prologue to *Testament*. She compares her task to that of Mrs Gaskell in writing Charlotte Brontë's biography; an interesting analogy for, though Brittain does not say so, one of the problems Mrs Gaskell faced was whether or not to reveal Brontë's unorthodox feelings towards M. Heger, a married man, not to mention how to deal with her passionate friendship for Ellen Nussey (see Chapter 2). Brittain comments on the double standard which has applauded friendships between men and ignored or despised friendships between women and assures her readers that such friendship strengthens rather than threatens the institution of heterosexuality: 'Loyalty and affection between women is a noble relationship which, far from impoverishing, actually enhances the love of a girl for her lover, of a wife for her husband, of a mother for her children'.[16]

In the Prologue Brittain writes that friendships between women have been 'mocked, belittled and falsely interpreted',[17] and this theme of the lesbian 'slur' is something she returns to several times in *Testament*. She writes of 'suspicions habitual among the over-sophisticated' and related that Holtby would say 'Too, *too* Chelsea' when some 'zealous friend related the newest legend current about us in the neighbourhood'.[18] Later she refers to 'a plentiful crop of rumours' about their 'unusual domestic arrangements',[19] and 'scandalmongers who invented for her [Winifred] a lurid series of homosexual relationships, usually associated with Lady Rhondda or myself'.[20] The combined effect of these references, which are not so frequent as to arouse the suspicions they are designed to allay and usually occur in a humorous rather than a self-righteous context, is to dismiss as laughable the idea that she and Winifred had a lesbian relationship. Having freed herself and Winifred from the 'taint' of lesbianism, she is able to quote a poem, 'The Foolish Clocks', in which Winifred writes of her loneliness on Vera's wedding night and refers to her as 'my love',[21] and parts of a letter in which Winifred analyses her love for Vera and writes 'And because you are you, there is part of me with which, in Marguerite's words to Faust, "I need thee every hour" '.[22] This strategy allows Brittain to acknowledge and even celebrate expressions of emotion between women, but at the price of endorsing the view that lesbianism is perverted sexuality.

But Brittain's *tour de force* is her treatment of Holtby's relationship with Harry Pearson, referred to as 'Bill' in *Testament*, with whom she was in love as a teenager and who drifted in and out of her adult life. Brittain presents the beginning of the love affair in 1916 when Bill came home wounded from the war and was nursed by Winifred. Bill wrote some love sonnets to Winifred, but out of embarrassment she rebuffed him, and Bill's reaction to this snub marred his future relations with her. Lest it should strain credulity to suppose that a woman's whole future emotional life could be blighted by an adolescent tiff, Brittain gives Bill a symbolic significance beyond his individual identity. As a survivor of the first world war Bill becomes a representative of that generation indelibly marked by the war. Like 'so many others', he had changed from 'an ardent idealist into a soul still benevolent but without purpose or integration, capricious, perverse, incalculable, a war casualty of the spirit'.[23] It is perhaps understandable that, given her own experience of loss of four young men who were close to her, including her brother Edward, in the first world war, Brittain should present Holtby as emotionally fixated on the associations of the war: 'For all the distinguished men that Winifred met later who would gladly have made her wife or mistress, she never outlived the compulsion of this memory – associated for her, with one individual.'[24] It is also true that Brittain is here producing a slightly more

148

psychologically sophisticated version of the classic 'her fiancé was killed in the first world war' which has done sterling service in explaining away women without men.

Not only does Brittain embellish *Testament* with references to the relationship with Bill, but the end of the biography is orchestrated to produce the climactic moment of the affair. As Winifred is dying, Bill and Vera take it in turns to sit with her. On the last morning of Winifred's life Vera leaves the nursing home and with her husband goes to St James's in Spanish Place where they were married ten years before. She remembers Winifred as a bridesmaid 'in her blue dress, golden, Madonna-like, reassuring'[25] – the apotheosis of heterosexual womanhood. On returning to the nursing home she learns that 'There was still just time for their [Winifred's and Bill's] strange, erratic story, constantly broken and as often resumed, to end in as much of contentment as most of us are destined to know.'[26] Reader, she almost married him.

Brittain, with the reputation of both herself and Holtby to consider and, perhaps, with some degree of confusion about her own feelings, produced a skilfully organised, highly self-conscious biography. Subsequent commentators have, incredibly, taken *Testament* as a straightforward factual account, apparently unaware that no biography, let alone one whose author is also a protagonist in the story, is completely objective. Vera Brittain's presentation of Holtby's life fits all too comfortably into these writers' heterosexist assumptions. Kenneth Young, writing in 1966, has clearly completely swallowed the Bill story:

> Yet in one sense it [the failure of the relationship with Bill] is not of prime importance for it released her both from the demands of sex and the needs of marital love. All that vast part of life was for her neatly packaged and put away in her mind with the label 'Love, hopeless'. It released her, too, for those strong and lifelong feminine friendships.[27]

Young shows some dim awareness here that marriage and mother-hood may not be unmixed blessings for a woman wishing to follow a creative or political career, but for him 'that vast part of life' must be heterosexual love, with which 'strong and lifelong feminine friendships' can never compete.

Much more shocking is Rosalind Delmar's Afterword to *Testament*, written in 1980. Delmar appears to subscribe to a view of sexuality current in the 1930s and shows no understanding at all of modern lesbian feminism when she writes that Brittain pointed to 'an extraordinary blindspot about relations between women which would reduce all its forms to being mere variants, suppressed or otherwise, of one particular mode of sexual practice'.[28] Paul Berry's introductory chapter on 'The Friendship' in the recently published collection of Holtby and Brittain's journalism makes available interesting new information, much of which could be used to support the view that the two women were involved in a lesbian relationship. Berry takes the orthodox line and in one extraordinarily muddled passage falls back on the good old British precept of minding one's own business:

> Except to those vicariously titillated by other people's sexual idiosyncracies, the individual's sexuality would seem to be important only as it affects his or her life and work, but to understand fully the friendship between Vera and Winifred it is none the less necessary to recognise that it was not a lesbian one.[29]

All the above commentators write as if friendship, love and sexuality were unproblematic concepts, with fixed definitions which have remained unchanged throughout history. In fact, as many feminist historians have illustrated, definitions of friendships between women and the social meanings of these relationships have, even in the last hundred years, undergone complex and radical changes. The lesbian feminist who wishes to discover how Holtby and Brittain saw their friendship is faced with an almost impossible task, coping as she must with the gaps and ambiguities in contemporary accounts and the heterosexist obfuscation of later commentators. One way of putting *Testament*

150

of Friendship into its historical context is to look at the ideas current about lesbianism in the 1930s and where Vera Brittain placed herself in relation to them.

The most widely known image of the lesbian in the 1930s was the male-identified Stephen Gordon in Radclyffe Hall's *The Well of Loneliness* (1928). Hall drew many of her ideas from the late nineteenth-century sexologists and her novel has a brief introduction by Havelock Ellis. By the 1930s Freudianism with its emphasis on psychological influences rather than biological impulses had become popularised, but Faderman argues that Freudianism helped to validate the role divisions beloved by the sexologists:

> In 'The Sexual Aberrations' Freud divided women who love women into 'butches' and 'femmes' no less than Hall did with her 'invert' and 'mate of the invert'. He declared that 'the active invert' generally exhibited both physical and mental masculine characteristics and looked for femininity in her love object.[30]

When Vera Brittain reviewed *The Well of Loneliness* in *Time and Tide* in August 1928 she welcomed Hall's plea for 'the extension of social tolerance, compassion and recognition' to homosexuals, but her view of the nature of homosexuality is essentially that of the sexologists. She writes of the 'biologically abnormal woman' and those who suffer under 'one of Nature's cruellest dispensations' in contrast to whom 'the emotions of normal men and women seem so clear and uncomplicated.'[31]

However, by the time Brittain published *Testament of Friendship* in 1940, other views of lesbianism far less stigmatising than those of the sexologists would have been available to her. M. Esther Harding in *The Way of All Women: A Psychological Interpretation* (1933) and Laura Hutton in *The Single Woman and Her Emotional Problems* (1935) both discuss close friendships between women in very positive terms. It is useful to compare their justification of female friendship with Brittain's. As we have seen, the complete separation of sexual love, and love in friendship is essential to Brittain's presentation of her relationship with Holtby in *Testament*. But both Harding and Hutton accept that there is a sexual element in any close friendship. The Jungian Harding comments: 'Thus from a broader point of view it must be recognised that the emotion involved in such friendships is instinctual or sexual in character.'[32] Freudian Hutton comments: 'It is is to be expected, however, that sexuality will play some part of any intense emotional relationship, and where this is understood (and indeed it is frequently not even recognised) emotional conflicts and tensions will inevitably arise.'[33] Hutton advocates: 'The first prerequisite for the management of the sexual element in any friendship is its frank recognition and acceptance.'[34]

Whereas Brittain presents close friendship between women as enhancing rather than threatening marriage, Harding, who saw women at the time she was writing as more psychologically evolved than men, states that men 'are still for the most part, quite unable to give women the kind of emotional satisfaction and security which they can find with their women friends'.[35] She comments that in choosing to marry rather than continue to live with a woman friend, a woman will be influenced by 'the weight of conventional evaluation which works from within the individual psyche no less than through the opinion of society'.[36] While Brittain argues that female friendship benefits marriage, Hutton cautiously proposes that lesbianism benefits society:

All that is intended is a suggestion that friendships between responsible women of the type just described – i.e. involving (perhaps only very occasionally, or during a transitory phase of the friendship) some sexual expression may indeed play quite a useful part in society at the present day.[37]

Both Harding and Hutton strenuously resist the view that lesbianism is perverted. Harding says that women involved in sexual relationships with other women 'cannot be considered perverted if their actions are motivated by love'.[38] Hutton warns against categorical assertions on the causes of homosexuality: 'it would seem wiser to refrain from adopting either the congenital or the psychogenic theory to the exclusion of the other'.[39] She carefully dissociates lesbianism from both perversion and pathology: 'It is fairer to describe such a woman as sexually abnormal (or anomalous) rather than perverted, bearing in mind always that the abnormal is not necessarily the diseased.'[40]

Brittain never allowed herself the flexibility of either Harding or Hutton. She maintained a rigid distinction between sexual and emotional feeling. In a letter to Sybil Morrison she wrote: 'I am a markedly heterosexual woman whose relations with men have been many and complicated, but who has had none with women.'[41] Speaking of Holtby to Sarah Gertrude Millin, she said: 'No one has ever been mentally and spiritually nearer to me, nor ever now, I imagine will be again.'[42] That this dichotomy was not always easy to live with is indicated by a scribbled note found among her papers after her death in 1970: 'I loved Winifred, but I was not in love with her.'[43]

It is relevant to ask why Brittain was not willing to go further and admit the possibility of some sexual element, even at a subconscious level, in the relationship, since she would, inevitably, invite suspicion from some quarters by merely celebrating a friendship with another woman. Of course writing about relationships on a distanced, academic level as Harding and Hutton did is very different from revealing one's own personal, intimate feelings and those of a dead friend, but I think Brittain was motivated by other factors than a wish simply to safeguard her privacy. As Muriel Mellown points out, Brittain advocated a more open and equal system of marriage and saw her own 'semi-detached marriage'[44] as exemplary. *Testament of Friendship* indicates that Holtby made a significant contribution to Brittain's marriage, as a companion and in more practical areas, such as childcare. Hints of lesbianism would not only embarrass Brittain personally, but sully the image of her pioneering experiment in flexible matrimony.

The myth of Winifred Holtby which, at its crudest, presents her as a sexually unattractive woman sublimating her unrequited love for a man through good works and literary activity, established itself soon after her death. Even the reticent Evelyne White begins her biography with a reference to Winifred and her sister Grace as children reciting a poem which contained the line, 'One is for use, the other for show', and comments: 'Winifred said how she longed to be asked sometimes to take the part of the good-looking, attractive person, but, no, that was always Grace's part and she had to reconcile herself to be the person for service.'[45] Brittain feels no compunction in endorsing this view of her friend. In *Testament of Experience* she quotes a remark her husband made about Holtby: 'I suspect great sexual diffidence passed off as a joke on "outsizes".'[46] But women frequently saw Holtby differently. Hilda Reid regarded her as beautiful,[47] and Jean McWilliam described her as 'beautiful and glowing'.[48]

Holtby acquiesced in the view of herself as unattractive to men and later commentators have uncritically reproduced and accentuated this 'plain as pikestaff' image.[49] Paul Berry, for example, crassly contrasts Winifred's and Vera's appearance to produce a version of 'the pretty girl and her ugly friend' stereotype. We could speculate that a woman who was ill at ease with heterosexual romance would not find 'a personality completely devoid of sexual attraction' an unsupportable burden.[50] Through the 1920s Holtby makes various references to her lack of enthusiasm for heterosexual love. Sometimes these comments are lighthearted: 'I really shall be disappointed if I go through life without once being properly in love. As a writer, I feel it is my duty to my work – but they are all so helpless, and such children. How can one feel thrilled?'[51] Sometimes there is a more serious tone: 'I can't even love as we usually speak of love'.[52] Even on Bill, the great romance of her life, she is less than passionate:

> Curious how, although I do not love nor respect as lovers love I yet feel my personality so strangely linked to him. I do not particularly want to see him, and in his company I am a little bored, but the thought of disaster to him oppresses me beyond words.[53]

It is perhaps significant that when she did express a desire for conventional attractiveness, it was not to gain lovers for herself but to remove them from Brittain. She promises to be Brittain's 'bulwark for as long as you want me. I regret that I have no Syren charms to entice away embarrassing suitors.'[54]

By the mid-1930s a vehemently anti-Freudian note is sounding in Holtby's writing. As we have seen, in *Women and a Changing Civilisation* she deplored the emphasis on sexual activity which she saw as one of the results of the popularisation of Freud's ideas. This attitude is repeated in her introductory chapter to her study of Virginia Woolf – as a result of the new emphasis on psychology: 'A woman she [i.e. Woolf] was told, must enjoy the full cycle of sex-experience, or she would become riddled with complexes like a rotting fruit.'[55] In an article in *Time and Tide* on George V's Jubilee celebrations, she comments on the changes in popular ideas about sexuality which had taken place in her lifetime:

> Today, there is a far worse crime than promiscuity: it is chastity. On all sides the unmarried woman today is surrounded by doubts cast not only upon her attractiveness or her common sense, but upon her decency, her normality, even her sanity.[56]

From one perspective, of course, this could be seen as merely the defensive rantings of a virgin spinster, regretting that 'maiden ladies' were no longer seen as sexually uncomplicated. I think it is far more likely that, unlike Vera Brittain who simply ignored Freud, Holtby realised that the new emphasis on the psychology of sex would put relationships such as the one she enjoyed with Brittain under critical scrutiny.

How should modern lesbian feminists see Winifred Holtby and her relationship with Vera Brittain? There are no cut and dried answers, but various options are open to us. We could see *Testament of Friendship* as a totally straightforward, factual account of a close friendship. As I have argued, *Testament* shows too much evidence of careful arrangement and wording to be simply a naive account. We could see *Testament* as a clever cover-up of a long-term lesbian affair. This is tempting, but there is no external evidence available at present which would absolutely corroborate this theory. Holtby and Brittain could have been conducting a classic romantic friendship in an age when such relationships could no longer be taken at their face value. According to this view, *Testament* is open to misinterpretation by those whom Brittain would term 'over-sophisticated'. Perhaps the most likely explanation is that both Holtby and Brittain recognised a sexual element in their relationship whether or not they acted on it. Vera Brittain, with the ideal of 'semi-detached marriage' to protect, had good reason for putting as much distance as possible between lesbianism and herself. Winifred Holtby for more complex reasons, among them a desire not to harm Brittain's reputation, was unable to take on a lesbian identity in the direct way chosen by some of her friends and contemporaries, for example Ethel Smyth. Of course, this is merely supposition, but until Holtby and Brittain's private papers are available for the use of historians and critics it will be difficult to make a more definite and detailed argument.

It is significant that despite the disclaimers and despite Bill, many of Brittain's contemporaries read against the text and saw *Testament* as a record of a lesbian relationship. Brittain says that 'many correspondents wrote me enthusiastically as a fellow homosexual'.[57] To the end of her days Brittain stuck to her rigid separation of sexual and emotional feeling. In her book on the trial of *The Well of Loneliness* she wrote of the 'intensity of love which can exist between woman and woman' and which she saw as existing 'between mother and daughter, sister and sister, or friend and friend; its distinction lies in its intensity, and its freedom from selfishness or the desire to possess'.[58] Ironically, Brittain is here anticipating Adrienne Rich's description of the 'lesbian continuum' which she defines as including 'a range – through each woman's life and throughout history – of woman-identified experience; not simply the fact that a woman has had or consciously desired genital sexual experience with another woman'.[59] She expands her definition to include 'many more forms of primary intensity between and among women, including the sharing of a rich inner life, the bonding against male tyranny, the giving and receiving of practical and political support'.[60] Although emotionally appealing to many women, I think Rich's 'lesbian continuum' is too vague and all-embracing to be of much practical use to lesbian historians. Nevertheless, it would be tragic if our sole criterion for allowing a woman a place in lesbian history becomes proof that she had or wanted to have genital sexual contact with another woman. If we apply this narrow standard to Holtby, we distort her life and contribute to the vicious irony of heterosexism which makes it more acceptable for her primary emotional attachment to be to a man with whom she had no viable relationship for fifteen years, than to a woman with whom she shared 'sixteen incomparable years'[61] of life and work.

8
Butch and Femme: Now and then

Sheila Jeffreys

An earlier version of this piece appeared in Gossip *No. 5, 1987.*

In the late 1960s and early 1970s a feminist critique was developed of butch and femme roleplaying in lesbian relationships. Such roleplaying had never been general in the lesbian community and in the 1960s when there was a move away from gender fetishism in heterosexual couples there was a similar shift amongst those lesbians who had been involved in roleplaying. In lesbian–feminist circles and in those parts of the community which saw themselves as radical and progressive, lesbians avoided identifying themselves as butch or femme in the 1970s, though doubtless there was roleplaying alive and well in less trendy areas, geographically and politically, of the lesbian subculture which had been less affected by gay liberation and lesbian feminism.

It was a shock to many lesbians in the 1980s to find that some lesbians in the US who could be seen as the leaders of their community, who were involved in recording our history, as novelists and writers on sexuality, were identifying themselves again as butch and femme. They were not only adopting roles cheerfully but reclaiming roleplaying in lesbian history as well as the lesbian present as revolutionary and positive. I will be looking at the writings of these lesbians here. Most of my sources are from the US because the revalidation of roleplaying is only just beginning to become fashionable in Britain. Butch and femme identified lesbians today criticise feminists for having disapproved of roleplayers, and most importantly, for having distorted lesbian history by playing down the importance of roleplaying or recording it in a negative light. Some lesbian historians who are chronicling lesbian roleplaying in history treat roleplayers with unqualified admiration. Davis and Kennedy, who have compiled the oral histories of lesbians in Buffalo, New York State from the forties and fifties, write of the lesbian roleplayers they interviewed:

> We suspected that these women were heroines who had shaped the development of gay pride in the twentieth century by forging a culture for survival and resistance under prejudicial conditions and by passing this sense of community on to newcomers; in our minds, these are indications of a movement in its pre-political stages.[1]

To such chroniclers it is that very roleplaying which lesbians in the Gay Liberation Front and lesbian feminism had rejected which was the radical foundation of lesbian liberation.

But there are many lesbians who experienced roleplaying in this period who did not and do not see roleplaying as positive. Such lesbians, like Julia Penelope, who abandoned roleplaying as they developed a feminist critique of the practice, regard the current reclamation and validation of butch and femme identities with alarm. Penelope sees this reclamation as part of a backlash against feminism:

> The impulse to revive the labels 'butch' and 'femme' and inject some political respectability into their meaning (however belatedly) by talking about 'gut feelings', 'intuitions', and

159

'power' is the lesbian manifestation of the contemporary right wing backlash, further encouraged by 50's nostalgia ('Happy Days'), and the illusion of security we get by going back to what we imagine to have been 'better days', (usually because we didn't live through them), and talking about 'reclaiming our heritage'.[2]

Clearly there is an important issue here for lesbian historians and all lesbians interested in our history. The territory under discussion – 1940s, 1950s, 1960s – is close enough for many lesbians to be able to enter this debate from their own experience, yet far enough away for some young lesbians to seem like quite distant history about which they wait to be informed. As Penelope suggests, before lesbians speak of reclaiming our 'heritage' as 'though it were behind us', 'Let's admit that there are millions of lesbians alive today who never once considered abandoning their roles' (p. 18). She points out that 'There's a difference between writing history and rewriting it, between documentary and romanticising', and it's that difference I intend to look at here. Using the writings of lesbians who give a glowing picture of roleplaying in the lesbian past and those who see roleplaying then and now as negative and restricting for lesbians I will try to work towards a 'documentary' which will illuminate both what roleplaying meant in the fifties and sixties and why some lesbians are seeking to reclaim it today.

I am not neutral in this debate and see the reclamation of roleplaying as a dangerous political development for lesbians. I didn't experience lesbian roleplaying myself in its heyday but I see that patterns of lesbian relating and identifying based on dominance and submission and gender fetishism are certainly present in the lesbian community today. My interest in roleplaying in the lesbian past stems from my anxieties about roleplaying in the present and my belief that the version of the past we are being given by promoters of butch and femme today is misleading. This chapter will look at the 'what' and the 'why' of roleplaying in the fifties and at what contemporary chroniclers have made of it.

What

Merrill Mushroom writes pieces of autobiography and short stories about being a butch dyke in the 1950s. She explains that there was a variety of roles which could be played within the framework of butch and femme. Butches could be average butches or 'strict' butches who never went with femmes, drag butches who passed as a man in various aspects of their lives, stone butches who did not let their partners touch them or 'femmie-looking' butches who looked enough like a femme to be mistaken for one. Femmes had rather fewer options and could be average femmes or 'butchie-looking' femmes. Lesbians who played either role depending on who they were with were called ki-ki. These terms were not necessarily the accepted version within all areas of the lesbian community. Ethel Sawyer, in a University of Washington essay written in 1965 on the Black lesbian community of Saint Louis, Missouri, tells us that the terms stud and fish were in use instead of butch and femme. Interestingly the word 'fish' is a term of insult used by gay men about women in general and is supposed to refer to the way women's genitals smell.

There was a hierarchy built into butch roleplaying, leaving aside the obvious hierarchy of butch and femme. In the accounts and personal testimony there is most honour and status accorded to the role of stone butch. Mushroom explains that butches or femmes who managed to make love to a butch won a victory over her and often turned this into a public humiliation.

A great deal of public ridicule and embarrassment came down on a butch who 'went femme', mainly because of the demeaning social attitudes towards femaleness. The derision shown toward those few butches who had been flipped was enough to prevent many of us, especially those of us who were not yet secure about our sexuality from letting our partners

161

touch us during lovemaking.[3]

The hierarchy was based on a scale of femaleness and maleness. The most male behaviour, and therefore most worthy of respect, was never to allow a woman to lay hands upon you.

The social pressures towards and pride involved in being a 'stone butch' could lead lesbians to distort their personal histories. Davis and Kennedy's narrators divided into butches who claimed they had always been untouchably 'stone' and those who had the reputation of being untouchable but claimed that that was really impossible.

> One, when asked if she were really untouchable replied, 'Of course not. How would my woman stay with me if I was? It doesn't make any sense. . . . I don't believe there ever was such a class – other than what they told each other.'[4]

This narrator was completely untouchable on the first night but would sometimes allow a lover to touch her during a long-term relationship because the lover desired it, not because she, the butch, experienced pleasure from it. Ethel Sawyer tells us that most studs started their lesbian career as fish but felt it necessary to deny this thereafter:

> . . . many studs do not like to admit that they were ever anything but stud. They have the tendency to play down all of their female characteristics to the point of insisting that they have been studs since entering the life.[5]

Why

Some of the stone butches in the 1950s, and those who remain stone butch today, see themselves as physically and biologically stone butch. One of the lesbians who spoke to Davis and Kennedy explained: 'I've tried to have my lover make love to me, but I just couldn't stand it. . . . I really think there's something physical about that.'[6] According to Sawyer the Black studs in St Louis 'almost invariably attribute their homosexuality to their own personal characteristics and attributes'.[7]

Since the propagation of sexological ideas of the 'real' lesbian in the late nineteenth and early twentieth century, i.e. mannish, able to whistle and so on, it is butch lesbians who have adopted the identity of 'real' lesbians; the realness of femmes has always been in doubt. Havelock Ellis distinguished between the 'actively inverted' woman and the 'women to whom the actively inverted woman is most attracted'.[8] The former had 'one fairly essential character: a more or less distinct trace of masculinity'. The latter were 'always womanly'. This assertion of roleplaying by the sexologists, based upon their belief that it was by definition a 'masculine' prerogative to make sexual advances to women so that a woman who did this would have to be abnormal and 'masculine', had formed the basic template for ideas of butch and femme in the twentieth century. It can be no comfort to us that the sexologist prescription is being so religiously obeyed by some lesbians who see themselves as feminists today. It may be argued that the sexologists did not so much prescribe as describe the actual situation of lesbians as they observed it, i.e. roleplaying was actually going on among the lesbians they encountered. Though there may have been some lesbians living out such patterns, the case studies Ellis gives by no means support this. The clearly mythological nature of many of his assertions would suggest that he is more than likely to have derived his roleplaying ideas from the less than reliable source from which he obtained much of his evidence on lesbian practice, i.e. contemporary male erotica.[9]

Davis and Kennedy do not say that butch and femme are biologically defined but do see roleplaying as being 'authentically' lesbian. It is difficult to know what 'authentic' lesbianism consists of unless we employ some concept of biological determinism. This idea implies that those who abjure roleplaying as best they are able, are somehow 'inauthentic'. They write 'although these women (butch and femme couples) did draw on models in heterosexual society, they transformed those models into an authentically lesbian interaction'.[10] Their concluding sentence employs the word 'authentic' again. 'As part of a long tradition of creating an authentic lesbian culture in an oppressive society, butch-fem roles remain, for many lesbians, an important code of personal behaviour in matters of either appearance, sexuality, or both.'[11]

The recorded experience of 1950s roleplayers lends no support to a biological determinist explanation. The motivations mentioned are much more prosaic. In Sawyer's study most of the studs had clearly started out as fish: 'most studs were first fish, and fish are the first to divulge this information'.[12] It is difficult indeed to imagine any other scenario – sexual initiation is a stud characteristic. So at the time when future studs are brought out they will almost certainly be fish. Sawyer's informants make it clear that stud and fish are social roles that were quite consciously chosen:

> One fish expressed the desire to turn stud but had certain reservations. Her reasons for wanting to turn stud were that she wanted 'to be the aggressor, to pick and choose, and to do the protecting'. On the other hand, she felt that she could not live up to the idealised social role of a stud. 'I don't feel that I would be able to support someone. I feel that a stud should be the provider and protector and right now, I'm not able'.[13]

Studs might have to be fish first as a kind of apprenticeship, to learn how to be studs: 'I had to get started as a fish first and then when I learned my way, I said, "I'm ready to be a stud now" '.[14] Another reason for not choosing to be a stud might be the difficulty of 'passing' as a stud and the social unacceptability of stud apparel. One fish explained: 'I wouldn't want my children to see me in pants all of the time'.[15]

Mushroom provides us with a good list of reasons for the adoption of the butch role in which biology is never mentioned. She associates the stone-butch role with lack of confidence about her own attractiveness and fear of vulnerability.

> Although as a stone butch I didn't let my partner touch me
> sexually I expected her to try, at least at first; and I was insulted
> if she didn't. I took these attempts to be indications of my own
> desirability, since I felt unattractive enough to believe that
> another woman wouldn't really be wanting to make love to
> me.[16]

Mushroom provides a very practical explanation for the wearing
of 'full drag'. She explains: 'It was safer to go out on a date with a
femme to a straight place if we could pass. . . . Men sometimes
beat up lesbians on the street.'[17] Butches, she says, did not want to
'be men' but wanted the 'goodies' which men had, 'the freedom,
the pride, the power, and the legitimacy to be with the women we
loved'. She attributes roleplaying overall to the fact that 'the only
models we had for our relationships were those of the traditional
female–male heterosexual couple, and we were too busy trying to
survive in a hostile world to have time to create new roles for
ourselves'. The choice to be butch or femme related to what,
according to Mushroom, maleness and femaleness meant in fifties
heteropatriarchal culture, and which, I venture to suggest, they still
mean in the dominant culture today:

> Maleness was equated with power, strength, pride and free-
> dom. Femaleness was equated with weakness, dependency
> and obedience. Female images were used in ways that were
> shameful and degrading.[18]

The reality of roleplaying

The contemporary proponents of roleplaying are offering a
romanticised version of the lifestyle of fifties roleplayers.
According to writers like Nestle, one of the founders of the New
York Lesbian Archives, roleplaying was a form of erotic prefer-

ence. It does not seem from the accounts we have available that roleplaying in the fifties was positively chosen for its erotic advantages. It is clear that both the butch and femme roles had serious disadvantages attached to them which make the revalidation of these roles today particularly difficult to understand.

The femme

Let us look first of all at the role of the femme. She seems to have experienced the social disadvantages in the lesbian community normally faced by the underclass of women in the heterosexual world. One was low status, which extended from being simply unimportant in the world of butches to being the object of scorn and contempt. Nestle explains:

> Fems were deeply cherished and yet devalued as well. There were always fem put-down jokes going around the bar, while at the same time tremendous energy and caring was spent courting the fem women, . . . We were mysterious and practical, made homes and broke them up, were glamorous and boring all at the same time.[19]

In St Louis, Missouri, the fish role was certainly inferior. The scale of values involved should be clear from the very titles 'stud' and 'fish'. Sawyer explains the hierarchy of stud and fish thus:

> Studs as a result of having attained the ultimate in homosexuality (as is perceived by members of this group) are therefore privileged with a higher status within the subculture than that which is accorded the fish, who on the other hand enjoy the situation of marginality.[20]

The disadvantage of the fish's marginality was that the researcher found it difficult to find fish to interview. The studs were astonished that she should wish to speak with fish. A party arranged by the researcher to get to know lesbian respondents

166

had only studs present, they had not invited fish. Sawyer comments:

> This status discrepancy between studs and fish in Jim's group is sufficiently strong that if I felt there might be some difficulty in interviewing a fish, I was able to work it through her stud.[21]

The marginality of the fish was evident in the fact that:

> Their association more frequently involves persons who are not homosexuals; their heterosexual relations are much more extensive; and in general, they are less committed to the life socially, sexually and psychologically.[22]

Today the same problem exists for researchers wanting to find femmes from the 1950s to interview. Davis and Kennedy had this problem in Buffalo. They explain that their 'information on fem sexuality is not as extensive as that on butch sexuality because we have been able to contact fewer fem narrators'.[23] But they were able to use 'comments by butches who sought them out and loved them'. In fact a discussion of butch sexuality dominates the Davis and Kennedy piece and the voice of the femme is almost entirely absent. This is uncannily like the difficulties of researching women's history generally where women are elusive but there are plenty of men to speak for women and explain them. The analogy is clearly not exact but there are problems here for lesbian historical research. Do we accept that the butch is the archetypal lesbian as most writings about roleplaying suggest, even those written by such femmes as Nestle? Do we accept that the femme is marginal and existed mainly, perhaps still does exist, as a mirror through which the butch might realise herself? Certainly there is evidence that the femme role was not and is not an equal but different choice of lifestyle. Femmes were seen as not 'real' lesbians, inauthentic, subordinate, marginal.

The butch

What were the advantages and disadvantages for the butch? An advantage must have been the superior status. Amidst all the hatred directed at lesbians by the straight world, butch lesbians were at least able to feel superior to someone, the femme. But besides this rather limited ego enhancement there were, according to most accounts, serious disadvantages. One butch narrator explained to Davis and Kennedy why she had always gone to bed with her clothes on:

What it came to was being uncomfortable with the female body. You didn't want people you were with to realise the likeness between the two.[24]

Julia Penelope states 'that the emotional and sexual damage I experienced from living within the limitations of my butch role has taken years for me to identitfy, comprehend, and disengage myself from. . .'.[25] Penelope describes the difficulty of the struggle to disburden herself of the remnants of the butch role, but the struggle led to the realisation of some potent pleasures that had been inaccessible to her as a butch: 'I've learned the exquisite pleasure of allowing another Lesbian to touch me and to let my feelings move through my body and to be aware of my feelings.'[26]

Cherrie Moraga, in her discussion with Amber Hollibaugh, despite joining in an attack on the prudish, anti-sex lesbian feminists who don't understand the joy of roleplaying, shows considerable ambivalence about the sexual problems created by butchness. She explains:

I am seriously attracted to butches sometimes . . . I have never totally reckoned with being the 'beloved' and, frankly, I don't know if it takes a butch or a femme or what to get me there. I know that it's a struggle within me and it scares the shit out of me to look at it so directly. I've done this kind of searching emotionally, but to combine sex with it seems like very dangerous stuff.[27]

Moraga's explanation of the behaviour of stone butches is not glamorous. She, like the interviewee in the Davis and Kennedy study who needed to keep her clothes on, sees 'stone' behaviour as resulting from discomfort with having a female body. Such a stone butch, Moraga states:

> doesn't want to feel her femaleness because she thinks of you as the 'real' woman and if she makes love to you, she doesn't have to feel her own body as the object of desire. She can be a kind of 'bodiless' lover. So when you turn over and want to make love to her and make her feel physically like a woman, then what she is up against is QUEER.[28]

Stone butchness here is identified as being about internalised lesbophobia, an attempt to avoid recognising oneself as a lesbian. Many lesbians who came out in the 1950s and 1960s recount that they had no choice about roleplaying; they were forced into it by the failure of the lesbian scene to accept that any lesbian was not one or the other. Luchia Fitzgerald describes how she was forced into roleplaying when she came out on to the gay scene in Manchester in the 1960s:

> Shocked I was that some women were dressed as men. I couldn't understand that because I fucking hated them, and I couldn't understand how women like you or me, that had the same feelings as me towards other women, were dressed up like men. I wasn't accepted at first on the gay scene because I was fancying women dressed up as men and I was fancying feminine women as well, so people used to call me an in-betweener. But after about six months of that I couldn't stand it any more, so I thought, I look ridiculous in a fucking skirt so I went and had the crop like. . . . I was pushed into it. If I had been left on me own I would have been all right, but I was pushed into this role.[29]

Penelope explains her 'stone' butchness as having been partly to do with her incest experience. Adopting the façade of a butch protected her from having to deal with the consequences emotionally and sexually of that experience, such as her 'utter inability to be intimate'.[30] Participation in an incest survivors' group helped Julia Penelope in 'Coming to terms with the ways in which my incest experiences distorted and atrophied my sexual and emotional responses. . .'.

As a lesbian–feminist movement we have explored the issue of incest well and courageously but have generally drawn to a stop before considering the implications of abuse for the construction of our sexuality. We can't afford to make this halt and lesbians like Penelope are pioneers of a new sexual frankness, not the kind of bravado so dear to practitioners of sadomasochism, but a frankness about our hurts and pain and what they do to us.

It might seem that the disadvantages of butch sexuality are clear but this is not so for those keen to reinvent roleplaying today. These very restrictions on sexual expression that roleplaying imposes, Davis and Kennedy see as having turned into an 'authentic lesbian sexuality'. Davis and Kennedy explain that their 'research counters the view that butch femme roles are solely an imitation of sexist heterosexual society'. It was true that the butch was the physically active partner,

> Yet unlike the dynamics of many heterosexual relationships, the butch's foremost objective was to give sexual pleasure to a fem; it was in satisfying her fem that the butch received fulfillment. . . . As for the fem, she not only knew what would give her physical pleasure, but she also knew that she was neither object of nor receptacle for someone else's gratification. The essence of this emotional/sexual dynamic is captured by the ideal of the 'stone butch', or untouchable butch, that prevailed during this period. A 'stone butch' does all the 'doin' and does not ever allow her lover to reciprocate in kind. To be untouchable meant to gain pleasure from giving pleasure. Thus, although these women did draw on models in heterosexual society, they transformed those models into an

170

authentically lesbian interaction. Through roleplaying they developed distinctive and fulfilling expressions of women's sexual love for women.[31]

If the very restrictions of roleplaying sexuality are 'authentic' for lesbians, then lesbians who seek to overcome the restrictions and expand their sexual choice and experience must be 'inauthentic'. There's not much hope here for changing anyone's sexuality. Who would purposely wish to pursue inauthenticity? Fortunately many butches have made and continue to make the decision to expand their sexual horizons.

Lesbian history

Joan Nestle of the New York Lesbian History Archives states that feminist writings have distorted lesbian history through their unwillingness to recognise the existence of roleplaying.

In their early pages, these books usually had a disclaimer about butch fem Lesbians or the bar culture and seldom ever considered these people and these places as more than expressions of internalised oppression. Passing women, Lesbian sex workers or working class Lesbian 'married' couples were either completely missing or dismissed as examples of victimisation.[32]

From an unwillingness to recognise forms of lesbian behaviour which were seen as politically embarrassing, Nestle argues, lesbian–feminist historians 'created a history of middle and upper class role models'. Feminist historians, she argues, have embraced the 'romantic friends of the 1800s through the literary salons of France in the first quarter of the twentieth century to the Lesbian feminists of the early 70s whilst neglecting the history of working class lesbians'.

Such a statement throws us into a nettle bed of problems. Lesbian history must, indeed, include the experience of

171

working-class lesbians, but the assumption that working-class lesbians were more prone to roleplaying than middle-class lesbians is not well substantiated and could lead to the creation of false stereotypes of the working-class butch or femme. The literary salons of the 1920s included plentiful examples of roleplaying and it is likely that there were many working-class lesbians who rejected roleplaying as some of their middle-class contemporaries did. There has been an unfortunate tendency amongst the detractors of feminism over the last few years to exploit the issue of class in inappropriate ways to support anti-feminist ideas and practice.

The implication of Nestle's writing is that somehow feminists imposed egalitarian forms of relationship upon lesbians in the late sixties and early seventies. This suggests that the feminist prescription came from outside the lesbian community, from political theorists who knew nothing about roleplaying from the inside. In fact roleplaying and dress were an issue for lesbians long before feminism introduced its own critique.

Del Martin and Phyllis Lyon write in *Lesbian/Woman* about the Daughters of Bilitis lesbian organisation which predated this wave of feminism. They tell of a butch femme couple who joined DOB:

> . . . one of D.O.B.'s goals was to teach the Lesbian a 'mode of behaviour and dress acceptable to society'. What D.O.B. meant by such a suggestion was that all persons should be free enough to dress, and feel at ease, in the appropriate attire for any situation, from evening gowns to bathing suits. We knew too many Lesbians whose activities were restricted because they wouldn't wear skirts . . .[33]

Joan Nestle's effeminised lesbian would have fitted quite well into this scene since it was clearly butch rather than femme clothing which was criticised. A similar debate over clothing took place in the London Minorities Research Group in the early 1960s and in their newsletter, *Arena 3*. Some lesbians attending the group's meetings above a pub were embarrassed that lesbians in full drag went through the main section of the pub to get to the meeting. Lesbians in the newsletter discussed the pros and cons of exaggeratedly butch attire. There was a debate at the Minorities Research Group meeting reported in the September 1964 issue of the newsletter. The motion was 'That this House considers the wearing of male attire at MTG meetings is inappropriate'.[34] Twenty-five voted for the motion and twenty-eight against, with six abstentions.

It is interesting that it is fems who find a feminist climate most restricting towards their sartorial style these days. Butches don't have so much of a problem. Feminist lesbians do not react to clothing on the basis of fearing exposure from the 'outness' of other lesbians. Feminists find effeminate clothing more difficult to stomach on the grounds that it is an ever-present symbol of the degraded condition of women and of the internalised self-hatred of lesbians.

Roleplaying as well as clothing was a debated issue in the fifties and sixties, not a settled and accepted way of life for the lesbian community. Penelope tells of lesbians who wouldn't consider having a relationship with her because she identified as a butch.

> More than one lesbian acquaintance told me to my face: 'If I wanted a man, I'd go out and get a real one. Who wants a bad imitation? I like women.' As far as I know, there have always been lesbians who attacked roles and disapproved of other lesbians who were 'into' them: there were those who felt comfortable with them and defended them, and those who didn't care one way or another.[35]

Martin and Lyon describe the process they worked through before they had a feminist analysis, away from butch femme roles which didn't seem to fit the reality of their relating in any way, towards 'acting as people, as ourselves, as women rather than as caricatures in a heterosexual marriage. But it took us a while.'[36]

It would seem that Nestle is distorting lesbian history in

stating that it is mainly feminists who have found roleplaying unacceptable. Her writings suggest that she is hostile to feminism and it suits her therefore to attribute any discomfort with roleplaying only to feminists.

Not only did lesbians before the impact of feminism criticise roles, but within gay liberation roles were subjected to severe criticism. Unfortunately very few British lesbians have written accounts of their experience within gay liberation but we do have a collection of the writings from *Come Together*, the British gay liberation magazine. The aims and principles in the early days contained strong pro-feminist commitments and a commitment to eliminating gender roles. The way this ideal was put into practice by some lesbians involved was over-zealous and not tactful. In 1970 when some London Gay Liberation Front (GLF) lesbians went to distribute leaflets at the Gateways club they seem to have been little affected by the embryo women's liberation movement. They still referred to themselves as 'girls' rather than as women or lesbians. But they had adopted wholesale the GLF enthusiasm that lesbians and gays should make themselves anew and overnight eject any behaviour or attitudes that GLFers found embarrassing. The writer was horrified by the roleplaying of the proprietors and by their ideas about lesbianism. She identifies Smith, one of the proprietors, as butch and concludes as follows on their conversation:

> Although we tried to argue with her it was obvious that she simply could not listen or take in anything we said – that's how rooted her attitudes are. The really sad thing is her negative attitude to her own lesbianism; she came back many times to the statement 'We are abnormal.' I would include as part of her negative attitude and distorted self-image the rigidly sex-defined roles she and her girlfriend feel compelled to play – 'butch' and 'femme', as among the most traditionalist heterosexual couples. This is not a personal attack, but it is another indication of the unliberated state of this as of very many other lesbian couples in which one partner plays the submissive 'feminine' role, as exploited as

many married women.[37]

This is of course a personal attack, arrogant and patronising and showing no respect for or interest in an older lesbian's experience and views. But this viewpoint comes squarely from within Gay Liberation. I don't expect that this was the standard attitude to roleplayers among GLF lesbians but it should cause those lesbians to hesitate who are currently engaging in feminist-bashing and uphold Gay Liberation as much more revolutionary and sexy. Davis and Kennedy see roleplaying lesbians in Buffalo as precursors of gay liberation, not lesbian feminism. This admiration for gay liberation seems to be based upon the fact that gay men who see themselves as part of gay liberation now glorify forms of sexual practice which appeal to such lesbians and are indeed subjected to a savage political critique by lesbian feminists. We must remember that in the first couple of years of gay liberation such forms of behaviour were analysed politically and found wanting. As the radicalism of gay liberation died and lesbians deserted in large numbers for lesbian feminism, gay male theorists of liberation turned around and began to promote as revolutionary practices based upon internalised homophobia, gender fetishism, eroticised power imbalance and sexual objectification.

Chris Bearchall, a Canadian lesbian, explains in 1983 why she is a gay liberationist and why she wholeheartedly rejects radical feminism:

Many dykes, including those who call ourselves feminists, are compulsive rule-breakers. We take women to beaches, or find them there, and head for the dunes. Or take bar-room tricks to bathroom cubicles for quickies. We reject Playboy lesbianism because it isn't hot enough and get our polaroids out instead. We seek out lovers we can trust for SM theatre, or choose to play sexual games because they involve certain risks. We are irresponsible tomboys who refused to grow up and who now refuse to leave out of our lives, including our love and sex lives, a kindred spirit because she happens to be

175

15 or 16 years old. It isn't true that public sex, porn, SM and child-adult sex are not lesbian issues. . . .[38]

Roleplaying could well be added to this list. Perhaps the only reason it isn't is that this is so obviously a male gay sexual freedom agenda and gay men are not clamouring to roleplay butch and femme. But it is from such male gay sexual politics that contemporary lesbian promoters of roleplaying get such theoretical support as exists.

So did lesbian feminists write pejoratively about roleplaying in early works on lesbian liberation? Martin and Lyon certainly did. They comment thus on the view of a butch lesbian who saw herself as 'psychologically heterosexual':

> Strangely, it is women who feel that they are 'born butch' who tend to ape all the least desirable characteristics of men. In this case one may well say to these butches, 'Up against the wall, male chauvinist pig!'[39]

They present the butch lesbian as a male impersonator but do so from no outsider position but from within their own conflict and process as two lesbians who have questioned their own roleplaying and rejected butch and femme stereotypes for themselves.

Butch and femme and lesbian feminism

It is a basic building block of feminist theory that women's oppression is maintained by the social construction of masculine and feminine roles. Of these roles, that which is defined as 'feminine' is used as a trap to restrict women's lives and opportunities and is seen as inferior and subordinate. Whence does this notion of gendered roles or 'difference' stem? According to the Canadian radical lesbians, Brunet and Turcotte, the concept exists to validate and is the foundation of the institution of heterosexuality. They write:

From heterosexuality flow all the other oppressions. Hetero-sexuality is the cornerstone on which men have grounded the norm, located the source and the standard for defining all relationships. The concept of difference, institutionalised as heterosexuality, rests on a value system where one is superior and the other inferior, one is dominant and the other dominated.[40]

This clear and convincing analysis sees the concept of difference as the heart, not just of the oppression of lesbians and therefore all women, but of all systems of oppression. Such an approach forces us to consider the contemporary revalidation of roleplaying as something rather different from good clean fun since it is upon the concept of difference that roleplaying is based.

Janice Raymond also sees the concept of difference, which she defines as 'male–female polarity' as that which upholds the oppressive system of hetero-reality and hetero-relations and becomes the 'stuff of the cosmos':

> . . . hetero-reality and hetero-relations are built on the myth of androgyny. 'Thou as a woman must bond with a man' to fulfill the supposed cosmic purpose of reunifying that which was mythically separated into male and female. Arguments supporting the primacy and prevalence of hetero-relations are in some way based on a cosmic male–female polarity in which the so-called lost halves seek to be rejoined. In a hetero-relational world view, the overcoming of such polarity requires the infusion of all life with the comings-together of the separated halves. All of life's relations are then imbued with an androgynous energy and attraction that seeks to reunite the selves divided from each other, forever paired in cosmic complementarity. . . . Hetero-relational complementarity becomes the 'stuff of the cosmos'.[41]

This is a particularly concise exposition of the problem inherent in the idea of androgyny. Any concept of there being 'masculine' and 'feminine' attributes, even such as in Jungian theory, where males are allowed a sprinkling of 'feminine' qualities and vice versa, is totally geared to the support of what Raymond calls a 'hetero-relational' political system. Androgyny is not a benign concept for feminists. It is the acceptable face of the hetero-patriarchy, allowing a little bit of leeway within crude gender divisions. It is based upon that very 'male–female polarity' which supports the heteropatriarchal system which maintains women, and most sharply and clearly, lesbians, in subjection.

This is why it is so shocking and distressing to find lesbians, and lesbians who see themselves as feminists, finding no problem with the concept of 'male–female' polarity, in fact embracing it and cheerfully fitting themselves into it. Merrill Mushroom provides us with an excellent feminist political analysis of why she and other lesbians felt compelled to live roles in the 1950s yet she proceeds to validate them. She ends her article thus:

> I have learned how to touch and appreciate both the butch and the femme qualities of my lovers and my friends. Over the years, I have worn different tags and taken different images, and by now I can take them or leave them. But as I think back through all of the roles I have played and either kept or left behind, I know that deep down in my most secret heart of hearts . . . I am still the butch.[42]

Joan Nestle writes 'I am a fem and have been for over 25 years'.[43] Davis and Kennedy define roleplaying as 'authentic' lesbian sexuality. How is this to be explained?

What is the attraction of roleplaying today?

Since the concept of difference or 'male–female polarity' is the organising principle of the heteropatriarchy it is not surprising that it should so profoundly have shaped the consciousness even of many lesbians, that they are unable to think 'same' and can

178

only think 'different'. But explanation for the current revalidation of roleplaying must go further than that. As Brunet and Turcotte and Janice Raymond point out, the concept of difference is not benign. When sexists put down feminists with the slogan 'vive la différence' they are stating something profound about the way sexual desire is organised under male supremacy. It is not difference they are afraid to lose – the world is full of cultural differences which provide rich variety; it is power. The 'male–female polarity' is a polarity of dominance and submission. That is why difference in this context cannot be benign. Under male supremacy it is the subordination of women and male power that are eroticised. Sexual attraction is constructed around 'difference', i.e. dominance and submission. Those lesbians who are revalidating butch and femme are not discovering that they are innately butch or femme, they are engaging in an erotic communication based on sado-masochism, the eroticising of power difference.

This is clear from the writings of Merrill Mushroom. Mushroom has given up being a stone butch and engages in relationships in which her lovers do make love to her. But she still sees herself as a butch and her sexual relationships are organised clearly around the eroticising of dominance and submission. The language she uses to describe sex is the language of SM apologist literature and SM pornography with the catchwords 'power, trust, vulnerability'.

> The basic dynamics of butch–femme relating involve power, trust, vulnerability, tenderness and caring. When I as a butch demand of my lover 'Give it to me, baby, now', being as deep inside her as I can penetrate; and she completely releases herself and flows out to me. . . . Sometimes I want her to take me right away, and then I seduce her the way a femme seduces a butch – seduce her into taking me instead of wanting me to take her. Sometimes her own butch streak will dominate, and she will Have Her Way with me, and I will let her.[44]

179

Mushroom's concept of sexuality is limited to roleplaying but allows a little role-swapping to take place. She uses a Jungian approach in which 'butch streak' is presumably something like the animus. The feminine partner would be allowed to have a streak only because Mushroom was still the butch.

The circumstances in which lesbians find themselves today, especially if they are big-city lesbians, are very different from those of the fifties which prompted the adoption of roles that we have seen above. This would suggest that we should look for different motivations. It is not too difficult to understand the attraction of the butch role and in fact the butch model seems totally to have permeated lesbian culture today – skirts are rare, short hair and non-effeminate dress are the norm. Feminists spent great energy rejecting the clothing which symbolised the second-class status of women and painfully restricted or humiliatingly exposed women's bodies for the sexual titillation of men. This felt like such a great triumph that the appearance within the lesbian community of femmes who celebrate their femininity is a phenomenon difficult to sympathise with. Yet the most vociferous proponents of roleplaying today are femmes. What could cause the voluntary adoption of a role whose meaning, as defined by Mushroom, was 'weakness, dependence and obedience'?

Two American lesbians, Joan Nestle and Amber Hollibaugh, who was a founding member of the San Francisco Lesbian and Gay History Project and an editor of *Socialist Review*, have reiterated in various articles the same basic argument about the glory of femmeness, or is it femininity? What is the appeal of femmeness since it doesn't have the obvious attractions of maleness, i.e. power and privilege, associated with it? Nestle writes about being a femme in the late 1950s. For her the main attraction seems to be a masochistic sexual response to the power and privilege of the butch. She did not go in for relationships with stone butches but her erotic love was composed of the worshipful admiration which the underclass of women is trained to feel for the superior class of men:

180

there was and still is a butch sexuality and a fem sexuality, not a woman-acting-like-a-man or a woman-acting-like-a-woman but a developed, Lesbian, specific sexuality that has a historical setting and a cultural function. For instance, as a fem I enjoyed strong, fierce lovemaking; deep, strong givings and takings; erotic play challenges; calculated to call forth the butch-fem encounter. . . . Dress was a part of it – the erotic signal of her hair at the nape of her neck, touching the shirt collar; how she held a cigarette; the symbolic pinky ring flashing as she waved her hand. . . . Deeper than the sexual positioning was the overwhelming love I felt for their courage, the bravery of their erotic independence.[45]

Nestle expresses her sadness that femininity is not seen as acceptable by feminists. Nestle wants to make femmeness acceptable now. Despite the fact that the dominant culture has scarcely begun to redefine its understanding of the feminine, we are told that as lesbians we can change the meaning of feminine symbolism around. Though Nestle is convinced that butch and femme roleplaying is 'specific' to lesbianism it is difficult to imagine where the characteristics of butch and femme could have come from independently of heterosexual roleplaying.

It seems clear that the revalidation of butch and femme roleplaying today is a rather different phenomenon from the roleplaying of the fifties and sixties. Lesbians like Nestle, Cherrie Moraga and Amber Hollibaugh are part of an extensive lesbian community in which few lesbians overtly roleplay so the pressure to take up roles is not strong. This lesbian community has developed a feminist critique of masculinity and femininity which these writers are well aware of though they choose to reject it. Such a critique was not available in the bar scene of the 1950s. The present lesbian community has courageous survivors of the roleplaying of the fifties, like Julia Penelope, who are prepared to analyse in detail their roleplaying and how they came to abandon it as a result of the impact of feminism upon their lives. Moreover, 'femininity', i.e. skirts and frilly underwear, high-heeled shoes, makeup etc., is no longer so necessary

181

in heteropatriarchal culture in order to escape censure. Straight women can get away with short hair, flat shoes and trousers. So the outburst of the proud femmeness is hard to explain and does not rely upon any of the determinants advanced by other lesbians to explain roleplaying in the fifties. Severed from any obvious explanation connected with socioeconomics, gender and historical specificity, we are reduced to understanding this contemporary glorification of butch and femme in terms of sadomasochism.

The writing of Moraga and Hollibaugh demonstrates the connection between contemporary butch and femme and sadomasochism. Hollibaugh identifies as a femme, attacks feminists for not being happy about her being a femme and clearly associates femmeness with sexual sadomasochism:

> For example, I think the reason butch/femme stuff got hidden within lesbian-feminism is because people are profoundly afraid of power in bed. And though everybody doesn't play out power the way I do, the question of power affects who and how you eroticise your sexual need. And it is absolutely at the bottom of all sexual inquiry. Given the present state of the movement, it's impossible to say I'm a femme and I like it – no apologies – without facing the probability of a heavy fight.[46]

When Moraga asks for a definition of what femmeness means to her Hollibaugh replies in the erotic language of SM pornography. 'Give me a way to be so in my body that I don't have to think; that you can fantasise for the both of us. You map it out. You are in control.'[47] There are many resonances in what Hollibaugh has to say with the old power game of heterosexual courtship that any lesbians with heterosexual experience will recognise. Hollibaugh sees the butch identity, like the masculine identity, as fragile. A femme must not make a too direct sexual approach to a butch lest it undermine the butch's dominance. Hollibaugh and Moraga explain this as follows:

A.H. . . . with butches you can't insist on them giving up their sexual identity. You have to go through that identity to that other place. But you don't have to throw out the role to explore the sexuality. There are femme ways to orchestrate sexuality . . . quite often what will happen is I'll simply seduce her. Now, that's very active. The seduction can be very profound, but it's a seduction as a femme.

C.M.: What comes to my mind is something as simple as you comin over and sittin on her lap. Where a butch, well, she might just go for your throat if she wants you.[48]

The language here is similar to that in Marabel Morgan's *Total Woman*, a very reactionary heterosexual bible. Morgan quotes Lois Bird who wrote *How to be a Happily Married Mistress*, 'Would he pick you for his mistress? A mistress seduces. A housefrau submits. We all know who gets the most goodies.' Morgan gives further details of the mistress role. 'She never refuses her body or talks about her headache. She never criticises or belittles. He is always the boss. She builds up his ego. She makes sex exciting.'[49] We are instructed by the promoters of butch and femme not to compare 'specific' lesbian roleplaying with heterosexual examples but it is difficult not to when the language and values are so similar.

Hollibaugh describes herself as a feminist but has a profound hostility to feminism. She writes:

Still, while lesbianism is certainly accepted in feminism, it's more as a political or intellectual concept. It seems feminism is the last rock of conservatism. It will not be sexualised. It's prudish in that way. . . . Sometimes, I don't know how to handle how angry I feel about feminism.[50]

There are theoretical problems in this analysis which would not worry the proponents of libertarian theory who pursue 'being what they are' and 'doing what feels good' and 'feeling what they feel' while regarding it as dangerously uncivilised and heretical to suggest that any doing, being or feeling could be subjected to

183

political analysis. Feminists have been savagely pilloried and attacked throughout this wave of the movement for criticising the concepts of masculinity and femininity by the whole of the heteropatriarchal world. Surely it's ironic that we should be called 'conservative' for that criticism. It's not as if in 20 years we have brought down the edifice of gender fetishism and are in a position to be rebelled against as the makers of a new dominant ideology.

The other problem with Hollibaugh's logic is that in saying feminism won't be 'sexualised' she makes categorically clear that she cannot imagine sex that is not organised around power differentials and gender fetishism. She is saying that we cannot build a sexuality which is about equality and mutuality. It is difficult to reconstruct our sexuality when we have been raised, and learned our emotions and sexual feelings, in a heteropatriarchal context of dominance and submission. But this is the feminist project. Men have attacked feminists, in both waves of feminism, as anti-sex prudes for failing to appreciate the obvious pleasure and excitement of SM sex. You might think that contemporary lesbian detractors would be able to recognise the negative value of using these male weapons against feminism.

The refusal to see any kind of sex without dominance and submission as possible, rules out the feminist adventure in the total transformation of sexuality with the object of eliminating sexual violence and the objectification of women, almost before it's begun. It also denies the real pleasures of a sexual relationship in which two lesbians, full of the double-takes and wounds of all their female and lesbian experience, seek to meet each other and make love without roles. It can be more alarming than a simple reversion to roles but it is also more intense and astonishing; a real adventure which takes courage.

'Male–female polarity' is so fundamental to the way we conceptualise and experience sexual desire, i.e. in the form of eroticised power imbalance, that those of us who criticise this form of sexuality are constantly accused of being anti-sex. For such accusers sex only means eroticised dominance and submission. Is there then any other form of sex? Can we have homo sex, based on sameness, mutuality, equality? Julia Penelope describes the difficult process of retraining her sexuality so that she could change from being a stone butch to having homo or lesbian sex. Contrary to the constant taunt that any sex not based on dominance and submission must be either 'not sex' or vanilla, bambi, boring, Penelope describes a much more intense sexual life:

> I have learned that my intense feelings when I make love, that combination of heat, strength, elation and euphoria that wells up from my gut and fills my body is JOY. What I'm experiencing is joy, not 'power'. Likewise, when my lover makes love to me, I now know myself to be really 'in control' when I am most present to her, when I am able to let go of my need to control and experience fully the ways she pleasures me. When I was a stone butch, I believed that I was 'in control'; now I know that I was being controlled by my past. . . .[51]

The context in which lesbians like Nestle, Moraga and Hollibaugh are promoting roleplaying is that of a massive and co-ordinated onslaught upon feminism. In the US this is represented by the contributors to the Barnard conference on sexuality in 1982, whose papers are collected in a volume entitled *Pleasure and Danger: Exploring Female Sexuality*.[52] Nestle writes in this volume about being a 'fem' (a new spelling of femme, adopted, I suspect, to conceal the roots of the word in the sex gender system). Hollibaugh and Moraga are here too, plus numerous writings which promote sadomasochism, such as the contribution of Gayle Rubin, which rename child sexual abuse as intergenerational sex, and hurl abuse at just about every feminist that we in Britain are likely to have heard of, including Andrea Dworkin, Robin Morgan, Sally Gearhart, and Kathleen Barry. The main thrust of the book is to redefine the feminist project as the eroticising of power imbalance and feminists are attacked for resisting such a project. The intention of the collection is well represented in the title, which states that female sexuality is composed of both pleasure and danger, a sadomasochistic formula similar to the title of the Havelock Ellis work in which he sets out his theory that all sex is about sadomasochism, women's masochism and men's sadism. The Ellis volume is entitled *Love and Pain*.[53] Another collection representing the same anti-feminist tendency was published in Britain as *Desire: The Politics of Sexuality*.[54] Nestle, Moraga and Hollibaugh appear in this volume too. In the US FACT, the Feminist Anti Censorship Task Force, is organised to fight against those feminists who persist in campaigning against pornography and the lesbians involved in eroticising power imbalance are well represented within it. In Britain the antifeminist backlash is not quite so well organised, but it is present. So we can expect the revalidation of butch and femme to take off here as well.

An example of the redefinition and undermining of feminism that such writers are engaged in is the way in which Hollibaugh and Moraga redefine the purposes of consciousness-raising. In the conclusion of their article they argue as follows:

> We would like to suggest that, for dealing with sexual issues both personally and politically, women go back to consciousness-raising (CR) groups. We believe that women must create sexual theory in the same way we created feminist theory. We simply need to get together in places where people agree to suspend their sexual values, so that all of us can feel free to say what we do sexually or want to do or have done to us.[55]

This is not what feminists ten or fifteen years ago ever understood CR to be about. In CR, feminists share experience in order to analyse it and form a critique of male supremacy. We intended to change ourselves and the world, not to worship the status quo. The redefinition made here is profoundly worrying. Of course if a group of lesbians sit together and discuss honestly their sexual feelings, we will hear about SM fantasies, about the ability to get sexual pleasure from fantasied or real humiliation and so on. A CR approach is to ask why this is so – to direct anger at the source of the problem, male supremacy, and to seek

186

to change it and ourselves. The purpose of CR is change and revolution.

The contemporary revalidation of butch and femme we have been looking at above makes roleplaying into an SM erotic fantasy and practice. It is quite different in kind from the roleplaying of the 1950s which was not the play-time fantasy of privileged lesbians but the enforced survival tactics of a lesbian community. Eroticised dominance and submission may have had a part to play in fifties roleplaying but, as is clear from the work of Sawyer in St Louis and the writings of Julia Penelope and many others, an individually chosen and fulfilling eroticism was what roleplaying conspicuously did not offer. For many butches and femmes roleplaying was sexually very restrictive, or even a disaster. To get to the nitty gritty of roleplaying in lesbian history, and it is important that we do, we have to emerge from the seduction of butch and femme as an SM fantasy, into asking all kinds of searching questions about roleplaying life.

It is a problem that at present some lesbians seem unable to break free from a hero-worship of butches based upon a masochistic sexual attraction which makes historical investigation a difficult task. Complete objectivity is neither possible nor desirable but it would be helpful if writers would state their bias. Davis and Kennedy pretend to innocence about what they will find out about roleplaying whilst referring copiously to the writings of Nestle, Moraga and Hollibaugh in their notes. Bias enters into oral history as much if not more than into other approaches, and writers should state their perspective clearly. Work such as that of Davis and Kennedy is marred and restricted by the inability of the researchers to clamber out of the romance they are having with the concept of butchness in order to ask interesting and searching questions, and to seek the 'femme' point of view. Such work does a disservice to lesbian roleplayers in history and shows disrespect for their experience. By labelling lesbian roleplaying as 'authentic' lesbian sexuality they do a great disservice to those lesbians who rejected or were indifferent to roles throughout lesbian history to the present.

9

An Introduction to Books for Lesbian History Studies

Avril Rolph, Linda Kerr and Jane Allen

Revised by Avril Rolph and Jane Allen, February 1993

The following list is a selection of titles for anyone interested in learning more about lesbian history. It is limited to titles which are likely to be available through public libraries and in good bookshops; in addition many of the books and bibliographies of other relevant material which enable the interested reader to follow up a topic in more depth.

The list is selective and a number of titles have not been included, particularly biographies of individuals. There are many works about Virginia Woolf, for example, some of which claim to be definitive, but none adequately reflect her feminism nor her love of women. Is it worth including biographies where the author goes to pains to obscure or even deny any hint that the subject could be a lesbian?

One of the major reasons for such determined attempts is undoubtedly the extremely limited and frequently negative definition of what 'lesbian' means, as shown for example by

Rosalind Delmar in her Afterword to the Virago edition of Vera Brittain's *Testament of Friendship* (1980). Discussing the friendship of Vera Brittain and Winifred Holtby she writes:

> Such friendships are not unique ... They show great complexity of feeling and richness of associations. The tenacity with which they are attributed to a hidden lesbianism is therefore all the more remarkable. Vera Brittain alludes to contemporary gossip and speculation about her relationship with Winifred Holtby and in denying it points to an extraordinary blind spot about relations between women which would reduce all its forms to being mere variants, suppressed or otherwise, of one particular mode of sexual practice. (p. 446)

Elizabeth Mavor makes similar comments in her introduction to *The Ladies of Llangollen* (1973) where she describes two women eloping from their native Ireland, living together for over 50 years, sharing their lives and their bed, and leaving a written record of their deep caring and commitment for each other, but denies that this is a lesbian relationship. Is this because she, like Rosalind Delmar, defines lesbian relationships simply as 'one particular mode of sexual practice' rather than everything to do with women making primary commitments to each other?

Novels, plays and poetry have not been included, although there is much to learn from literature for anyone interested in lesbian history. In revising the list for the new edition, we have been faced with the dilemma of removing titles in exchange for new ones. Although relevant new books are published frequently, older books are also very important in studying lesbian history, and we feel that most of our original titles are still worth including. We have therefore limited ourselves to a small number of books published between 1989–1993.

The list is divided into the following sections, since these seemed most appropriate to the study of lesbian history as it is at present:

General: books which deal with lesbian history in its broadest sense
Black lesbian history
Lesbian history before the mid-nineteenth century
Visible lesbian history – from c. 1850 to Stonewall and the Women's Liberation Movement
Lesbian feminism and gay liberation – modern lesbian history
Autobiographies
Lives: nineteenth and twentieth century

General

Evelyn BLACKWOOD (ed.), *The Many Faces of Homosexuality: Anthropological Approaches to Homosexual Behaviour*
(Harrington Park, 1986) 0 918393 20 5
Papers on anthropological research into lesbian and gay male behaviour in a number of different cultures.
Not all the authors are lesbians or gay men, and some of the conclusions are based on assumptions which lesbian feminists would question.

Martin DUBERMAN, Martha VICINUS, George CHANEY Jr. (eds), *Hidden from History: Reclaiming the Gay and Lesbian Past* (Penguin, 1991) 0 14 014363 7
The wide chronological and cultural range of these articles gives insights into many aspects of lesbian history, including 'Lesbian sexuality in medieval and early modern Europe'; 'Lesbians in American Indian Cultures'; 'She even chewed tobacco: a pictorial representation of passing women in America' (interesting use of pictorial sources); 'The Mythic Mannish Lesbian: Radclyffe Hall and the New Woman'; 'A Spectacle in Color: lesbian and gay subculture of jazz age Harlem'. Although other articles

190

report research into gay and lesbian history from the Ancient World to the present, many of them make only token gestures towards lesbian history.

Michael ELLIMAN and Frederick ROLL, *Pink Plaque Guide to London* (GMP, 1986) 0 85449 026 4
Biographical sketches of lesbians and gay men involved in London life over the last 500 years. The lesbians whose profiles are presented come from all walks of life – the arts, medicine, women's rights campaigners, soldiers, musicians. This is a particularly useful book for lesbian history students since it includes information on *Fictional portraits* (e.g. Natalie Barney is portrayed as Valerie Seymour in *The Well of Loneliness*), *Memorabilia* (e.g. collections of letters available in the Fawcett Library), *Portraits* (mainly in the National Portrait Gallery), and a select bibliography.

Lillian FADERMAN, *Surpassing the Love of Men: Romantic Friendship and Love between Women from the Renaissance to the Present* (The Women's Press, 1985) 0 7043 3977 3
A detailed study of love, sex and friendship between women in America, Britain, Germany and France from the sixteenth to the twentieth century. Lillian Faderman traces society's changing attitudes to lesbianism – as a useful prelude to heterosexual sex, as idealised romantic friendships and as the logical result of first-wave feminism. But the publication of French pornographic novels, the development of anti-feminism, and the sexologists' 'discovery' of lesbianism as a disease, led to lesbians being seen as sick, evil and debauched. This stereotype was used to discourage independence and friendship between women. In the first half of the twentieth century lesbians internalised this image, as shown in *The Well of Loneliness*. These ideas have been replaced in the 1970s, Lillian Faderman says, by lesbian feminists who have analysed their lives without reference to male 'authorities'.

191

An essential historical overview of Western lesbianism with plenty of source notes. The one criticism is that such a study can only draw on written sources, which limits the history to that of white, middle-class, literary lesbians, and lesbian prostitutes, as described by male writers.

Jeannette H. FOSTER, *Sex Variant Women in Literature* (Naiad, 1985) 0 930044 65 7
Barbara Grier says 'this is the pioneer bibliography in this field and is essential to any collection of Lesbian literature'. Jeannette Foster attempts to document 2600 years of lesbian history beginning with Sappho, and analyses books written, efforts to achieve publication, and lesbian lives. This edition also has an Afterword by Barbara Grier which includes a list of titles of special interest published after the book's first publication in 1956, up until 1984.

Judy GRAHN, *Another Mother Tongue: Gay Words, Gay Worlds* (Beacon Press, 1984) 0 8070 6717 2
Entertaining eclectic collection, blending legend, autobiography, poetry and etymology to produce a 'fascinating account of gay life throughout history'.

Judy Grahn uses wide-ranging sources 'dictionaries and history, anthropology and sociology, poetry and the occult' interspersed with stories of her own life to formulate the history and, especially, the culture of lesbians and gay men, which she concludes is 'old, extremely old, and it is continuous'. As *Sojourner* describes it, the book is 'a multi-level historical presentation of gay life, past, present, and future'.

Barbara GRIER, *The Lesbian in Literature: a Bibliography* (Naiad, 3rd edn 1981) 0 930044 23 1
'The most complete listing of writing by or about lesbians that exists . . .'. Listing began in 1958 when Marion Zimmer Bradley produced brief booklists for the American

lesbian magazine, *The Ladder*. The current edition is a treasure-house of c.7000 titles, both fiction and non-fiction; not annotated, but given codings (letters and asterisks) indicating extent of lesbian interest. There are some oddities amongst the ratings, but this is inevitable in any list which tries to make value judgements.

Elaine HOBBY and Chris WHITE (eds), *What Lesbians Do In Books: Lesbians as Writers, Readers and Characters in Literature* (The Women's Press, 1991) 0 7043 4288 X
The first British collection of explicitly lesbian essays on literature. 'Lesbian books' focuses on lesbian readings of lesbian texts, including the poetry of Sappho, the work of Edith Ellis (1861–1916) and a fresh look at how Radclyffe Hall and Virginia Woolf related to and moved beyond contemporary sexology. 'Lesbians reading' deciphers lesbian meanings and lesbian moments in texts that are not explicitly lesbian, such as a short story by Katherine Mansfield, *The Chinese Garden* by Rosemary Manning, and the possibility of lesbian motifs in Sanskrit myth. 'Lesbians writing' includes Dorothea Smartt's select bibliographies and short biographies, *From my eyes . . . zamis publishing poetry 1984–1988*, and an examination of the work of Katherine Philips, seventeenth-century lesbian poet.

Monika KEHOE (ed.), *Historical, Literary, and Erotic Aspects of Lesbianism* (Harrington Park Press, 1986) 0 918393 21 3
A wide-ranging collection of articles and book reviews, first published as Vol. 12, Nos 3/4 of the *Journal of Homosexuality*. They include Kathryn Kendall on the treatment of lesbianism on the English stage from the late seventeenth to the mid-nineteenth century; Manny Hall investigates the position of working lesbians and the strategies they use to deal with hostile working environments; Joanna Russ considers the lesbian identity of Willa Cather; two articles examine sexuality, including

the 'treatment of (lesbian) sexual dysfunction'; and more on lesbian history and older lesbians.

Dolores KLAICH, *Woman Plus Woman: Attitudes Towards Lesbianism* (Naiad Press, rev. ed. 1989) 0 941483 28 2
A book directed especially to those who automatically, with little actual knowledge, condemn. It offers some background notes toward a social history of lesbianism, and examines past and present attitudes: Part 1 outlines some of the sexual, medical, psychological research; Part 2 discusses the lives of lesbians in history who chose not to be silent, from Sappho to the poetry and fiction of Colette, Gertrude Stein, Virginia Woolf; Part 3 listens to 'contemporary voices'.

Jane LEGGETT, *Local Heroines: a Women's History Gazetteer of England, Scotland and Wales* (Pandora, 1988)
0 86858 193 5
Featured in this gazetteer are a wide range of achievements and activities of women who are so often hidden from traditional male-dominated history. Jane Legget records birthplaces, workplaces, homes, schools, memorials and so on associated with feminist achievements. While recording 'women's history', Jane Leggett is however reticent about naming women as lesbians although there are many lesbians in the biographical index, including Hannah Snell, Sophia Jex-Blake, Frances Power Cobbe, Nancy Spain, Emily Faithfull and Geraldine Jewsbury.

Dell RICHARDS, *Lesbian Lists: A Look at Lesbian Culture, History and Personalities* (Alyson, 1990) 1 55583 163 X
Lists of lesbian history, culture and personalities from ancient history till now, including lesbian novelists, lesbians who died young, spinsters who need to be rescued, famous Black American lesbian singers and entertainers, women who passed as men, banned lesbian books and works of art . . . and many more.

194

Its main value is as a 'dip-into' book which creates interest into finding out more. Some of the entries are of doubtful accuracy and need checking further, but it includes a bibliography which lists the sources used, and is an entertaining and wide-ranging spin around the lesbian universe.

Jane RULE, *Lesbian Images* (Crossing Press, 1982; 1st edn, 1975) 0 89594 088 4
Well-written study of literature which has images of a wide range of lesbians. Twelve well-known authors are examined in detail: Radclyffe Hall, Gertrude Stein, Willa Cather, Vita Sackville-West, Ivy Compton-Burnett, Elizabeth Bowen, Colette, Violette Leduc, Margaret Anderson, Dorothy Baker, May Sarton, Maureen Duffy.
   Jane Rule also looks at other books written in the last four decades which have been important in reflecting and changing lesbian images: from *Patience and Sarah*, *Torchlight to Valhalla* and *Nightwood*, to *Rubyfruit Jungle*, and *Lesbian Nation* by Jill Johnston.

Dale SPENDER, *Women of Ideas and What Men Have Done to Them: from Aphra Behn to Adrienne Rich* (Ark, 1983) 0 7448 0003 X
Women of Ideas details the work of numerous women, many of whom are lesbian (from Anna Jameson and Frances Power Cobbe to Cicely Hamilton and Adrienne Rich), who have contributed to feminist political thought. In a very energetic and provocative manner, Dale Spender examines how 300 years of women's ideas and theories have been removed from historical and literary records by men.

Julie WHEELWRIGHT, *Amazons and Military Maids: Women who Dressed as Men in Pursuit of Life, Liberty and Happiness* (Pandora, 1989) 0 04 440356 9
Julie Wheelwright describes some of the very large numbers of women who cross-dressed as men from the eighteenth

century until around 1920. These seem to have been surprisingly numerous: as 'men', working-class women could earn a living as navvies, grooms etc; at least 400 women fought as men in the American Civil War; and women boxers were common in South London in the early nineteenth century. The author makes clear the different social attitudes over the period and also the problems for women in trying to be 'one of the boys'.

Bonnie ZIMMERMAN, *The Safe Sea of Women: Lesbian Fiction 1969–1989* (Beacon, 1990; Onlywomen Press, 1992) 0 906500 42 7
Bonnie Zimmerman provides a fascinating overview of lesbian fiction, published by alternative feminist presses (over 200 titles), in the 1970s and 1980s, to identify what the lesbians of these decades believe to be the 'truth' about lesbian existence.

Black lesbian history

CARMEN, GAIL, NEENA and TAMARA, 'Becoming Visible: Black Lesbian Discussions', in *Sexuality: a Reader*, edited by Feminist Review pp. 216–44 (Virago, 1987) 0 86068 802 X
Four women talk about coming out and how different it is for them as Black lesbians in a predominantly white Britain. They discuss their experiences in their work environment, how to challenge racism, and their relationships with white women in the white women's liberation movement.

Anita CORNWELL, *Black Lesbian in White America* (Naiad, 1983) 0 930044 41 X
Anita Cornwell, Black lesbian activist, wrote from the early 1960s with both a political analysis of racial and sexual

oppression, and a radical feminist perspective. An inspiring and thought-provoking collection.

Shabnam GREWAL, Jackie KAY, Liliane LANDOR, Gail LEWIS, Pratibha PARMAR (eds), *Charting the Journey: Writings by Black and Third World Women* (Sheba, 1988) 0 907179 33 9
An anthology of stories, poems, essays and interviews which describe the experiences, the emotional and physical journeys, of Black and Third World women in Britain. Several contributions are of particular interest for lesbian history.

'From the Inside Looking In' is a reappraisal by Sisters in Study (a group which looks at issues affecting Black women and Black people) of *Heart of the Race*, a history of Black women's lives in Britain. They acknowledge its values as the history of one segment of Black women's experiences but also point out some significant omissions, e.g. the experiences of Asian women from the Caribbean, and the debates which took place in the Black women's movement around Afro-Asian unity. The issue of sexuality, and specifically of lesbianism, was also omitted from *Heart of the Race*, an omission rightly challenged by Sisters in Study: 'our discussions were about . . . the need for the *whole* of the Black community to take on board the considerations raised by the fact that lesbians exist as part of the community'.

There are interviews with Audre Lorde, and with Mo Ross who talks about her life, and specifically her experience as a lesbian mother.

Gloria T. HULL, Patricia Bell SCOTT, Barbara SMITH (eds), *[All the Women are White, All the Blacks are Men] But Some of us are Brave: Black Women's Studies* (Feminist Press, 1982) 0 912670 95 9
This collection 'illuminates and provides examples of recent research and teaching about Black women . . . [and] fulfills

a long-term need for a reference text and pedagogical tool'. Useful bibliographies and bibliographic essays include Afro-American women 1800–1910, Afro-American women poets of the nineteenth century, novels by selected Black women, Black women playwrights from Grimké to Shange, and American Black women composers. Lesbian clues include a letter written in 1957 by Black playwright and political activist Lorraine Hansberry to *The Ladder*, and perhaps Undine Moore's use of a poem by Sappho for the lyrics of the art song for soprano and piano 'Love let the wind cry . . . how I adore thee.'

Bruce KELLNER (ed.), *The Harlem Renaissance: a Historical Dictionary for the Era* (Routledge, 1984) 0 7102 1422 7
This dictionary is a useful source of information on Black women connected in some way to the Harlem Renaissance between 1917 and 1935. The information on individuals has been collected from many sources (which are listed) and could be used as a starting point for further research, revealing specific lesbian references as well as possibilities.

Audre LORDE, *Sister, Outsider* (Crossing Press, 1984) 0 89594141 4
These essays and speeches show that Audre Lorde's voice was central to the development of contemporary feminist theory. White Western patriarchy requires an inherent conflict between poetry and theory but Audre Lorde's writing is an impulse towards wholeness, a blending of knowing and feeling.

Audre LORDE, *Zami: a New Spelling of my Name* (Sheba, 1984) 0 907179 26 6
Zami is Audre Lorde's autobiographical novel which begins with her life in Harlem in the 1950s. As a young child, her near-sightedness caused her much frustration until the day a 'library lady', taking pity on her anger at not being

able to join her two older sisters for story hour, introduced her to the world of books, after which 'I was sold on reading for the rest of my life'.

In the fifties, she became a 'gay girl' in Greenwich Village and describes what it was like to be one of the few gay Black women, and a Black student at Hunter College: 'Downtown in the gay bars I was a closet student and an invisible Black. Uptown at Hunter, I was a closet dyke and a general intruder. Maybe four people altogether knew I wrote poetry . . .'

Audre Lorde gives her perceptions of Pearl Harbor and of the McCarthy era within the novel. The book's title reflects the strength of her mother, her aunts and of the women of her mother's homeplace: 'Zami. A Carriacou name for women who work together as friends and lovers.'

Audre Lorde died in 1992 after a long battle with cancer. She wrote movingly and powerfully about this struggle in *The Cancer Journals* (Sheba, 1985, 0 907179 34 7).

Cherrie MORAGA and Gloria ANZALDÚA (eds), *This Bridge Called my Back: Writings by Radical Women of Color* (Kitchen Table, 1981) 0 913175 03 X
A wide-ranging collection of articles, interviews, essays, journal entries, letters and poems, many by lesbians, documenting 'particular rites of passage. Coming of age and coming to terms with community – race, group, class, gender, self . . . And coming to grips with its perversions – racism, prejudice, elitism, misogyny, homophobia, and murder . . .'.

J.R. ROBERTS (comp.), *Black Lesbians: a Bibliography* (Naiad, 1981) 0 930044 21 5
' . . . a comprehensive guide to materials by and/or about Black lesbians in the United States.'

Recognising that so much of the material on Black lesbians is hidden or unidentified, J.R. Roberts (a white lesbian) includes every reference she has managed to find, however small. Photographs and other illustrations are also noted, and a number of photographs are included in the book. Some of the American sources might prove difficult to obtain in Britain, but the book is an invaluable resource.

Barbara SMITH (ed.), *Home Girls: a Black Feminist Anthology* (Kitchen Table: Women of Color Press, 1983)
0 913175 02 1
Many of the 34 contributors are lesbian. They pinpoint some of the realities of Black lesbians and the oppressions of racism, sexism and homophobia.

A large section is called *Black Lesbians – Who Will Fight for Our Lives But Us?* and includes work by Cheryl Clarke, Pat Parker, Barbara A. Banks, Becky Birtha, Beverley Smith and Donna Allegra. The section on artists includes Gloria T. Hull's article, ' "Under the Days": the buried life and poetry of Angelina Weld Grimké', a Black lesbian poet (1880–1958) whose works were published during the Harlem Renaissance of the 1920s.

Lesbian history before the mid-nineteenth century

Judith C. BROWN, *Immodest Acts: the Life of a Lesbian Nun in Renaissance Italy* (Oxford University Press, 1986)
0 19 503675 1
The life of the Abbess of a convent in a small town near Florence in the first quarter of the seventeenth century, who began to have visions of both a religious and erotic nature and to suffer considerable physical pain. To help her cope she was assigned a young nun as a companion. Eventually the church authorities became suspicious of her claims of supernatural contacts with Christ, and they carried out their own investigations, which revealed that

she and her companion had been involved in a sexual
relationship for years.

Judith Brown pieces together the story of women's lives
within the convent at that period, of their economic and
sexual options, and of the life of Sister Benedetta Calini,
the Abbess, who was a religious visionary and mystic and,
as such, a threat to the church establishment.

Lillian FADERMAN, *Scotch Verdict* (Quartet, 1985)
0 7043 0089 3
Scotch Verdict illuminates a critical moment in lesbian
history. It tells the story of two schoolteachers in
Edinburgh who were, in 1809, accused of lesbianism by
one of their pupils. They sued for libel, and, after ten
years, received about £1000 in damages; but their
friendship and careers had been destroyed.

Faderman researched the court transcripts, and also
includes a first-person 'partly autobiographical' narrator
to discuss the case with the reader as she researches it. She
speculates from a twentieth-century lesbian perspective on
what is a complicated and confusing issue for the
'judges'.

This case was the source for the play *The Children's Hour*
by Lillian Hellman.

Elizabeth MAVOR (comp. and ed.), *A Year with the Ladies of
Llangollen* (Penguin, 1984) 0 14 006976 3
Two aristocratic Irish women, Eleanor Butler and Sarah
Ponsonby, ran away in 1778 from their respective families
to live together in a cottage in Wales. Their dedication to
a life of simplicity and learning was much admired and
attracted many famous and literary visitors. They gradually
transformed their cottage into a mansion which is now a
museum.

This book is a selection from the journal that Eleanor
Butler kept of their life together, with previously
unpublished letters.

Elizabeth Mavor also wrote a biography based on the same material: *The Ladies of Llangollen: a Study in Romantic Friendship* (Penguin, 1973) 0 14 003708 X

Fidelis MORGAN with Charlotte CHARKE, *The Well-known Trouble Maker: a life of Charlotte Charke* (Faber, 1988) 0 571 14743 7

Charlotte Charke (1713–60) was the youngest daughter of Colley Cibber, the Poet Laureate. Much of this book is based on her own work *A Narrative of the Life of Mrs Charlotte Charke* (1755) which is divided up into periods followed by Fidelis Morgan's biographical notes on Charlotte Charke's life. Charlotte Charke had an extensive stage career, particularly in male roles, as well as attempting to earn her living in other ways (as a grocer and oil seller in Long Acre, pastry-cook in Bristol). She dressed in men's clothes from the age of three, freely admitted that women were attracted to her, and lived with the actress who played the Queen to Charlotte's Lorenzo in *The Spanish Fryar*. She is referred to as 'Mrs Brown', Charlotte takes the name of 'Mr Brown', and they obviously lived together as husband and wife. However, Fidelis Morgan takes pains in her 'biographical notes' to try to prove Charlotte was not a lesbian. Worth reading to form your own conclusions from Charlotte Charke's own words.

Helena WHITBREAD (ed.), *I Know My Own Heart: the Diaries of Anne Lister (1791–1840)* (Virago, 1988) 0 86068 840 2

The diaries highlight the fact that women have been involved in passionate relationships with other women throughout history. They cover eight years of Anne Lister's life, from 1817 to 1824, when what she wanted above all was 'a fit companion to dote on, to beguile the tedious hours'.

Transcribed (from code), edited and annotated by Helena Whitbread, the diaries build up a clear picture of Anne

202

Lister's everyday domestic life: what food she eats, how much her purchases cost, and her outings – both local and further afield – to visit the Ladies of Llangollen and to Paris.

She writes with great frankness and much emotion about her affairs and flirtations with women, and about provincial Yorkshire society, where she considered herself 'like no-one in the whole world'. Anne Lister encountered problems very similar to those facing lesbians today: and the diaries make compelling reading.

'Visible lesbian history' – from c. 1850 to Stonewall and the Women's Liberation Movement

Shari BENSTOCK, *Women of the Left Bank: Paris, 1900–1940* (Virago, 1987) 0 86068 925 5
The author claims that the contributions of two dozen American and English expatriate women – writers, publishers, booksellers, 'salonières' – to the life of literary Paris between 1900 and 1940, 'nurtured the development of literary Modernism's powerful culture'. This detailed examination of the lives and works of these women, along with the 'misogyny, homophobia, and anti-Semitism that indelibly mark Modernism', challanges and reinterprets many of the prevailing myths about the lives of Natalie Barney, Gertrude Stein, Margaret Anderson, Jane Heap, Jean Rhys, Edith Wharton, Bryher, Nancy Cunard, and many others.

BRIGHTON OURSTORY PROJECT, *Daring Hearts: Lesbian and Gay Lives of 50s and 60s Brighton* (Brighton, Queenspark Books, 1992) 0 904733 31 9
Forty lesbians and gay men speak openly about their lives in Brighton in the 1950s and 1960s when the town had a

reputation as a gay capital, but when male homosexuality was totally illegal, and attitudes to lesbians and gay men were generally hostile and ill-informed. The contributions create a strong picture of place, period, pressures and pleasures, and give a clear and moving picture of many aspects of lesbian and gay life, supported by contemporary photographs and other illustrations including book jackets.

Kaier CURTIN, *We Can Always Call Them Bulgarians: the Emergence of Lesbians and Gay Men on the American Stage* (Alison, 1987) 0 932870 36 8
During the first half of this century a number of plays with lesbian and gay themes were successful on Broadway; this was despite legal prohibitions, police raids, and the arrest of playwrights, producers and performers.

Kaier Curtin has documented the reactions of actors, critics and theatre-goers, used passages from the plays plus photographs and bound them into a fascinating and informative narrative.

During the period when Broadway audiences saw identifiable lesbian roles, they were usually those of aggressive characters attempting the seduction of younger, seemingly heterosexual women, and it is a pity that Kaier Curtin, in concluding that the lifestyles of lesbians and gay men can now be portrayed as they really are, does not mention any of the positive portrayals of lesbians in plays of recent years.

Lillian FADERMAN *Odd Girls and Twilight Lovers: A History of Lesbian Life in Twentieth-Century America* (Columbia University Press, 1991; Penguin, 1992) 0 14 017122 3
Detailed and very readable, using a variety of sources – journals, unpublished manuscripts, songs, news accounts, novels, medical literature, personal interviews – to give a decade-by-decade account of her perception of the journey for North American lesbians from romantic friendship in

the late nineteenth century to the politics of 'Queer Nation' in the 1990s.

Janet FLANNER, *Darlinghissima: Letters to a Friend; edited and with commentary by Natalia Danesi Murray* (Pandora, 1988) 0 86358 248 6

Janet Flanner was an American journalist who sent a *Letter from Paris* on European cultural, social and political life to the *New Yorker* magazine almost every week from 1925 to 1975. The letters here are the hundreds of private ones she wrote to her friend and lover, Natalia Danesi Murray, who writes that 'Janet entered my life unexpectedly on a lively New York afternoon in early January 1940, and there she remained until her death at dawn on that sad November day (1978, aged 86). I realised how unique our relationship was, worth sharing with the world not only for the value of the letters per se, but also as a demonstration of how two women surmounted obstacles, trying to lead their personal and professional lives with dignity and feeling.'

Public figures, writers and artists are encountered in these letters, which are a fascinating record not only of their relationship, but also of their experiences and perceptions of events worldwide from 1944 to 1975.

Gillian HANSCOMBE and Virginia L. SMYERS, *Writing for their Lives: the Modernist Woman 1910–1940* (The Women's Press, 1987) 0 7043 4075 5

Detailed analysis of the network of women writers who were writing innovative and influential literature in the early years of this century, and who have been relatively overlooked in comparison with their male counterparts. The book chronicles in fascinating detail how writers like Dorothy Richardson, H.D., Djuna Barnes and Amy Lowell formed networks with each other.

In her Preface, Gillian Hanscombe writes 'The overview we trace presents two themes which seem to us particularly significant: one is the importance of women's patronage, both directly financial . . . and literary . . . The second theme is what appears to be a clear connection between literary endeavour and the shunning of conventionally heterosexual lives . . .'. The authors make clear that for these women 'the need to find emotional satisfaction had somehow to be balanced against the need to pursue independence of vision': they chose to do this in various ways, including open lesbian relationships, passionate friendships, and complicated triangles with men. But all of them shared an emotional connectedness to women which gave them the intellectual freedom they needed.

Sheila JEFFREYS, *The Spinster and Her Enemies: Feminism and Sexuality 1880–1930* (Pandora, 1985) 0 86358 050 5
Stimulating examination of the development of feminist sexual politics in the nineteenth century. Sheila Jeffreys looks at the ways in which women's actions around prostitution and other 'Purity' campaigns were ignored or ridiculed as reactionary when, in reality, they were strong attacks on male sexual power, and very similar in many ways to radical feminist thought today.

She is highly critical of the role of male sexologists in supposedly 'supporting' feminism; they were generally hostile to independent women and put forward very negative and inaccurate images of lesbians which we have been trying to overcome ever since.

There are some horrifying examples of prejudice and distortion, including some by contemporary feminists, but the book is an inspiration to lesbian feminists trying to gain a clearer picture of the reality of women's struggles and ideas in an important period for the development of contemporary feminist thought.

Judith SCHWARTZ, *Radical Feminists of Heterodoxy: Greenwich Village 1912–1940* (New Victoria, 1986) 0 934678 08 1
In her autobiography, writer Mabel Dodge Luhan,

described Heterodoxy as 'a club for unorthodox women . . . women who did things and did them openly'. It was a luncheon club which flourished for nearly 30 years; its members were amazingly diverse in ages, attitudes and lifestyles but most were strongly feminist, and many were well known in American life at the time.

Judith Schwartz, co-founder of New York Lesbian Herstory Archives, describes her attempts to research the history of this fascinating club which is almost never mentioned in modern published history, and details something of the lives of its individual members. Appendices include a bibliography of relevant material, including books and articles by Heterodoxy members.

Martha VICINUS, *Independent Women: Work and Community for Single Women, 1850–1920* (Virago, 1985) 0 86068 570 5
Detailed study into the lives of so-called 'superfluous' single middle-class women showing how major their role was for the women who followed them, in opening up new professions for women, improving education, and asserting women's political and economic rights. Over sixty years, independent women and their institutions changed and developed despite the constraints of their own weaknesses and the power of established traditions and social opinion.

Andrea WEISS and Greta SCHILLER, *Before Stonewall: the Making of a Gay and Lesbian Community* (Naiad, 1988) 0 941483 20 7
Andrea Weiss explains how she attempts to uncover 'the visual artefacts of a largely invisible subculture' through both national archive material (as represented by the dominant heterosexual culture) and home movies, photo albums etc. of lesbians and gay men.

Using interviews as oral history, the film and the book cover the period from early twentieth century to the Stonewall riots of 1969, looking at the New Women and Harlem Renaissance of the 1920s, the Depression of the

1930s, the relative tolerance of the second world war period through the intolerance of the McCarthy era. Among the lesbians interviewed are Barbara Grier, Ann Bannon, Audre Lorde and Maua Adele Ajanaku.

Andrea WEISS, *Vampires and Violets: Lesbians in the Cinema* (Cape, 1992) 0 224 03575 4

Andrea Weiss focuses on the periods in the twentieth century when the most significant changes in the visual representation of lesbianism occurred and on the meanings behind those changes for the viewers she identifies as 'lesbian spectators'. She suggests that early cinema did not directly subscribe to prevalent medical theories of 'female inversion', and, under the influence of women directors, such as Leontine Sagan and Dorothy Arzner, and early female stars like Louise Brooks and Greta Garbo, it combined with the longings of lesbian spectators to create role models for a lesbian subculture. Andrea Weiss suggests that, despite the Motion Picture Production Code of 1934 which prohibited references to homosexuality in the cinema until the 1960s, a lesbian dynamic can still be perceived as the unspoken character motivation in films such as *Johnny Guitar* and *Rebecca*. She examines post-war European art cinema's representation of lesbians, and sees a silent film *Borderline* (1930) starring H.D. and her lover Bryher, as pointing to a long tradition of lesbian film-making at the margins of cinema, culminating in the growing number of lesbian independent films made in the 1970s and 1980s.

Lesbian feminism and gay liberation – Modern lesbian history

Sidney ABBOTT and Barbara LOVE, *Sappho was a Right-on Woman: a Liberated View of Lesbianism* (Stein & Day, 1985;

1st edn, 1972) 0 8128 2406 7
The first serious non-fiction account of the lesbian
experience from an authentic, inside perspective and the
first book on the relationship of lesbianism to feminism.
Isabel Miller wrote that 'this is the most complete and
honest book about Lesbians I ever read. At first I was afraid
the authors were just saying the same things the Enemy
says about our pains and how they damaged us. We'd have
to be idiots to choose this contempt and punishment . . .
But then came why. Joy, pleasure, equality, energy, heroism.
I am very glad this book exists.'

Bob CANT and Susan HEMMINGS (eds), *Radical Records:
Thirty Years of Lesbian and Gay History, 1957–1987*
(Routledge, 1988) 0 415 00201 X
Radical Records collects together a number of personal
accounts of involvement in lesbian and gay politics. The
diversity of experiences is reflected in the many different
perspectives from which the pieces are written: from the
successes and failures of co-operation with gay men in
the Campaign for Homosexual Equality, the Gay
Liberation Front, and on the London Lesbian and Gay
Switchboard, through to lesbians who argue for
separatism. Irish, Black and Chinese lesbians write about
the racism encountered in the British Women's Liberation
Movement and the problems of 'living in the fringe'.
Lesbian mothers and lesbians with disabilities describe the
initiatives undertaken in organising for legal action.

Rosemary CURB and Nancy MANAHAN (eds), *Lesbian
Nuns: Breaking Silence:* (The Women's Press, 1993)
0 7043 4374 6
Fascinating collection of personal experiences by American
women who have been, or still are nuns, and who define
themselves as lesbian. A number of important points are
considered: what the definition of 'lesbian' means for
individual women; the extent to which sexual activity is

compatible with the vow of celibacy; the importance of spirituality, even when it becomes distorted in the convent by patriarchal channelling; the strength and love often experienced in the convent, which they want to see replicated in women's lives outside. The sense of repression, of pettiness, of racism, is also brought out, as is the sense of strength and commitment to women which underlies the various stories, and which has led so many of the women into active participation in lesbian politics.

HALL CARPENTER ARCHIVES, LESBIAN ORAL HISTORY GROUP, *Inventing Ourselves: Lesbian Life Stories* (Routledge, 1989) 0 41502959 7
Fifteen women talk about their lives from the 1930s to 1987. The contributors comprise: Jewish lesbians, including one who fled Germany in 1939; Black women; a physically disabled woman; and women of different class backgrounds. They recount experiences ranging from the pacifist movement of World War 2, involvement with CND and with Greenham; life in the army; butch–femme; the formation of organised lesbian groups in the 1960s and the beginnings of gay liberation; the search for a political and emotional base for Black lesbians; involvement in the Women's Liberation Movement.

These first hand accounts of life as a lesbian are valuable. As one contributor notes in her postscript 'I wanted to be in this book because if we don't put ourselves down in history no-one else will. I also want it to be known that no particular sort of woman is a lesbian, we have all kinds of backgrounds. Lastly I wanted to show that it's not all 'doom and gloom' – we can have very happy times.'

Sheila JEFFREYS, *Anticlimax: A Feminist Perspective on the Sexual Revolution* (The Women's Press, 1990) 0 7043 4203 0
Sheila Jeffreys convincingly demolishes the myth that the sexual revolution of the 1960s empowered women in this

critical study of the work of sexologists, therapists, pornographers, novelists and sex radicals, and the politics of sex in the 1940s, 1950s and 1960s.

The eroticising of power difference is examined critically: within heterosexuality, defined as a political institution through which male dominance is organised and maintained; in its domination of much male gay culture; and in the way it has had considerable influence on lesbian ideology over the past decade. Controversial and provocative, *Anticlimax* offers an important radical analysis of what is meant by 'the sexual revolution'. It concludes with Sheila Jeffreys' own vision of how to construct homosexual desire, offering a sexual future not based on the eroticisation of power.

Hannah KANTER, Sarah LEFANU, Shaila SHAH, Carole SPEDDING (eds), *Sweeping Statements: Writings from the Women's Liberation Movement 1981–1983* (The Women's Press, 1984) 0 7043 3930 7
An historically important compilation of articles previously published in feminist magazines and newsletters.
Lesbian-feminist politics are conveyed in papers on lesbian mothers and the law, sexuality, and anti-lesbianism in the women's movement. Gives the background to current key issues in feminist politics.

Love Your Enemy? the Debate between Heterosexual Feminism and Political Lesbianism (Onlywomen, 1981) 0 906500 08 7
A now famous collection of letters and papers which debates the place of sexuality in feminist theory and practice.

'Political Lesbianism: the Case against Heterosexuality' was originally written as a conference paper produced by Leeds Revolutionary Feminists in 1979; then published in *WIRES*, the internal newsletter of the Women's Liberation Movement, where it aroused immense controversy. Most of the letters published in *WIRES* as a result are reprinted

here, together with an Afterword by the Leeds
Revolutionary Feminists.

Del MARTIN and Phyllis LYON, *Lesbian/Woman* (Bantam
Books, rev. edn. 1983) 0 553 23597 4
The personal experiences of the two lesbians who, in 1955,
founded The Daughters of Bilitis, the first lesbian
organisation in the USA. As pre-feminist movement
lesbians, Del and Phyllis initially 'made up the rules as
they went along', including roleplaying since they had no
other experience to guide them, but gradually became
aware of the possibilities and potential to evolve new ways
for women to relate to each other as lesbians and as
feminists. A book well ahead of its time when it first
appeared in 1972, this revised edition includes a section
on what they see as the gains and setbacks for lesbians in
the US during the past ten years.

Suzanne NEILD and Rosalind PEARSON, *Women Like Us*
(The Women's Press, 1992) 0 7043 4285 5
Interviews with 19 older lesbians from different races,
regions, class backgrounds, with and without disabilities,
and living in a variety of situations. Most of the interviews
were used in an acclaimed Channel 4 documentary which
illustrated the reality and diversity of lesbian lives, and
created a personal history of the changing face of lesbian
life and culture in Britain from the 1920s to the present
day.

Julia PENELOPE, *Call Me Lesbian: Lesbian Lives, Lesbian
Theory* (Crossing Press, 1992) 0 89594 496 0
Brings together nine provocative articles and lectures from
the late 1980s in which the author reflects on lesbian
identities, politics, issues, sexuality, language and semantics,
from a radical feminist perspective. She raises questions
located in her direct lesbian experience which informs her
analysis and opinions of lesbian life and politics.

Julia PENELOPE and Sarah Lucia HOAGLAND (eds), *For Lesbians Only* (Onlywomen, 1988) 0 906500 28 1
The first anthology of American lesbian separatism is informed by political fervour and autobiographical insight. It ranges from theoretical analyses to short stories and poetry, with contributions from well-known feminist theoreticians, Mary Daly, Marilyn Frye and Monique Wittig; novelists Lee Lynch and Anita Cornwell; musicians Alix Dobkin and Linda Shear. There are statements from the beginning of the Women's Liberation Movement and many of the radical writings of the seventies and eighties, hitherto only available in small, local newsletters published 'for lesbians only'. It concludes with a useful chapter on resources, though most of the references are from the US.

Autobiographies

Valentine ACKLAND, *For Sylvia: an Honest Account* (Methuen, 1986) 0 413 60610 4
After 19 years as a 'secret drinker', Valentine Ackland experienced a 'mystical crisis' which she felt meant that she would be able to conquer her alcohol problem. Following this crisis, she wrote this account for Sylvia Townsend Warner, her lover of many years. Valentine discusses her life: a childhood plagued by the antagonism of her older sister; her early lesbian experiences and her parents' prejudice. She became a Catholic and attempted a loveless (and unconsummated) marriage. She describes a long-standing relationship with 'X' and her life with Sylvia, in which she says she blundered from 'shame to shame'.

Barbara DEMING, *A Humming Under My Feet: a Book of Travail* (The Women's Press, 1985) 0 7043 3952 8
In the first chapter, written in 1952, Barbara Deming relates

her experience of travelling in Europe in the early 1950s, when she discovered many things about herself and her women friends, after visiting the matriarchal sites of Greece, where she experiences the force of women's history quite literally as 'a humming under her feet'.

However, the friends to whom she showed this chapter and notes for the rest of the book were embarrassed by it, and suggested that, if she must write it, it should be in the third person, with more humour . . . She left it alone until finding it again in 1971, when she felt compelled to complete it, which she did in 1984, shortly before her death.

Barbara Deming was America's foremost writer on women and peace, feminism and non-violence, and this book is both a gentle and a powerful story of love and discovery.

Rosemary MANNING, *A Corridor of Mirrors: An Autobiography* (The Women's Press, 1987) 0 7043 4054 2
A Time and a Time: an Autobiography (Calder & Boyars, 1982) 0 7145 2746 7
Rosemary Manning, who died in 1988, reflects on her life, politics, work and relationships with friends and lovers. She wrote several novels including *The Chinese Garden* and the *Dragon* books for children. Her autobiography *A Time and a Time* was first published in 1971 under the pseudonym Sarah Davys, because she was then running a private school for girls and felt it necessary to keep her identity secret. The book begins with her suicide attempt, and tells of her loneliness and depression, caused at least in part by the need to keep her lesbian identity secret. She explores ways of surviving and maintaining her integrity and creativity, rather than denying herself and the validity of her feelings.

In 1980, at the age of 70, she declared on ITV that she was a lesbian. *A Corridor of Mirrors* is an inspiring account by a woman who until then had kept the central fact of her life a secret. Each decade brought her new interests, new friends, new perspectives; and the book ends with an image of great optimism.

Alice B. TOKLAS, *What is Remembered: an Autobiography* (North Point, 1986; 1st edn, 1963) 0 86547 180 0
Alice B. Toklas' own account of her life with Gertrude Stein, which reveals her as stronger and more dynamic than she has been portrayed in other books. She emerges here as a competent organiser with positive views of her own, despite the staccato nature of her writing.

Val WILMER, *Mama Said There'd Be Days Like This: an Autobiography* (The Women's Press, 1989) 0 7043 5040 8 (hb), 0 7043 4120 4 (pb)
Val Wilmer is a respected photographer and writer on jazz, who not only reveals the struggle to establish herself as a professional jazz commentator in an otherwise all–male world, but also explores her own personal conflicts while coming to terms with her identity as a writer and photographer, and as a lesbian. Her personal revelations include valuable snippets about London lesbian life from the early 1960s.

Charlotte WOLFF, *Hindsight: an Autobiography* (Quartet, 1980) 0 7043 2253 6
Autobiography of the author of the pioneering study of lesbianism *Love between Women* (1971) and *Bisexuality: A Study* (1977).

Charlotte Wolff was born in Poland and studied medicine at various German universities, including Berlin during the period of the Weimar Republic. She describes the experience of living in this period when culture flourished, homosexual bars for women and men proliferated but inflation soared out of control.

She fled from Berlin to Paris in 1933 when she was dismissed from her job as a doctor. Her lover had left her, partly because of the danger she faced if she continued to share her life with a Jewish woman. In France she met Aldous and Maria Huxley and became interested in hand-reading, a study in which she later became world-famous. She eventually settled in England where she undertook the research which was to lead to *Love between Women* and *Bisexuality*.

The book contains much material of interest to students of lesbian history; Charlotte Wolff is frank in discussing her own views and the ways these changed throughout the years, including a reassessment in the late 1970s when she was invited to Berlin by German feminists.

Lives: nineteenth and twentieth century

Lilian BARKER (1874–1955)
Elizabeth GORE, *The Better Fight: the Story of Dame Lilian Barker* (G. Bles, 1965)
Lilian Barker began her working life as a teacher. While away from full-time employment for seven years to nurse her mother she met her lifelong partner, Florence Francis. In the course of a varied and distinguished career she set up an experimental evening institute in London; became superintendent of Woolwich Arsenal in 1916 with the responsibility for the change-over to a female work-force; and was governor of the first girls' Borstal Institution at Aylesbury – a job which she undertook so successfully (particularly in terms of improving conditions and building up the self-esteem of young women held there) that she was appointed the first woman Prisoner Commissioner for England and Wales in 1935.

She and Florence (whose role was very much that of a traditional housewife) retired to Devon on Lilian's retirement in 1943. In 1944 Lilian was created a DBE.

Djuna BARNES (1892–1982)

Andrew FIELD, *The Formidable Miss Barnes: a Biography of Djuna Barnes* (Secker and Warburg, 1983) 0 436 15595 8
Now mainly remembered for her classic novel *Nightwood* (1936), Djuna Barnes was an American who lived in Greenwich Village where she published her first item *The Book of Repulsive Women*, a booklet with eight poems and five drawings clearly portraying lesbianism. After a number of relationships with men, she went to Paris in 1919 and joined its circle of expatriate writers and artists, where she met Thelma Wood, an American sculptor, who became her lover for ten years. She also had a brief affair with Natalie Barney.

In 1929 she published *Ladies Almanack*, a comic picture of the expatriate lesbians of Paris. When her affair with Thelma Wood finally broke down in 1931 she began work on *Nightwood*, which was in part the story of their romance.

As well as describing Djuna Barnes' life and work, the author also attempts a 'psychological portrait', drawing heavily on Freud and on the fact that she hated her father, but the book has interest in slotting another figure into the lesbian networks of the 1920s and 1930s.

Natalie BARNEY (1876–1972)

George WICKES, *The Amazon of Letters: the Life and Loves of Natalie Barney* (W.H. Allen, 1977) 0 491 01608 5
When Natalie Barney died in 1972 at the age of 95, she apparently left well over 40,000 letters. This biography contains much interesting information on her long and fascinating life, but like many biographies of famous women it tends to trivialise ('Natalie Barney was a poetess and a writer but her notoriety stems more from her being unquestionably the leading lesbian of her time') and does not take Natalie Barney's 63 years of varied writing, including verse, plays and essays, seriously. Natalie Barney's many lovers (who invariably remained her close friends)

included poet Renée Vivien, Dolly Wilde (niece of Oscar) and Romaine Brooks who remained the greatest love of her life until their final split when Natalie was 85, which she never fully accepted. Hopefully, given the complexity of her long life and the wealth of documentary material, other feminist-orientated books will appear in due course.

Sylvia BEACH (1887–1962)
Noel Riley FITCH, *Sylvia Beach and the Lost Generation: a History of Literary Paris in the Twenties and Thirties* (Souvenir Press, 1984) 0 285 64997 3
In 1919 Sylvia Beach opened Shakespeare & Co., the first English-language bookshop and lending library in Paris, which was to become famous throughout the literary world: it was frequented by all the major writers of the time. Sylvia Beach undoubtedly had a major influence on the course of modern literature, and her decision to publish James Joyce's *Ulysses* in 1922 brought her even greater fame.

Her literary fame was shared with French writer and publisher Adrienne Monnier with whom she had a very long relationship which lasted from 1917 until 1955 when Adrienne, unable to cope with effects of Ménière's syndrome (aural disturbance of the inner ear causing delusional noises), took an overdose of sleeping tablets and died. The author (a woman) writes 'Personal happiness went with the death of Adrienne, who for thirty-eight years had been a sister, lover, mother and mentor. The rest of Sylvia's life . . . was marked by mere literary awards.'

Romaine BROOKS (1874–1970)
Meryl SECREST, *Between Me and Life: a Biography of Romaine Brooks* (Macdonald & Jane's, 1976) 0 356 08382 9
Romaine Brooks died in 1970 at the age of 96. She was recognised as one of the finest painters of her generation,

though her reputation declined from around 1945 until a major retrospective exhibition of her work was held in New York and Washington in 1971.

She was part of European intellectual society (according to Bryher, ' . . . was inclined to know the conventional French and was already considered a bit too Right Bank and smart . . .'), knew Gertrude Stein and Alice B. Toklas, was a friend of Una Troubridge (she painted Una's portrait showing her in severely tailored clothes, wearing a monocle), attended Sylvia Beach's gatherings at the Shakespeare Bookshop, lived for a time on Capri and was caricatured in Compton Mackenzie's spiteful novel *Extraordinary Women*. Her major relationship, with writer Natalie Barney, lasted for 50 years until jealousy over Natalie's last love affair at the age of 85 made her refuse to have any further contact. There is much interesting information in the book but the author puts forward trite psychological interpretations of Romaine Brooks' character.

COLETTE (1873–1954)
Nicole Ward JOUVE, *Colette* (Harvester Key Women Writers, 1987) 0 7108 0637 X
A detailed look at Colette's work and life from a feminist perspective. The author, a Frenchwoman herself, argues that Colette's work has been seriously undervalued. Various authors have dealt superficially with the facts of her life including her strong lesbian relationships, and paid little consideration to the effect of her provincial French background. In addition, translation from the original French weakens its impact.

Edith CRAIG (1869–1947)
Joy MELVILLE, *Ellen & Edy: a Biography of Ellen Terry and her Daughter, Edith Craig, 1847–1947* (Pandora, 1987) 0 86358 078 5
Edy Craig was a theatre producer, costume designer and

suffragette who lived with two women, Christopher St John, and Clare (Tony) Atwood, from 1916 until her death in 1947. The book tells of their everyday lives and loves and gives a fascinating picture of these remarkable women.

It also focuses on the often stormy relationship with Ellen Terry, Edy's mother, and starts with a biographical account of the unconventional life of this famous actress.

H.D. [Hilda DOOLITTLE] (1886–1961)

Barbara GUEST, *Herself Defined. The Poet H.D. and Her World* (Collins, 1985) 0 00 272312 3

A biography of the American poet, Hilda Doolittle, written by the poet Barbara Guest, who gives an intimate portrait of H.D. and the circle of novelists, artists and poets who were her friends.

It seems that Barbara Guest does not approve of H.D.'s relationships with women and like many other biographies of lesbians, tends to give more weight to relationships with men. She even concludes that 'No matter that she [H.D.] declared herself thankful she had not married Ezra [Pound], because "he would have destroyed me and the center they call 'Air and Crystal' of my poetry". An afterthought. Despite her moth wings, the young Hilda would have married Pound.'

GLUCK (1895–1978)

Diana SOUHAMI, *Gluck: Her Biography* (Pandora, 1988) 0 86358 236 2

Born Hannah Gluckstein into the close-knit Jewish family which founded the J. Lyons catering empire, Gluck 'no prefix, no quotes' was always a rebel. She dressed in male clothes from an early age, had passionate love affairs with society women (including Constance Spry, Sybil Cookson, Nesta Obermer and Edith Shackleton Heald), and exhibited her paintings only in (highly praised) 'one man shows'. Yet she never entirely broke away from her family and remained financially dependent on them.

The biography, which draws on unpublished letters, diaries and manuscripts, draws a fascinating portrait of a woman who was undoubtedly one of the major painters of the twentieth century. Diana Souhami describes Gluck's personality and life in an entertaining and positive way: 'Throughout her adult life she dressed in men's clothes, pulled the wine corks and held the door for true ladies to pass first . . . Her father, a conservative and conventional man, was utterly dismayed by her "outré clobber", her mother referred to a "kink in the brain" which she hoped would pass, and both were uneasy at going to the theatre in 1918 with Gluck wearing a wide Homburg hat and long blue coat, her hair cut short and a dagger at her belt.'

Radclyffe HALL (1880–1943)
Michael BAKER, *Our Three Selves: a Life of Radclyffe Hall* (GMP, 1985) 0 85449042 6
Radclyffe Hall is possibly the most famous of all British lesbians, mainly as a result of the publicity surrounding her novel *The Well of Loneliness* which was banned as 'obscene' in a sensational court case in 1928. Her early attachments to women, and her relationship with singer Mabel Veronica Batten (Ladye), 23 years her senior, which was to change her from a 'half-educated young cub who ignored all the important aspects of a civilized existence and preferred hunting to literature, music or the arts' to a serious woman who began her writing career and also became a convert to Catholicism, are described with constant references to source materials including letters and diaries.

Her 28-year partnership with Una Troubridge, her writing career, their interest in psychic research and in breeding dogs, and her infatuation with a Russian nurse Evguenie Souline which almost destroyed her relationship with Una are similarly described.

221

Radclyffe Hall was clearly a complex character, sometimes absurd, sometimes arrogant and unlikeable but also deeply courageous and compassionate, and *Our Three Selves* conveys something of this complexity.

For readers interested in Radclyffe Hall, it is informative to compare this biography with two other books about her. The first is Una Troubridge's *The Life and Death of Radclyffe Hall* written in 1945 but not published until 1961 (Hammond) when many of the people written about were dead, which omits and distorts a great deal in order to draw 'John' in the best possible light.

The other is Lovat Dickson's *Radclyffe Hall at the Well of Loneliness: a Sapphic Chronicle*, Collins, 1975, a sensational and very nasty picture by the man Una had been unwise enough to appoint her literary executor and entrust with writing a biography of her beloved 'John'.

Cicely HAMILTON (1872–1952)

Lis WHITELAW, *The Life and Rebellious Times of Cicely Hamilton: actress, writer, suffragist* (The Women's Press, 1990) 0 7043 4225 1

Cicely Hamilton was a celebrated playwright, novelist, actress, suffragist and peace campaigner. She was friends with major figures of the time, Ellen Terry, Vera Brittain, Winifred Holtby, H.G. Wells, Lilian Baylis, George Bernard Shaw, and was closely involved with the feminist periodical *Time and Tide*, which began in 1920 following the success of women's franchise. She is mainly remembered today for her part in the suffrage movement.

Her book *Marriage as a Trade* (1909, reprinted by The Women's Press, 1981) is probably her most influential work – a witty and at times caustic critique of the way women have been forced into marriage through economic necessity, and the limiting and often stultifying effect this has on them. It had a profound effect on many women when it was published and is still relevant and interesting today.

In her introduction Lis Whitelaw touches on some of the problems she encountered in writing this biography, including the absence of personal papers, and the reticence Cicely Hamilton showed in her autobiography where some of her closest friends are not mentioned at all. She analyses possible reasons for this, and pays much attention to Cicely's friends and colleagues and her relationships with them, since these were clearly of immense importance in her life.

Charlotte MEW (1869–1928)

Penelope FITZGERALD, *Charlotte Mew and Her Friends* (Collins, 1984) 0 00 217008 6

Virginia Woolf described the poet Charlotte Mew as 'very good and interesting and unlike everybody else'. Penelope Fitzgerald views Charlotte Mew as a strange, reserved woman who acted as a dutiful daughter in Victorian Bloomsbury, where she and her sister cared for their difficult mother and concealed the family's financial difficulties by renting part of the house to pay for the institutional care of two schizophrenic siblings.

On the surface Charlotte (Lotti) was witty and clever, but she was a melancholic and repeatedly fell in love with the 'wrong' woman. The first of these was Lucy Harrison, headmistress of Gower Street School which Lotti, then 14, attended. This typical unrequited schoolgirl passion proved to be a pattern constantly repeated for her, and she later fell in love with Ella D'Arcy, one of the editors of *The Yellow Book*, and author May Sinclair with similar frustrating results.

This is a detailed and compassionate biography of a talented and complex woman.

Vita SACKVILLE-WEST (1892–1962)

Victoria GLENDINNING, *Vita: the Life of V. Sackville-West* (Penguin, 1984) 0 14 007161 X

Vita Sackville-West was a writer, poet, gardener of great

imagination and vision, broadcaster, aristocrat, and lover of women. She married diplomat Harold Nicolson, a homosexual himself who was possibly her closest friend, and had two sons who appear to have been rather peripheral in her life.

She had several passionate relationships with women, the most famous being Virginia Woolf: Vol. 3 of Virginia Woolf's *Letters* and Vol. 3 of her *Diaries* give a detailed picture of the relationship. The biography is detailed and succeeds in portraying something of the powerful personality of Vita Sackville-West, but yet again tends to be patronising about her lesbianism and about the women who were attracted to her.

Ruth SLATE (1884–1953) and Eva SLAWSON (1882–1916)
Tierl THOMPSON (ed.), *Dear Girl: the Diaries and Letters of Two Working Women, 1897–1917* (The Women's Press, 1987) 0 7043 4026 7
The diaries and letters (with Tierl Thompson's excellent introduction and summaries) provide a unique record of a friendship between Ruth Slate, a clerk in a City grocery firm, and Eva Slawson, a legal secretary from Walthamstow. They met in 1902 and formed a loving friendship which Ruth called 'the foundation of my life'. Ruth did not marry until after Eva's death, while Eva's diaries reveal her intense passion and physical relationship with Minna Simmons. Writing over 20 years, the two women give first-hand accounts of some of the great suffrage rallies and of leaders like Christabel Pankhurst and Charlotte Despard. They became gradually disenchanted with orthodox religion, committed to pacifism during the first world war, and discuss the merits of 'free love'. In spite of poverty, sickness and loss, the women continued to read, learn and contribute to the issues of their time, and to maintain a lifelong friendship.

Ethel SMYTH (1858–1944)
Louise COLLIS, *Impetuous Heart: the Story of Ethel Smyth*
(Wm Kimber, 1984) 0 7183 0543 4
Dame Ethel Smyth is one of the major British composers,
and was also closely involved in the suffrage movement
(she composed 'March of the Women'). She fell in love
with a number of women – Edith Somerville, Winaretta
Singer, Virginia Woolf (the last great love of her life)
amongst others. But Louise Collis says 'Her most lasting
attachment was to an American, Harry Brewster . . .'.
However she had the good sense not to marry him when
his wife died and had earlier written to a friend 'no
marriage, no ties, I must be free. I love my own loves, my
own life. I thank God for teaching me to know my own
mind in some few things that matter.'
   The book includes a select bibliography and information
on manuscript sources (Ethel Smyth's unpublished
letters).
Some of Ethel Smyth's own writings are available in *The
Memoirs of Ethel Smyth*, abridged and introduced by
Ronald Crichton, Viking, 1987, 0 670 80655 2.

Edith SOMERVILLE (1858–1949) and Martin ROSS
(1862–1915)
Gifford LEWIS, *Somerville and Ross: the World of the Irish
R.M.* (Viking, 1985) 0 670 80760 5
Biography of Irish cousins and writers Edith Somerville
and Martin Ross (real name Violet Martin) who together
produced popular fiction reflecting Anglo-Irish experiences
in late nineteenth and early twentieth centuries. When
Martin Ross died in 1915, Edith Somerville claimed to
continue to communicate with her spiritually and her
cousin's name continued to appear on the title pages of the
books.
   This book looks at their work and lives, including their
relationship. The author (a woman), goes to some pains
to point out that 'when we come to define their love for

each other, one fact stands out clear: there was no passion in it'. Her reasons for deciding this are not strikingly convincing (they often use affectionate rudeness to each other in their letters – 'This is not the language of a Sapphic sexual love'), but worth considering in a critical context.

Una TROUBRIDGE (1887–1963)
Richard ORMROD, *Una Troubridge: the Friend of Radclyffe Hall* (Cape, 1984) 0 224 02179 6
In spite of the title (Una acted very much as 'wife', certainly more than 'friend' to Radclyffe Hall) the book doesn't just cover her life with 'John' (as Radclyffe Hall was known to her friends) but also her early years, when she studied sculpture at the Royal College of Art and produced a bust of Nijinsky while he was in London with Diaghilev's Russian Ballet in 1913; and the period after 'John's' death when her love of music is expressed. The author obviously admires Una and takes trouble to show her as a loyal, deeply caring and also interesting woman in her own right and not just as the partner of the one love of her life, 'my John'.

Sylvia Townsend WARNER (1893–1978)
Claire HARMAN, *Sylvia Townsend Warner: A Biography* (Chatto & Windus, 1989) 0 7011 29387
Wendy MULFORD, *This Narrow Place: Sylvia Townsend Warner and Valentine Ackland: Life, Letters and Politics 1930–1951* (Pandora, 1988) 0 8635 826 2
Sylvia Townsend Warner and Valentine Ackland met in Dorset in 1926, and lived together for nearly 40 years, during which time they developed their literary careers, and were actively involved in the left-wing cultural activity of the 1930s and 1940s.

Claire Harman's biography was in preparation when Wendy Mulford's book was published with the result that only Claire Harman had access to important unpublished sources in the Sylvia Townsend Warner and Valentine

Ackland Collection in Dorset County Museum, including the diaries of Sylvia Townsend Warner from 1927–78 and those of Valentine Ackland from 1925–69. She makes considerable use of these sources and presents a full and detailed picture of Sylvia Townsend Warner's life, making clear the importance to Sylvia of Valentine Ackland, and their shared life and interests.

Wendy Mulford concentrates particularly on the lives of the two women during the 21 years when they were most creatively and politically active. She explains 'the combination of the quality and liveliness of Sylvia's writing, the two writers' political commitment, and their lives together as women living in Dorset . . . made me want to investigate further . . . [and] discover how two women writers of this period lived their lives: as writers and political people . . . and how their experiences as women living together differed from those passed down to us from the assumed, central, male point of view.'

Comparison of the two books, and also with Valentine Ackland's autobiography *For Sylvia* [qv] is an interesting exercise in examining the documented lives of a lesbian couple as they are interpreted by different authors.

Endpiece

We'd like to complete this book by identifying the paths which we in the Lesbian History Group have taken so far, and suggest possible fruitful avenues for further research.

The writing of lesbian history is always a political process, and cannot but be informed by our own current experiences as lesbians and feminists. For each of us in different ways, our interest in lesbian history has arisen from our present concerns: as teachers of literature, librarians, feminist activists, local history enthusiasts and so on. Analysing the relationship of our lesbian past to our present politics, and unpicking the bias of male heterosexist accounts of women's history is one essential strand of our work.

Allied to this is a second, the reworking of traditional biographical sources about women and creating new accounts. While we should attempt to avoid hagiography, we need to understand how our lesbian heroines of the past perceived themselves, and the constraints on their lives.

A third area represented in this book links together the knowledge of individual women in order to trace lesbian networks of the past. Inevitably this kind of research largely throws light on middle-class lesbians, literary and professional women of their times, who left some (though still limited) sources of documentation about their lives.

This observation highlights the obvious gaps in our collection – the absence of working-class lesbian history and Black and ethnic minority lesbian history. To our knowledge, there is as yet very little work in these areas in Britain, though considerably more in the USA. We need to re-think our questions imaginatively in order to discover the Black and working-class lesbians in our past.

One source for the recent history of Black and working-class lesbians is oral history, and some testimonies have been collected by lesbian and gay archives. This material and approach needs to be developed, and also written up and made available.[1]

A very different kind of absence is the historical relationship between lesbianism and the women's movement. We need to build on our scanty collection of Cicely Hamilton, Christabel Pankhurst and other feminist lesbians and ask more searching and general questions about how lesbians saw feminism. Feminism, apart from a brief turn-of-the-century suffrage phase (and then unclearly) seems to have skirted nervously around the subject of lesbianism, inversion, and even romantic friendship. But what might be revealed if we take a closer look at the feminist politics concerning single women?

This brings us back to the present-day relationship between lesbianism and feminism. As historians, we believe that there has to be more interchange between lesbian history and feminist history – we cannot develop the one without the other. Feminist history has notoriously ignored lesbians and it's crucial that it is forced to take on heterosexuality as historically problematic rather than as an automatic assumption. On the other hand we also must remember to link back into feminist history to make sense of the context for our lesbian history. As lesbian historians, however, we are able to explore in a particularly insightful way a rather obscure area which feminist history has failed to tackle adequately – that is, the area of single women, women who were outside heterosexuality, women in institutions, female friendship, independent women, and certain strands of the history of feminism. Obviously this isn't entirely new ground for lesbian feminists[2], but the potential here is huge. It's essential, however, that we attempt to distinguish this, a lesbian view of history, from the history of lesbians. We don't believe that all women can be placed on a lesbian continuum; however, we do believe that a lesbian perspective can illuminate the history of women and of male power.

Since the first edition of *Not A Passing Phase* was published in 1989, the status of lesbian studies in the United Kingdom has perceptibly changed. After years of being confined to adult education classes and small specialist publishers, with the occasional appearance on women's studies courses, lesbian studies are now, apparently, becoming respectable. Publishers' lists – including those of mainstream houses like Penguin – now feature lesbian studies books[3]; women's studies conferences routinely allocate space to lesbian studies[4]; some women's studies courses in universities offer whole modules on lesbian studies[5]; there are even postgraduate degrees in lesbian and gay studies.[6] Television dramas about lesbians (*Oranges are not the only fruit*, *Portrait of a Marriage*) and series intended for gays and lesbians (for example, the *Out* programme on Channel 4) have drawn large audiences.

But just as the subject's former relative obscurity had advantages as well as drawbacks – quite radical work could go on, unmonitored but influential – so the greater acceptance and publicity given to lesbian studies, in many ways a phenomenon to be welcomed, invite potential dangers. In an academic milieu dominated by postmodernist ideas we must be careful to ensure that lesbian experiences are not reduced to one simple category within a checklist of 'differences', thereby losing their political significance. Another danger is that lesbian studies will be subsumed in gay (male) studies, just as women's history used to be subsumed in men's.[7] There is already some evidence that lesbian history is being rewritten to fit into categories drawn from gay men's history, in which any critique of patriarchy is almost inevitably absent.[8]

These scholarly trends – which mirror not only the structures and norms of the academic world, but also popular cultural movements among gays and lesbians – need to be recognised and resisted. We can never make sense of our past, let alone seek to change the present, if we confine ourselves within frames of reference imposed by masculine scholarship. Our pursuit of lesbian history has been made possible, and indeed we've been fired to do it, by the existence of and our participation in the lesbian and feminist movements of the last twenty years. Our writing of our history validates our existence – it is our own history and it's also a step towards our future.

Notes

Introduction

1. London Feminist History Group (eds), *The Sexual Dynamics of History*, Pluto Press, London, 1983.
2. Criminal Law Amendment Bill 1921. This clause proposed that 'An act of gross indecency between female persons shall be a misdemeanour and punishable in the same manner as any act committed by male persons under section eleven of the Criminal Law Amendment Act, 1885'.
3. Local Government Act 1988. Section 28 states that 'a local authority shall not intentionally promote homosexuality' and that 'a local authority shall not promote the teaching in any maintained school of the acceptability of homosexuality as a pretended family relationship'.
4. See, for example, Chapters 4 and 7 in this book.
5. Rich, Adrienne, *Compulsory Heterosexuality and Lesbian Existence*, Onlywomen Press, London, 1981, p. 29.
6. For example, Viscountess Rhondda, *This Was My World*, Macmillan, London, 1933; Hamilton, Cicely, *Life Errant*, Dent, London, 1935; Robins, Elizabeth, *Both Sides of the Curtain*, Heinemann, London, 1940.
7. Thompson, Tierl (ed.), *Dear Girl*, The Women's Press, London, 1987.
8. See Firth, Catherine B., *Constance Louisa Maynard, Mistress of Westfield*, Allen & Unwin, London, 1949; and Vicinus, Martha, *Independent Women: Work and Community for Single Women, 1850–1920*, Virago, London, 1985, Chapter 4.
9. Powell, Tristram, Preface to Julia Margaret Cameron, *Victorian Photographs of Famous Men and Fair Women*, 1973.
10. Lewis, Gifford, *Somerville and Ross: the World of the Irish R.M.*, Viking, 1975.
11. White, Evelyn, *Octavia Hill*, 1957; Bell, E. Moberly, *Octavia Hill*, Constable, London, 1942.

12. Webb, R.K., *Harriet Martineau. A Radical Victorian*, Heinemann, London, 1960, p. 51.

13. Mavor, Elizabeth, *The Ladies of Llangollen*, Penguin, Harmondsworth, Middx, 1973, p. xii.

14. For example, Rosalind Delmar's afterword to the Virago edition of Vera Brittain's *Testament of Friendship*, Fontana/Virago, London, 1980. See Chapter 7 in this book.

15. See Vicinus, Martha, op. cit.

16. See Chapter 6 in this book.

17. Carpenter, Edward, *Love's Coming of Age*, Methuen, London, 1906, p. 124.

18. Ellis, Havelock, *Sexual Inversion*, 3rd edn. 1913, p. 127. First published 1897.

19. See Grosskurth, Phyllis, *Havelock Ellis, A Biography*, Allen Lane, London, 1980. See also Jackson, Margaret, 'Sexology and the social construction of male sexuality (Havelock Ellis)', in Lal Coveney et al. (eds), *The Sexuality Papers*, Hutchinson, London, 1984; and Jeffreys, Sheila, *The Spinster and Her Enemies*, Pandora, London, 1985.

20. Stopes, Marie, *Enduring Passion*, Hogarth Press, London, 1923, p. 29.

21. Freud, Sigmund, 'Female Sexuality' (1931); 'Some Physical Consequences of the Anatomical Distinction Between the Sexes' (1925); 'Femininity' (1933). All three essays can be found in Jean Strouse (ed.), *Women and Analysis*, Laurel, New York, 1974.

22. See Chapter 5 in this book.

23. See Rich, op. cit.

24. Whitbread, Helena (ed.), *I Know My Own Heart: the Diaries of Anne Lister 1791–1840*, Virago, London, 1988, p. x.

Chapter 1. Does It Matter If They Did It?

1. Faderman, Lillian, *Surpassing the Love of Men: Romantic Friendship and Love between Women from the Renaissance to the Present*, The Women's Press, London, 1985.

2. Ibid., p. 18.

3. Ibid., p. 329.

4. Ruehl, Sonja, 'Sexual Theory and Practice: Another Double Standard', in Sue Cartledge and Joanna Ryan (eds), *Sex and Love*, The Women's Press, London, 1983.

5. Rich, Adrienne, 'Compulsory Heterosexuality and Lesbian Existence', in Ann Snitow et al. (eds), *Desire: The Politics of Sexuality*, Virago,

London, 1984.

6. Faderman, Lillian, *The Scotch Verdict*, Quartet, London, 1985.
7. Ibid, p. 246.
8. Ibid., p. 247.
9. Leeds Revolutionary Feminist Group, 'Political Lesbianism: The Case Against Heterosexuality', in Onlywomen Press (eds), *Love Your Enemy*, Onlywomen Press, London, 1981.

Chapter 2. Through All Changes and Through all Chances: The relationship of Ellen Nussey and Charlotte Brontë

1. Benson, E.F., *Charlotte Brontë*, Longmans Green, London, 1932, Chapter 4, pp. 37–48.
2. Quoted in Glendinning, Victoria, *Vita: The Life of Vita Sackville-West*, Penguin, Harmondsworth, Middx, 1984, Chapter 15, p. 168.
3. Raymond, Ernest, *In the Steps of the Brontës*, Rich and Cowan, London, 1948, Chapter 7, p. 77.
4. Foster, Jeanette, *Sex-Variant Women in Literature*, The Naiad Press, Florida, USA, 1985, Chapter 5, p. 130.
5. Wise, T.J. and Symington, J.A., *The Brontës: Their Lives, Friendships and Correspondence*, 4 Vols, Shakespeare Head, Oxford, 1932, Vol. IV, p. 127.
6. The collection edited by Wise and Symington comes nearest to a comprehensive published collection although this is regarded as somewhat unsatisfactory because of its dating and number of omissions. It is hard to find outside specialist libraries.

   The name of this collection is abbreviated in following notes as SHB (Shakespeare Head Brontë).
7. Gérin, Winifred, *Charlotte Brontë: The Evolution of Genius*, Clarendon Press, Oxford, 1967, Chapter 13, p. 191; Chapter 27, pp. 544–5; Chapter 5, p. 75. (Referred to in following notes as WGEG.)
8. SHB Vol. I, p. 148.
9. Ellen Nussey to Arthur Bell Nicholls, November 1854, SHB Vol. IV, p. 157.
10. Mary Taylor (1817–93) was a very close friend of both Charlotte Brontë and Ellen Nussey. The three friends met at Roe Head School in 1831 and remained on intimate terms until Mary emigrated to New Zealand in 1845. While in New Zealand, Mary corresponded with Charlotte until the latter's death in 1855, and with Ellen until Mary's

return to England in 1859. Soon after Mary's return, she and Ellen quarrelled and thenceforth had little to do with each other. Mary Taylor wrote a series of strong and witty feminist articles for the Victoria Press between 1865 and 1870, published in one volume as *The First Duty of Women* (1870). She also wrote a novel, *Miss Miles*, published in 1890 by Remington and Co.

11. Mary Taylor to Ellen Nussey, from New Zealand 15 August 1850, SHB, Vol. III, pp. 136–7.
12. Charlotte Brontë to Ellen Nussey (abbreviated in following notes as C.B. and E.N.) SHB, Vol. I, pp. 139–40.
13. C.B. to E.N. (SHB Vol. I, p. 141).
14. C.B. to E.N. (SHB Vol. I, p. 153).
15. C.B. to E.N. (SHB Vol. I, p. 138).
16. C.B. to E.N. (SHB Vol. I, p. 146).
17. C.B. to E.N. (SHB Vol. I, pp. 138–44 and 159–61). Letter number: 43(145) 44(20) 45(21) 46(22) 47(23) 48(41) 63(38) 64(42).
18. Faderman, Lillian, *Surpassing the Love of Men: Romantic Friendship and Love between Women from the Renaissance to the Present*, The Women's Press, London, 1985, Chapter 3, pp. 254–63.
19. C.B. to E.N. (SHB Vol. I, pp. 173–5).
20. Gaskell, Elizabeth, *The Life of Charlotte Brontë* (with introduction and notes by Clement Shorter), John Murray, London, 1930, Chapter 8, pp. 168–9 (abbreviated in following notes as EGL).
21. C.B. to E.N. 4 March 1845 (SHB Vol. II, pp. 26–7).
22. C.B. to E.N. 26 July 1839 (SHB Vol. I, pp. 182–3).
23. SHB Vol. I, pp. 188–90.
24. C.B. to E.N. 28 December (SHB Vol. II, pp. 118–19).
25. C.B. to E.N. (SHB Vol. I, p. 227).
26. C.B. to E.N. (SHB Vol. I, p. 228).
27. C.B. to E.N. (SHB Vol. I, pp. 249–50).
28. EGL, Chapter 11, p. 217.
29. *Villette*, Penguin, Harmondsworth, Middx, 1985, Chapter 14, pp. 207–23 (first published 1853).
30. Ibid., Introduction, p. 35.
31. *Shirley*, Penguin, Harmondsworth, Middx, 1985, Chapter 12, pp. 221–2.
32. C.B. to E.N. (SHB Vol. II, pp. 198–9). See also SHB Vol. II, pp. 184–5 for further evidence of Charlotte's jealousy of Amelia.
33. SHB Vol. III, pp. 138–9. Joe Taylor was the brother of Mary Taylor (see note 10).

34. C.B. to E.N. 5 February 1850 (SB Vol. III, p. 74).
35. Benson, op. cit., Chapter 4, p. 47.
36. C.B. to Elizabeth Gaskell 25 March 1851, quoted from WGEG, Chapter 24, pp. 468–9, by courtesy of the Librarian, Manchester University Library.
37. C.B. to E.N. from Cliff House, Filey, 6 June 1852 (SHB Vol. III, p. 336).
38. C.B. to E.N. 24 September 1852 (SHB Vol. IV, p. 9).
39. C.B. to E.N. 9 October 1852 (SHB Vol. IV, p. 10).
40. Mary Taylor to E. N. (SHB Vol. IV, pp. 104–5).
41. C.B. to E.N. (SHB Vol. IV, pp. 112–13).
42. C.B. to Elizabeth Gaskell 18 April 1854 (SHB Vol. IV, p. 116).
43. C.B. to George Smith 25 April 1854 (SHB Vol. IV, pp. 118–19).
44. C.B. to E.N. 15 April 1854 (SHB Vol. IV, pp. 114–15).
45. C.B. to Margaret Wooler (SHB Vol. IV, p. 149).
46. C.B. to E.N. (SHB Vol. IV, pp. 133–4).
47. C.B. to E.N. (SHB Vol. pp. 145–6).
48. C.B. to Margaret Wooler 22 August 1854 (SHB Vol. IV, p. 148).
49. C.B. to E.N. 7 September 1854 (SHB Vol. IV, pp. 150–1).
50. C.B. to Margaret Wooler 19 September 1854 (SHB Vol. IV, pp. 152–3).
51. C.B. to E.N. (SHB Vol. IV, pp. 155–6).
52. *Brontë Society Transactions*, 1944. Mabel Edgerley (1868–1946) was born in Edinburgh into the Blackwood family. She was the great-niece of Thomas Blackwood of the Blackwood magazine. She studied medicine but at a time when women were not awarded degrees. She married a Dr Edgerley of Menston Asylum, York. She was Secretary of the Brontë Society from 1929 to 1946.
53. SHB Vol. IV, pp. 247–95.
54. Shorter, Clement, *Charlotte Brontë and Her Sisters*, Hodder, London, 1905, pp. 35 and 45.
55. Letter from J. Ridley, Pulham Rectory, Dorchester 23 June 1909.
56. Sinclair, May, *The Three Brontës*, Hutchinson, London, 1912, p. 88.
57. Ratchford, Fanny, *The Brontës' Web of Childhood*, Columbia University Press, New York, 1941.
58. WGEG, Chapter 5, pp. 74–5; Chapter 14, p. 217.
59. Gérin, Winifred, *Elizabeth Gaskell*, Clarendon Press, Oxford, 1977, Chapter 15, p. 164.
60. Lane, Margaret, *Brontë Society Transactions*, 1979, pp. 261–71. See also Margaret Lane's homophobic comments in *The Brontë Story*, Heine-

mann, London, 1953, pp. 86–7.

61. Moglen, Helene, *Charlotte Brontë: The Self Conceived*, University of Wisconsin Press, 1984, Chapter 5, p. 206.
62. Fraser, Rebecca, *Charlotte Brontë*, Methuen, London, 1988, Chapter 21, p. 456.
63. Ibid., p. 457.
64. Ibid.
65. Ibid.
66. Ibid., Chapter 6, p. 107.
67. Ibid.
68. See Whitbread, Helena (ed.), *I Know My Own Heart: The Diaries of Anne Lister 1791–1840*, Virago, London, 1988, pp. 97, 104–5, 121, 139, 281, 293, 351 and passim. The diaries were written in a secret code; even then, the euphemism 'kiss' was used for 'orgasm'.
69. Fraser, op. cit., Chapter 6, p. 107.
70. Ibid.
71. For example, Holtby, Winifred, *South Riding* (1936); Cather, Willa, *My Antonia* (1918); Warner, Sylvia Townsend, *The True Heart* (1929); and Woolf, Virginia, *To the Lighthouse* (1927).
72. C.B. to E.N. 5 September 1832 (SHB Vol. I, pp. 104–5).
73. Sinclair, op. cit., p. 91.

Material and quotations taken from *Brontë Society Transactions* are by courtesy of the Brontë Society.

Chapter 3. Edith Simcox and Heterosexism in Biography: a lesbian-feminist exploration

1. Simcox, Edith, *Autobiography of a Shirt Maker*, Bodleian Library (MS, Eng. Misc. d. 494), p. 141, 17 October 1887. The author gratefully acknowledges the permission of the Bodleian Library to quote from the diary. (Hereafter referred to as 'Bodleian ms'.)
2. McKenzie, K.A., *Edith Simcox and George Eliot*, Oxford University Press, Oxford, 1961, p. 118, 16 April 1882.
3. See Sarah, Elizabeth, 'Female Performers on a Male Stage: The First Women's Liberation Movement and the Authority of Men, 1890–1930', pp. 133–56 in Scarlet Friedman and Elizabeth Sarah (eds), *On the Problem of Men: Two Feminist Conferences*, The Women's Press, London, 1981; and Sarah, Elizabeth, 'Christabel Pankhurst; Reclaiming her Power', pp. 256–84 in Dale Spender (ed.), *Feminist*

Theorists, The Women's Press, London, 1983.

4. Vicinus, Martha, *Independent Women: Work and Community for Single Women, 1850–1920*, Virago, London, 1985, p. 6.

5. McKenzie, op. cit. pp. 1–3.

6. Ibid., p. 17.

7. Ibid., p. 11.

8. Ibid., p. 22.

9. Ibid., p. 23.

10. Simcox, Edith, 'Eight Years of Co-operative Shirtmaking', *Nineteenth Century*, June 1884, quoted in McKenzie, op. cit., p. 27.

11. McKenzie, op. cit., p. 38.

12. Ibid., p. 40.

13. Ibid., p. 55.

14. Bodleian ms, p. 82, 28 December 1880.

15. Ibid., p. 78.

16. See McKenzie, op. cit., p. 87.

17. Ibid., p. xv.

18. Ibid., p. xiv.

19. Ibid., p. xvi.

20. Ibid.

21. Ibid., p. 134.

22. Ibid., p. 102.

23. Ibid., p. 109.

24. Ibid., p. 32.

25. Allen, Walter, *George Eliot*, Weidenfeld & Nicolson, London, 1964, p. 74.

26. Laski, Marghanita, *George Eliot and Her World*, Thames & Hudson, London, 1973, p. 102.

27. McKenzie, op. cit., p. xvi.

28. Haight, Gordon S., *George Eliot: A Biography*, Oxford University Press, Oxford, 1968, pp. 458–9.

29. Laski, op. cit. p 100.

30. Smith-Rosenberg, Carroll, 'The Female World of Love and Ritual: Relations between Women in Nineteenth Century America.' *Signs*, Vol. I, No. I (Autumn 1975), pp. 1–29. Faderman, Lillian, *Surpassing the Love of Men: Romantic Friendship and Love between Women from the Renaissance to the Present*, Junction Books, London, 1981, p. 18; reissued by The Women's Press, London, 1985.

31. Weeks, Jeffrey, *Coming Out: Homosexual Politics in Britain, from the Nineteenth Century to the Present*, Quartet, London, 1977, p. 95.

237

32. Redinger, Ruby V. *George Eliot: the Emergent Self*, The Bodley Head, London, 1976, p. 94.
33. Ibid., p. 140.
34. Ibid.
35. Ibid., p. 201.
36. Ibid., p. 140.
37. Haight, op. cit., p. 494.
38. Ibid., p. 496.
39. Redinger, op. cit., p. 14.
40. Ibid., p. 361.
41. Vicinus, op cit., p. 158.
42. 17 September 1879 and 14 April 1879, quoted in McKenzie, op. cit., pp. 110–12.
43. 14 September 1879, in McKenzie, op. cit., p. 112.
44. 3 March 1881, in McKenzie, op. cit., p. 98.
45. 16 January 1878, in McKenzie, op. cit., p. 90.
46. 22 November 1878.
47. 9 March 1880.
48. See McKenzie, op. cit., p. 108.
49. Quoted in Haight, op. cit., p. 533.
50. Redinger, op. cit., p. 479.
51. Bodleian ms, p. 1.
52. For the chronology of this, see McKenzie, op. cit., p. 88.
53. Ibid., p. 95.
54. Bodleian ms, 18 January 1881, p. 88.
55. Ibid., 23 January 1881, p. 90.
56. 28 March 1881, in McKenzie, op. cit., p. 62.
57. 5 June 1880, ibid., p. 61.
58. 30 April 1882, ibid., p. 63.
59. Bodleian ms, p. 143.
60. Simcox's unsent letter stored with the Bodleian ms.
61. 2 January 1881, Bodleian ms, p. 84.
62. Faderman, op. cit., p. 208.
63. 1 February 1880.
64. 28 June 1889.
65. See Bodleian ms, pp. 141–6.
66. 13 June 1880, in McKenzie, op. cit., p. 134.
67. November 1887, ibid., p. 91.
68. 22 June 1878, Bodleian ms, pp. 13–14.
69. 9 March 1880.

70. 17 October 1885.
71. Allen, op. cit., p. 75.
72. 16 April 1882.
73. 15 October 1882.
74. 1898, in McKenzie, op. cit., 136.
75. Ibid., p. 7.
76. Vicinus, op. cit., pp. 186–7.

Other books consulted or referred to in the text:

Carpenter, Edward, *Love's Coming of Age: A Series of Papers on the Relation of the Sexes*, Allen & Unwin, London, 1948. First published 1896, rev. ed. 1906.

Cross, J.W., *George Eliot's Life as Related in her Letters and Journals*, Blackwood and Sons, 1885.

Eliot, George, *The Mill on the Floss*, Penguin, Harmondsworth, Middx, 1979. First published 1860.

Ellis, Havelock, *Psychology of Sex*, Pan Books, London, 1959. First published 1933.

Gissing, George, *The Odd Women*, Virago, London, 1980. First published 1893.

Haight, Gordon S. (ed.), *The George Eliot Letters*, 9 Vols, Yale University Press, New Haven and London, 1954–78.

Pankhurst, Sylvia, *The Suffragette Movement*, Virago, London, 1977. First published 1931.

Rowbotham, Sheila, and Jeffrey Weeks, *Socialism and the New Life: The Personal and Sexual Politics of Edward Carpenter and Havelock Ellis*, Pluto Press, London, 1977.

Simcox, Edith, *Episodes in the Lives of Men, Women and Lovers*, Trübner & Co, Ludgate Hill, 1882.

Strachey, Ray, *The Cause: A Short History of the Women's Movement in Great Britain*, Virago, London, 1978. First published 1928.

Chapter 4. By Their Friends We Shall Know Them: The lives and networks of some women in North Lambeth, 1880–1940.

1. Healey, Edna, *Lady Unknown. The Life of Angela Burdett-Coutts*, Sidgwick & Jackson, London, 1978, pp. 75–6.
2. The information for this section comes from Katherine Bentley Beauman, *Lady Margaret Hall Settlement. A Short History 1897–1980*, Friends

of the LMHS, n.d.; and from an unpublished manuscript by Katharine Thicknesse in the Minet Library, Lambeth.

3. See Maurice C. Edmund, *Life of Octavia Hill from her Letters*, London, 1913; Bell, E. Moberly, *Octavia Hill*, Constable, London, 1947; Hill, W.T., *Octavia Hill*, Hutchinson, London, 1956; Todd, Margaret, *The Life of Sophia Jex-Blake*, Macmillan, London, 1918; and Auchmuty, Rosemary, 'Women's Forgotten Friendships', *Revolutionary and Radical Feminist Newsletter*, 10 (Summer 1982), p. 9.

4. Jamison, E.M., 'Elizabeth Wordsworth', Appendix to Georgina Battiscombe, *Reluctant Pioneer*, Constable, London, 1978, p. 311.

5. See Benson, A.C., *Life and Letters of Maggie Benson*, John Murray, London, 1918; Benson, E.F., *Mother*, Hodder & Stoughton, London, 1925; and Askwith, Betty, *Two Victorian Families*, Chatto & Windus, London, 1971.

6. For example, Martindale, Louisa, *A Woman Surgeon*, Gollancz, London, 1951.

7. Smyth, Ethel, *Impressions That Remained*, Longman, London, 1921, Vol. II, pp. 188–247.

8. Lady Margaret Hall Settlement Jubilee Report, 1947. .

9. The building was situated within the county of Surrey at the time. Today a block of student residences, also called Surrey Lodge, stands on the site.

10. Baylis, Lilian, 'Emma Cons', in Cicely Hamilton, *The Old Vic*, Jonathan Cape, London, 1926, pp. 256, 258. See also Tabor, Margaret S., *Pioneer Women*, 2nd series, The Sheldon Press, London, 1927, on Emma Cons' friendship with Octavia Hill.

11. Webb, Beatrice, *My Apprenticeship*, Penguin, Harmondsworth, Middx, 1938, p. 315. First published 1929.

12. Unpublished letter from Lord Sandhurst to Channel 4 *Flashback*, 24 February 1984.

13. Richards, Denis, *Offspring of the Vic. A History of Morley College*, Routledge & Kegan Paul, London, 1958, p. 134. The Foreword to this book was written by the then President of Morley College, Harold Nicolson, husband of one of the most famous lesbians of the century, Vita Sackville-West.

14. Ibid., p. 31.

15. Today most of the students are women, and once again there is a woman Principal.

16. Richards, op. cit., p. 137.

17. Ibid., p. 106.

18. Ibid., p. 107.
19. Ibid., p. 16.
20. Oldfield, Sybil, *Spinsters of this Parish*, Virago, London, 1984, pp. 92–6.
21. See Chapter 6 in this book.
22. Tickner, Lisa, *The Spectacle of Women. Imagery of the Suffrage Campaign*, Chatto & Windus, London, 1987, p. 245.
23. Findlater, Richard, *Lilian Baylis. The Lady of the Old Vic*, Allen Lane, London, 1975, p. 12.
24. Ibid., p. 65.
25. Ibid., p. 92.
26. Ibid., p. 240.
27. See St John, Christopher, *Ethel Smyth*, Longmans, London, 1959 (esp. pp. 179, 228); Baker, Michael, *Our Three Selves: A Life of Radclyffe Hall*, GMP, London, 1985; Glendinning, Victoria, *Vita*, Penguin, Harmondsworth, Middx, 1983; Holledge, Julie, *Innocent Flowers. Women in the Edwardian Theatre*, Virago, London, 1981; Melville, Joy, *Ellen and Edy*, Pandora, London, 1987.
28. Adlard, Eleanor, (ed.) *Edy*, Muller, London, 1949, p. 25.
29. Findlater, op. cit., p. 241.
30. Holmes, Miss Gordon, *In Love With Life. A Pioneer Career Woman's Story*, Hollis & Carter, London, 1944, p. 140.
31. Ibid., p. 90.
32. Martindale, op. cit.
33. Riddell, Lord, *Dame Louisa Aldrich-Blake*, Hodder & Stoughton, London, 1926.
34. Woolf, Leonard, *The Journey Not the Arrival Matters*, Hogarth Press, London, 1969, p. 83; Spender, Dale, *Time and Tide Wait for No Man*, Pandora, London, 1984.

Chapter 5: 'Embittered, Sexless or Homosexual': Attacks on spinster teachers 1918–39

1. See Oram, Alison, 'Serving Two Masters? The Introduction of a Marriage Bar in Teaching in the 1920s', in London Feminist History Group (eds), *The Sexual Dynamics of History*, Pluto Press, London, 1983, pp. 134–48; and Oram, Alison, 'Inequalities in the Teaching Profession: the Effects on Teachers and Pupils', in Felicity Hunt (ed.), *Lessons for Life: The Schooling of Girls and Women 1850–1950*, Basil Blackwell, Oxford, 1987, pp. 97–119.

2. Tranter, N., *Population since the Industrial Revolution*, Croom Helm, London, 1973, pp. 101–8; Winter, J.M., 'Some Aspects of the Demographic Consequences of the First World War in Britain', *Population Studies*, Vol. 30, No. 3 (1976), 545–51.

3. See Bland, Lucy, 'Purity, Motherhood, Pleasure or Threat? Definitions of Female Sexuality 1900–1970s', in S. Cartledge and J. Ryan (eds), *Sex and Love*, The Women's Press, London, 1983, pp. 8–29; Jeffreys, Sheila, *The Spinster and Her Enemies*, Pandora Press, London, 1985, Chapter 5; Faraday, Annabel, 'Social Definitions of Lesbians in Britain, 1914–1939', unpublished PhD thesis, University of Essex, 1985. It is important to point out that while each of these writers identifies these effects of sexology, they vary in their approach and emphasis. Lillian Faderman, in *Surpassing the Love of Men* (The Women's Press, London, 1985), still the classic text of lesbian history, also discusses this change, while a British writer has argued the opposite case, that sexology stimulated the formation of a lesbian identity and subculture: Sonja Ruehl, 'Inverts and Experts: Radclyffe Hall and the Lesbian Identity', in R. Brunt and C. Rowan (eds), *Feminism, Culture and Politics*, Lawrence & Wishart, London, 1982, pp. 15–36.

4. Adrienne Rich's writing on the 'lesbian continuum', *Compulsory Heterosexuality and Lesbian Existence*, Onlywomen Press, London, 1981, is relevant here. While there is a danger of including heterosexual women as lesbians under the banner of sisterhood, nevertheless for the purposes of research into lesbian history it is useful to have a fairly broad definition, since 'lesbians' in the past do not often handily identify themselves as such, even if the term were available.

5. Oram, Alison, ' "Sex Antagonism" in the Teaching Profession: Equal Pay and the Marriage Bar, 1910–39', in G. Weiner and M. Arnot (eds), *Gender and the Politics of Schooling*, Hutchinson, London, 1987, pp. 276–89.

6. Jewsbury, Geraldine, *The Half Sisters* (1848), pp. 66–9 (a novel), quoted in Rosemary Auchmuty, 'Victorian Spinsters', unpublished PhD thesis, Australian National University, 1975, p. 63.

7. Bland, op. cit., p. 11.

8. Ballard, P., *The Changing School*, Hodder & Stoughton, London, 1925, p. 314.

9. Wilson, John Dover, quoted in the *Times Educational Supplement*, 28 March 1931, p. 113.

10. Association of Assistant Mistresses, *Annual Report*, January 1933.
11. *News Chronicle*, 21 March 1934.
12. Oram, 'Inequalities in the Teaching Profession', op. cit.
13. *Daily Herald*, 5 September 1935.
14. Jeffreys, op. cit., pp. 105–8.
15. Weeks, J., *Sex, Politics and Society*, Longman, London, 1981, pp. 116–7; Faraday, op. cit., pp. 210–25.
16. Lambertz, Jan, in 'Single but not Alone: Interwar Spinsters in England', unpublished paper, 1983, points out that older spinsters were likely to escape stigmatisation as lesbians, since they were not seen as sexual. For changes after 1928 in how female friendship was depicted in schoolgirl stories, see Chapter 6 of this book.
17. Gallichan, W., *Sexual Apathy and Coldness in Women*, T. Werner Laurie, London, 1927, p. 13, quoted in Jeffreys, S., 'Sex Reform and Anti-feminism in the 1920s', in London Feminist History Group (eds), *The Sexual Dynamics of History*, pp. 177–202.
18. *Times Educational Supplement* (*TES*), 26 April 1924, p. 180. NAS Conference.
19. *TES*, 15 April 1939, p. 142. Speeches at NAS Conference.
20. Other gains for women at the end of the first world war or shortly afterwards were the opening of the legal profession, divorce law reform and the greater availability of contraception.
21. *TES*, 3 April 1937, p. 112.
22. *Education*, 22 June 1923, pp. 401–2. Conference of Education Committees.
23. 'Why Are Teachers Unpopular?', *TES*, 6 August 1932, p. 301.
24. *TES*, 15 April 1939, p. 142. Speeches at NAS Conference. For a detailed discussion of the debate over 'men teachers for boys' see Oram, 'Inequalities in the teaching profession', op. cit., and Littlewood, Margaret, 'Makers of Men: the Anti-feminist Backlash of the National Association of Schoolmasters in the 1920s and 30s', *Trouble and Strife*, No. 5 (1985).
25. Bland, Lucy, 'Marriage Laid Bare: Middle-Class Women and Marital Sex c.1880–1914', in Jane Lewis (ed.), *Labour and Love: Women's Experience of Home and Family 1850–1940*, Basil Blackwell, Oxford, 1986, pp. 138–9; Jeffreys, op. cit., pp. 91–3.
26. Hamilton, Cicely, *Marriage as a Trade*, The Women's Press, London, 1981. First published 1909.
27. Bland, 'Definitions of Female Sexuality', p. 17; Jeffreys, op. cit., pp. 93–101, 115–21. See Introduction to this book.

28. Holtby, W., *Women*, The Bodley Head, London, 1934, pp. 125–33. See Chapter 7 of this book.
29. *News Chronicle*, 20 February 1930.
30. NUWT, *A Short History of the Union to 1956*, NUWT, London, n.d.
31. *The Woman Teacher*, 2 January 1920, p. 114; 30 January 1920, p. 150. The National Federation of Women Teachers changed its title to National Union of Women Teachers in 1920.
32. *Daily Herald*, 5 September 1935.
33. *The Woman Teacher*, 12 October 1934, p. 5.
34. *The Star*, 24 May 1935.
35. NUWT Archive, Box 176, Institute of Education Library, London. This exchange of letters took place between 27 and 31 May 1935.
36. *The Woman Teacher*, 12 October 1934, p. 5.
37. *TES*, 20 July 1935, pp. 257–8, for all the quotes in this paragraph.
38. Ibid.
39. NUWT Archive, Box 176. This exchange of letters took place between 7 and 20 July 1935.
40. For a discussion of some of the issues affecting lesbian teachers today, see Squirrell, Gillian, 'In Passing . . . Teachers and Sexual Orientation', in Sandra Acker (ed.), *Teachers, Gender and Careers*, Falmer Press, Brighton, 1989, and Carol Jones and Pat Mahony (eds), *Learning Our Lines: Sexuality and Social Control in Education*, The Women's Press, London, 1989.

Chapter 6. You're a Dyke, Angela! Elsie J. Oxenham and the rise and fall of the schoolgirl story

1. A shorter version of this chapter was published in *Trouble and Strife*, 10 (Spring 1987). I am grateful to the *T & S* collective, especially Cath Jackson, for their work on it, and for the title.
2. Oxenham, Elsie, J., *Jen of the Abbey School*, Collins, London, 1925, pp. 92–3.
3. Avery, Gillian, *Childhood's Pattern. A Study of the Heroes and Heroines of Children's Fiction 1770–1950*, Hodder & Stoughton, London, 1975, p. 228.
4. See McClelland, Helen, *Behind the Chalet School. Elinor Mary Brent-Dyer*, New Horizon, Bognor Regis, 1981, p. 146.
5. Brazil, Angela, *Answers* (1922), quoted in Gillian Freeman, *The Schoolgirl Ethic. The Life and Work of Angela Brazil*, Allen Lane, London, 1976, p. 18. See also Angela Brazil, *My Own Schooldays*, Blackie,

Glasgow, 1925.

6. Blyton, Enid, *The Story of My Life*, Pitkins, Andover, Hants, 1952. Readers interested in Blyton are referred to Barbara Stoney, *Enid Blyton: A Biography*. Hodder & Stoughton, London, 1974; Ray, Sheila, *The Blyton Phenomenon*, Deutsch, London, 1982; Mullan, Bob, *The Enid Blyton Story*, Boxtree, 1987.

7. Williams, Raymond, *The Long Revolution*, Penguin, Harmondsworth, Middx, 1965, p. 73.

8. *Chalet Club Newsletter*, extracts from readers' letters. Twenty issues were published by Chambers, Edinburgh, the last posthumously in 1969.

9. Walsh, Jill Paton, in Edward Blishen, (ed.), *The Thorny Paradise: Writers on Writing for Children*, Viking Kestrel, 1975, p. 59.

10. Leavis, Q.D., *Fiction and the Reading Public*, Chatto & Windus, London, 1965, p. 60. First published 1932.

11. Burstall, Sara A., *Retrospect and Prospect. Sixty Years of Women's Education*, Longman, London, 1933, p. 60.

12. Mason, Bobbie Ann, *The Girl Sleuth. A Feminist Guide*, Feminist Books, New York, 1975, p. 125.

13. *The Abbey Girls Win Through*, Collins, London, 1928, pp. 142–3.

14. *Queen of the Abbey Girls*, Collins, London, 1926, p. 81.

15. *The Abbey Girls on Trial*, Collins, London. 1931, pp. 185–6.

16. *The Abbey Girls in Town*, Collins, London, 1925, p. 308.

17. *The Abbey Girls Win Through*, p. 145.

18. *Queen of the Abbey Girls*, p. 284.

19. *The Abbey Girls in Town*, p. 80.

20. *The Abbey Girls Win Through*, p. 175.

21. *The Abbey Girls Go Back to School*, Collins, London, 1922, p. 163.

22. *The Abbey Girls Again*, Collins, London, 1924, p. 164.

23. *The New Abbey Girls*, Collins, London, 1923, p. 233.

24. See Faderman, Lillian, *Surpassing the Love of Men: Romantic Friendship and Love between Women from the Renaissance to the Present*, The Women's Press, London, 1985; also see the Introduction to the present book.

25. Cockshut, A.O.J., *Man and Woman: A Study of Love and the Novel 1740–1940*, Collins, London, 1977, p. 190.

26. Ibid., p. 189.

27. Cadogan, Mary and Craig, Patricia, *You're a Brick, Angela! A New Look at Girls' Fiction from 1839 to 1975*, Gollancz, London, 1976.

Chapter 7. 'The Best Friend Whom Life Has Given Me.' Does Winifred Holtby have a place in lesbian history?

1. Brittain, Vera, *Testament of Friendship*, Fontana in association with Virago, London, 1980, p. 179. First published 1940.
2. *Afterword* to *Testament of Friendship*, p. 450.
3. *Testament of Friendship*, p. 134.
4. See Spender, Dale, *Women of Ideas and What Men Have Done to Them*, ARK, 1983, pp. 623–7.
5. Holtby, Winifred, *Women and a Changing Civilisation*, Cassandra Editions/Academy Chicago Editions, 1978, p. 130.
6. *Testament of Friendship*, p. 214.
7. Holtby, op. cit., pp. 159–60.
8. Ibid., p. 192.
9. Holtby, Alice and McWilliam, Jean, (eds), *Letters to a Friend*, Collins, London, 1937, p. 145.
10. White, Evelyne, *Winifred Holtby as I Knew Her*, Collins, London, 1938, p. 93.
11. Ibid., p. 36.
12. Ibid., p. 147.
13. Berry, Paul, and Bishop, Alan, (eds), *Testament of a Generation – The Journalism of Vera Brittain and Winifred Holtby*, Virago, London, 1985, p. 6.
14. Ibid., p. 16.
15. *Testament of Friendship*, p. 4.
16. Ibid., p. 2.
17. Ibid.
18. Ibid., p. 118.
19. Ibid., p. 291.
20. Ibid., p. 328.
21. Ibid., p. 166.
22. Ibid., p. 262.
23. Ibid., p. 53–4.
24. Ibid., p. 52.
25. Ibid., p. 436.
26. Ibid.
27. From Introduction to *South Riding*, Collins, London, 1966.
28. Afterword to *Testament of Friendship*, p. 446.
29. *Testament of a Generation*, p. 13.

30. Faderman, Lillian, *Surpassing the Love of Men: Romantic Friendship and Love between Women from the Renaissance to the Present*, The Women's Press, London, 1985, p. 323.

31. 'Facing the Facts', *Time and Tide*, No. 12 (August 1928).

32. Harding, M. Esther, MD MRCP, *The Way of All Women: A Psychological Interpretation*, Longmans Green & Co., London, 1970, p. 103. First published 1933.

33. Hutton, Laura, *The Single Woman and Her Emotional Problems*, Baillière, Tindall & Cox, London, 1935, p. 28.

34. Ibid., p. 103.

35. Harding, op. cit., p. 100.

36. Ibid., p. 113.

37. Hutton, op. cit., pp. 120–1.

38. Harding, op. cit., p. 103.

39. Hutton, op. cit., p. 126.

40. Ibid., p. 131.

41. *Testament of a Generation*, p. 13.

42. Ibid., p. 15.

43. Ibid., p. 13.

44. Mellown, Muriel, 'Vera Brittain – Feminist in a New Age', in Dale Spender (ed.), *Feminist Theorists – Three Centuries of Women's Intellectual Traditions*, The Women's Press, London, 1983, pp. 321–2.

45. White, op. cit., p. 29.

46. Brittain, Vera, *Testament of Experience*, Fontana in association with Virago, London, 1979, p. 179. First published 1957.

47. *Testament of a Generation*, p. 7.

48. Holtby and McWilliam, op. cit., p. 8.

49. *Testament of a Generation*, p. 7.

50. Holtby and McWilliam, op. cit., p. 433.

51. Ibid., p. 325.

52. Ibid., p. 202.

53. *Testament of Friendship*, p. 171.

54. Brittain, Vera, (ed.), *Selected Letters of Winifred Holtby and Vera Brittain (1920–1935)*, pp. 29–30.

55. Holtby, Winifred, *Virginia Woolf*, Cassandra Editions/Academy Chicago Limited, 1978, p. 29.

56. *Testament of a Generation*, p. 91.

57. Ibid., p. 13.

58. Spender (ed.), *Feminist Theorists*, op. cit., p. 327.

59. Rich, Adrienne, *Compulsory Heterosexuality and Lesbian Existence*, Onlywomen Press, London, 1981, p. 20.

60. Ibid, pp. 20–21.
61. *Testament of Friendship*, p. 2.

Chapter 8. Butch and Femme: Now and then

1. Davis, Madeline, and Kennedy, Elizabeth Lapovsky, 'Oral History and the Study of Sexuality in the Lesbian Community: Buffalo, New York, 1940–1960', *Feminist Studies*, Vol. 12, No. 1 (Spring 1986), p. 7.
2. Penelope, Julia, 'Whose Past Are We Reclaiming?', *Common Lives, Lesbian Lives*, No. 13 (Autumn 1984), p. 18.
3. Mushroom, Merrill, 'Confessions of a Butch Dyke', *Common Lives, Lesbian Lives*, No. 9 (Autumn 1983), p. 42.
4. Davis and Kennedy, op. cit., p. 16.
5. Sawyer, Ethel, 'A Study of a Public Lesbian Community', *Washington University, Sociology–Anthropology Essay Series*, September 1965, p. 10.
6. Davis and Kennedy, op. cit., p. 16.
7. Sawyer, op. cit., p. 10.
8. Ellis, Havelock, 'Studies in the Psychology of Sex', Vol. II, *Sexual Inversion*, F.A. Davis, Philadelphia, 1927, p. 222.
9. See the chapter on 'Women's Friendships and Lesbianism', in Sheila Jeffreys, *The Spinster and Her Enemies: Feminism and Sexuality 1880–1930*, Pandora, London, 1985.
10. Davis and Kennedy, op. cit., p. 14.
11. Ibid., p. 24.
12. Sawyer, op. cit., p. 11.
13. Ibid.
14. Ibid., p. 12.
15. Ibid.
16. Mushroom, op. cit., p. 40.
17. Ibid., p. 41.
18. Ibid., p. 42.
19. Nestle, Joan, 'The Fem Question', in Carole Vance (ed.), *Pleasure and Danger*, Routledge & Kegan Paul, London, 1984, p. 237.
20. Sawyer, op. cit., p. 12.
21. Ibid., p. 13.
22. Ibid., p. 14.
23. Davis and Kennedy, op. cit., p. 16.
24. Ibid., p. 17.
25. Penelope, op. cit., p. 28.
26. Ibid., p. 31.

27. Hollibaugh, Amber, and Moraga, Cherrie, 'What We're Rollin Around in Bed With: Sexual Silences in Feminism', in Ann Snitow and Sharon Thompson, (eds), *Desire: The Politics of Sexuality*, Virago, London, 1984, p. 410.

28. Ibid.

29. Stewart-Park, Angela, and Cassidy, Jules, *We're Here*, Quartet, London, 1977, p. 124.

30. Penelope, op. cit., p. 31.

31. Davis and Kennedy, op. cit., p. 14.

32. Nestle, Joan, *Lesbian History Archives News*, 8 (Winter 1984), p. 15.

33. Martin, Del and Lyon, Phyllis, *Lesbian/Woman*, Bantam, New York, 1972, p. 66.

34. *Arena Three*, No. 9 (September 1964).

35. Penelope, op. cit., p. 16.

36. Martin and Lyon, op. cit., p. 63.

37. Walter, Aubrey, (ed.), *Come Together*, Gay Men's Press, London, 1980, p. 52.

38. Bearchall, Chris, 'Why I am a Gay Liberationist; Thoughts on Sex, Freedom, the Family and the State', *Resources of Feminist Research*, Vol. 12, No. 1 (March 1983), The Lesbian Issue, p. 59.

39. Martin and Lyon, op cit., p. 65.

40. Brunet, Ariane and Turcotte, Louise, 'Separation and Radicalism: An Analysis of the Differences and Similarities', *Lesbian Ethics*, Vol. 2, No. 1, p. 46.

41. Raymond, Janice G., *A Passion for Friends: Towards a Philosophy of Female Affection*, The Women's Press, London, 1986, p. 12.

42. Mushroom, op. cit., p. 45.

43. Nestle, op. cit., p. 232.

44. Mushroom, op. cit., p. 43.

45. Nestle, Joan, 'Butch–Fem Relationships', *Heresies*, No. 12, Sex Issue, pp. 22–3.

46. Hollibaugh and Moraga, op. cit., p. 407.

47. Ibid.

48. Ibid., p. 408–9.

49. Morgan, Marabel, *The Total Woman*, Hodder & Stoughton, London, 1975, p. 118.

50. Hollibaugh and Moraga, op. cit., p. 412.

51. Penelope, op. cit., p. 33.

52. Vance, Carole, (ed.), *Pleasure and Danger: Exploring Female Sexuality*, Routledge & Kegan Paul, London, 1984.

53. Ellis, Havelock, 'Studies in the Psychology of Sex, vol. III. Analysis of the Sexual Impulse', in *Love and Pain*, F.A. Davis, Philadelphia, 1923.
54. Snitow, Ann, Stansell, Christine and Thompson, Sharon, (eds), *Desire: The Politics of Sexuality*, Virago, London, 1984.
55. Hollibaugh and Moraga, op. cit., p. 413.

Endpiece

1. See Hall Carpenter Archive Oral History Group (eds), *Inventing Ourselves: Lesbian Life Stories*, Routledge, 1989; Brighton Ourstory Project, *Daring Hearts: Lesbian and Gay Lives of 50s and 60s Brighton*, Queenspark 28, Brighton 1992.
2. See, for example, Martha Vicinus, *Independent Women*, Virago, 1985; Janice Raymond, *A Passion for Friends*, The Women's Press, 1986; Rosemary Auchmuty, *A World of Girls: The appeal of the girls' school story*, The Women's Press, 1992.
3. See, for example, Martin Bauml Duberman, Martha Vicinus and George Chauncey Jr (eds), *Hidden from History: Reclaiming the Gay and Lesbian Past*, Penguin 1991; Lillian Faderman, *Odd Girls and Twilight Lovers: A History of Lesbian Life in Twentieth-Century America*, Penguin 1992.
4. For example, the Women's History Network conferences in London (1991) and Nottingham (1992), and the Women's Studies Network Conference in Northampton (1993).
5. Two such are the MAs in women's studies at the University of Kent at Canterbury and the University of Westminster in London.
6. At the University of Sussex in Brighton and the University of Melbourne, Australia.
7. See Rosemary Auchmuty, Sheila Jeffreys and Elaine Miller, 'Lesbian History and Gay Studies: Keeping a Feminist Perspective' in the *Women's History Review* 1/1 (1992), p. 89.
8. This tendency is evident in some of the articles in Dennis Altman et al (eds), *Which Homosexuality? Essays from the International Scientific Conference on Lesbian and Gay Studies*, Gay Men's Press, 1989; Duberman et al (eds), *Hidden from History*, op. cit.; and Lillian Faderman's most recent book, *Odd Girls and Twilight Lovers*, op. cit.

Notes on the Contributors

Rosemary Auchmuty was born in Egypt in 1950 and grew up in Australia, where she acquired a Ph.D in history with a thesis on Victorian spinsters. She has lived in London since 1978 and now teaches law and women's studies at the University of Westminster. A founder member of the Lesbian History Group, she is the author of *A World of Girls: The Appeal of the Girls' School Story* (The Women's Press, 1992) and a number of textbooks, articles, and short stories, two of which appeared in the anthology *Girls Next Door: Lesbian Feminist stories* edited by Jan Bradshaw and Mary Hemming (The Women's Press, 1985).

Sheila Jeffreys is a lesbian and a revolutionary feminist who has been active within the Women's Liberation Movement since 1973, mostly in campaigns against male violence and pornography. She was a founder member of London Women Against Violence Against Women (WAVAW) in 1980, and more recently helped to set up the London Lesbian Archive. She now lives in Australia where she teaches lesbian and gay studies at the University of Melbourne. She is the author of *The Spinster and Her Enemies: Feminism and Sexuality 1880–1930* (Pandora Press, 1985); of *Anticlimax: A Feminist Perspective on the Sexual Revolution* (The Women's Press, 1990); and *The Lesbian Heresy* (The Women's Press, 1993).

Pam Johnson was born in 1949. She lives in London and works in further education. During the early 1980s she contributed book reviews to *Spare Rib* and *Gay News*. The two pieces published here were originally written as essays for part of a women's studies course tutored by Rosemary Auchmuty. She would like to acknowledge Rosemary's encouragement and supportive criticism. Currently, she is working on critical discourse analysis of the representation of lesbians in newspaper reports.

Elaine Miller is a lesbian and a radical feminist who teaches English and women's literature in further and adult education. She was born in 1939 into a coalmining family in South Yorkshire and was brought up near Doncaster. She has been a member of the Lesbian History Group since 1986. Her most recent publication is a lesbian reading of the work of Mary Taylor, friend of Charlotte Brontë, which appears as a chapter in a new volume of lesbian literary criticism edited by Suzanne Raitt, *Volcanoes and Pearl Divers* (Onlywomen Press, 1993).

Alison Oram was born in 1956 in Southend-on-Sea. A feminist historian, she has published several articles on women teachers between the wars and is currently completing a book about women teachers and twentieth-century feminism. During the 1980s she taught women's studies and feminist history in adult education classes in the London area. She co-taught the first lesbian history course in London in 1985–87, run by the London University Extra-Mural Department, and was a founder member of the Lesbian History Group. She is now a senior lecturer in women's history at Sheffield Hallam University.

Avril Rolph, *Linda Kerr* and *Jane Allen* are librarians whose interest in lesbian history and culture led to their involvement in Lesbians in Libraries, a campaigning and support group of lesbians interested in books and other media, and who either use and/or work in libraries. Their publications include *Out on the Shelves: Lesbian Books into Libraries* (Association of Assistant Librarians, 1989) 0 900092 74 (a bibliography of lesbian literature with 226 annotated entries including fiction, poetry and plays, history, politics and periodicals).

Index

257

women's movement 20, 36, 57–8, 85, 88, 90, 91, 94, 113, 229; gains 107–8
Women's Social and Political Union 113
Wood, Thelma 218
Woods, Marianne 24–7
Wooler, Margaret 33, 47, 48, 49–50
Woolf, Virginia 54n, 90, 95, 96, 155, 188, 191, 223, 224, 225

Wordsworth, Elizabeth 80–1
work 56–7, 58, 77, 83, 107–9, 122, 194, 196; *see also* teachers
Workers' Educational Association 82, 87
Working Women's College 86–7, 88

Yorke, Harriet 5, 80
Young, Kenneth 149–50